THE COMPLETE FILMS OF
ORSON
WELLES

THE COMPLETE FILMS OF
ORSON WELLES

by James Howard

A CITADEL PRESS BOOK

Published by the Carol Publishing Group

A Citadel Press Book
Published by Carol Publishing Group
Citadel Press is a registered trademark of Carol Communica-
tions, Inc.

Editorial Offices: 600 Madison Avenue, New York, N.Y. 10022
Sales & Distribution Offices: 120 Enterprise Avenue, Secaucus,
N.J. 07094
In Canada: Musson Book Company, a division of General Pub-
lishing Co., Ltd., Don Mills, Ontario

Queries regarding rights and permissions should be addressed
to Carol Publishing Group, 600 Madison Avenue, New York,
N.Y. 10022

Carol Publishing Group books are available at special discounts
for bulk purchases, for sales promotions, fund raising, or educa-
tional purposes. Special editions can be created to specifications. For details contact: Special Sales Department, Carol
Publishing Group, 120 Enterprise Avenue, Secaucus, N.J.
07094

Designed by A. Christopher Simon

Manufactured in the United States of America
10 9 8 7 6 5 4 3 2 1

Library of Congress Cataloging-in-Publication Data

Howard, James, 1953-
    The complete films of Orson Welles / by James Howard.
        p. cm.
    "A Citadel Press book."
    ISBN 0-8065-1241-5
    1. Welles, Orson, 1915-1985. 2. Motion picture producers and
directors -- United States--Biography. 3. Actors--United States--
Biography. I. Title.
PN1998.3.W45H69   1991
791.43'0233'092--dc20   91-15920
                                                              CIP

This book is for Susie:
and Max, Charley, Buster, Daisy, Oscar, Kit,
Mickey, Betsy, Timmy, Pip and Tessy.

ACKNOWLEDGMENTS:

In researching this book, I owe a sincere debt of gratitude to the following individuals and organizations for their help, time, patience, and advice: Robert Arden, Frank Capra, Aaron Copland, Andrew Faulds, Sir John Gielgud, Gary Graver, Graham Greene, Charlton Heston, Gordon Jackson, Henry Jaglom, John McCallum, Michael Powell, Paul Scofield, Michael Winner.

Further contributions from some of those mentioned above were received too late for inclusion in the main body of the book. My thanks to Robert Arden for extra information concerning Orson Welles' work for BBC radio: "O.W. was an absolute master of the radio medium," says Mr. Arden. "And working on the two series . . . was an education in radio technique. The BBC would take two or three days to record a show. With Orson, we did two a day."

Gary Graver confirmed the current position concerning the unreleased films of Orson Welles: *The Other Side of the Wind* "is quietly resting in a vault in Hollywood." Shooting was completed, with "forty minutes edited by Orson Welles." Of *Don Quixote*, the film is again complete, though "sound and picture were not made into a composite release print."

It's All True exists as a twenty-minute documentary produced by Richard Wilson, available from the American Film Institute. "Paramount Pictures now owns the rest of the negative and it is a toss up between the Film Institute and Paramount regarding who will finish it," notes Mr. Graver. *The Deep*, or *Dead Calm*, is finished, even complete with promo trailer. "It may be shown in the future."

The major stumbling block with all of these projects—as was the case during Orson Welles' lifetime—is the lack of sufficient financing to complete and release the films. Mr. Graver writes, "From 1970, I worked with Orson Welles until his death. We made many projects. They were never publicized and are unknown to most people. Someday, I'll do a book on the last fifteen years."

I am also indebted to the Staff at the British Film Institute Library and Information Services; the BFI Stills and Poster Department, in particular Jane Byrne; Gill Gibbins and Barry Jafrato of W.H. Allen, Ltd., London; John Kobal, Dave Kent, and Martin Dives of the Kobal Collection, London; Tim Highsted of ICA, London; John Russell Taylor; World Famous Movie Stores, Manchester; Flashbacks, London.

And for permission to quote from sources:

An Open Book, the autobiography of John Huston, published by Macmillan. Reproduced by permission.

Vanity Will Get You Somewhere, the autobiography of Joseph Cotten, published by Avon Books.

An Actor and His Time, by John Gielgud, by kind permission of the author and UK publishers Sidgwick and Jackson Ltd.

Orson Welles, by Andre Bazin, published by Elm Tree Books.

The Actor's Life: Journals 1956–1976, by Charlton Heston, published by Penguin Books Ltd., by kind permission of Elaine Green Ltd., London and the author. Copyright © 1976, 1978 by Charlton Heston.

Also, Mr. Charlton Heston and the BBC for permission for quotes from the "Arena" special *The Orson Welles Story*, 1982, and a BBC Radio interview, 1985.

On the impossible subject of stills and illustrations, I am forever grateful to the British Film Institute. The publishers acknowledge the cooperation of the following production companies: Gate Theatre, Mercury Productions, RKO, International Rainbow Pictures, The Rank Organisation (*Ferry to Hong Kong, Return to Glennascaul*), British Film Institute (*Othello*), Twentieth Century-Fox, Warner Bros., Columbia, United Artists, Paramount, MGM, ORTF, CCC, Copernic, Cervantes Films, Janus Productions, London Films, Republic Pictures, British Lion, Universal Films, Lux Films, Rosa Film, Copernic, Cosmos, ITC, Mosfilm, Films la Boetie, Woodfall.

CONTENTS

THE COMPLETE FILMS OF

ORSON WELLES

Charlton Heston and
Orson Welles on the
set of *Touch of Evil*.

Robert Arden (left) with Welles
in a scene from *Mr. Arkadin*.

Michael Winner with Orson on the set of *I'll Never Forget What's 'Is Name* (1967).

ABOUT ORSON WELLES . . .

CHARLTON HESTON:

Orson was born a generation too soon. He was the first independent filmmaker in an era where there were no independent filmmakers. They gave him [in making *Citizen Kane*] freedoms that they were not to allow again for a generation, and in certain areas were never to allow again — Had he come along in 1960 I think he might well have had the richer career that his talents deserved.

— letter to the author, Beverly Hills, August 1989

ROBERT ARDEN:

For me, to have known Orson, to have worked with him, and to have maintained a friendship with him for thirty years is something that I will always be grateful for. He was a totally original creation — endowed with more gifts than any human has a right to expect or hope for. Unfortunately, among those gifts was a talent for self-destruction. Nobody suffered more than he from his own acts, but there can be no doubt that the modern cinema owes most of its grammar to the genius of Orson Welles.

— letter to the author, London, June 1989

Gordon Jackson, British stage and screen star who appeared in Orson's 1955 London stage production of *Moby Dick*.

11

MICHAEL WINNER:

Orson Welles was as nice and helpful an actor as I have ever worked with. He was kind and considerate to everybody. Responded very well to direction. Did not mind at all if his suggestions were not taken up. He was quite the kindest man I ever worked with.

— letter to the author, London, March 1990

GORDON JACKSON:

Needless to say I absolutely worshipped Orson — especially after *Kane* and *Ambersons*. A great genius of the cinema . . . He loved actors, and loved telling theatrical and film anecdotes. His note sessions on *Moby Dick* were like a cabaret act! Very entertaining!

— letter to the author, London, May 1989

Michael Powell, Britain's top director during the 1940s.

Orson Welles with close friend Henry Jaglom.

12

JOHN McCALLUM:

Orson had a brilliant streak, undoubtedly, but more gimmicky really, quirky. He was always thinking of effect; truth and reality came down the line. I got on well with him and quite enjoyed feeding his massive ego — it was so patently obvious it had a naïve charm . . . He was good company, even if his outpourings after a few drinks were all about himself! He had an obsession about makeup, especially noses — he hated his own little button of one. I sympathise now about all his efforts to raise money for films; I've been through it myself.

— letter to the author, Melbourne, Australia, March 1990

MICHAEL POWELL:

I only knew Orson in the way that two independent artists know each other, and recognise each other as both fighting for the same cause . . . When Orson came to London in those days of the forties and fifties, I met him . . . I saw, of course, his production of *Othello*, with the wonderful curtains that turned around and around, with exits and entrances. How commanding he was on the stage! How much he loved it!

— letter to the author, New York, June 1989

HENRY JAGLOM:

In the fifteen years I knew him, I'd say the two main lessons Orson taught me came early. The positive lesson was this: *Make movies for yourself.* "Make them as good as you can, so that you are satisfied, never compromising." . . . The negative lesson was simply this: *Never need Hollywood.* Never depend on *them* for your financing, for support, for your ability to make films . . . Co-existence cannot occur, as Orson's last two decades sadly showed. He needed them until the end, and they rejected him until the end. As a result, at least a half-dozen brilliant motion pictures never got made, and a magnificent artist could never get back to the canvas they had pulled from his reach.

— Article, "Lessons From Orson," reproduced by permission of Henry Jaglom

PAUL SCOFIELD:

I liked him. I wasn't bowled over by him but I recognised his authority and I sensed no one-upmanship. I did not feel in the presence of a mas-

Two giants of American cinema: Orson Welles with John Huston during the filming of *Moby Dick*.

ter, but I knew that he knew his limitations and I respected that.

— letter to the author, Sussex, April 1989

ANDREW FAULDS:

He wanted me to play Henry IV in the tour in Ireland of *Chimes at Midnight*. I think it was the thing I most regret in my career — I said "No." I'd just been offered some ghastly horror film that I was going to get £200 a week for, and I turned down the £30 a week to tour with him. Playing every night — not cutting and playing about as on a film — but actually playing on a stage with him would have been a marvellous opportunity. I've never regretted anything more.

— in conversation with the author, June 1990

JOHN HUSTON:

Orson has a wholly undeserved reputation for extravagance and unreliability . . . I have seen the way he works. He is a most economical filmmaker. Hollywood could well afford to imitate some of his methods . . . People are afraid of Orson. People who haven't his stamina, his force or his talent. Standing close to him, their own inadequacies show up all too clearly. They're afraid of being overwhelmed by him.

— from An Open Book, *reproduced by permission of the publishers, Macmillan Ltd.*

13

JEAN COCTEAU:

Orson Welles is a kind of giant with the look of a child, a tree filled with birds and shadow, a dog that has broken its chain and lies down in the flower beds, an active idler, a wise madman, an island surrounded by people, a pupil asleep in class, a strategist who pretends to be drunk when he wants to be left in peace . . . When I left Paris for New York, the morning of my departure Orson Welles sent me an automaton, an admirable white rabbit that could move its ears and play the drum . . . whenever an Oscar arrives from America, or in France I am awarded the little Victory of Samothrace, I think of Orson Welles' white rabbit as the Oscar of Oscars and as my true prize.

— *from* Orson Welles *by Andre Bazin,*
reproduced by permission

The boy Orson aged six with pet dog Caesar.

ORSON WELLES: THE CONFIDENCE OF IGNORANCE

"I started at the top and have been working my way down ever since."

The speaker may or may not have been Orson Welles concerning his own work in movies. As with so many aspects of Welles' extraordinary career(s), facts have become confused, tangled and lost over the years, perpetuated by an eager press who, it seems, were never more willing to "print the legend."

What stands unchallenged is that Orson Welles' very first movie, *Citizen Kane*, is consistently hailed as the best American film ever produced; yet almost as soon as it was completed, Hollywood was to deny him the freedom to create another like it. In a screen career stretching over forty-five years, Welles directed only twelve features — six of them in his first decade in Hollywood, appearing as actor in over seventy films, many frankly unworthy of his talents. Like Erich von Stroheim before him, Welles had been robbed of the basic materials with which to practice his art by the very people who, after his death in 1985, bemoaned the pitifully small catalogue of his work that remained.

On May 6, 1915, in Kenosha, Wisconsin, Beatrice Welles gave birth to her second son, to be named George Orson. A professional musician, Beatrice had married Richard Head Welles in the early years of the new century, eldest son Richard being born in 1905. Dick Welles Senior had been an inventor of small items, most successfully a bicycle and automobile lamp which he also manufactured before selling the entire business. An apparently unlikely couple, the Welleses' marriage came to an end when young Orson was six years old, the situation evidently not helped by the attentions of Dr. Maurice Bernstein who, when treating Mrs. Welles one day, claimed to have heard the eighteen-month-old youngest son exclaim, "It is the desire to take medicine that is one of the greatest features which distinguishes man from the animals!"

From then on, Dr. Bernstein was a familiar face at the Welles house, seemingly fascinated by mother and child alike.

This first legend concerning the child prodigy led to equally suspect stories. Orson's chosen bedtime reading was said to be Shakespeare's original

15

At sixteen, Welles set off for Ireland, soon to tread the boards of the Gate Theatre.

texts, Lamb's *Tales* having been rejected as inferior, with the boy reputedly giving a word-perfect rendition of *King Lear* at the age of nine.

In truth, Welles later dismissed most of these stories, despite the insistence of subsequent articles that he allowed them to stand unchallenged as a boost to his reputation. Nevertheless, he was undoubtedly a gifted child, a thoroughly accomplished pianist (largely through his mother's influence), and a stage performer at the age of five in *Samson and Delilah* and *Madama Butterfly* in Chicago, where the family had moved — followed by the ever present Dr. Bernstein.

The piano lessons ended abruptly with the death of Beatrice Welles shortly after Orson's ninth birthday. There then followed a somewhat undignified struggle between Dick Welles and Dr. Bernstein over the future education of the child, a compromise being reached when Orson was enrolled at the Todd School in Woodstock, Illinois. Elder brother Richard had already been expelled from the school, but Orson was to fare much better, striking a lasting friendship with tutor Roger "Skipper" Hill, who encouraged the boy's interests in Shakespeare and allowed him to produce successful school versions of *Richard III*, as well as other classics like *Dr. Jekyll and Mr. Hyde*.

Radio's highest paid unknown star.

In makeup as the young Charles Foster Kane.

The early Welles myth tells of one well-documented occasion where the Todd group was disqualified from a Chicago Drama League contest for allegedly hiring two professional actors for its version of *Androcles and the Lion*. Both parts had been performed by the fourteen-year-old Orson Welles.

One final reunion with his father took Orson on a trip to the Orient, but back in Chicago, Dick Welles died alone in a hotel room from heart and kidney failure, brought on by a serious drinking problem. Bernstein became Orson's legal guardian, although it was Roger Hill to whom the teenager turned for influence and guidance.

At sixteen, Orson left Todd and traveled alone to Ireland where he presented himself at the famous Gate Theatre as a member of New York's Theatre Guild, smoking his first cigar — bought earlier that day to make himself appear older — and claiming to be nineteen years old. Offered a role in the new production of *Jew Süss*, he was such a success that *The New York Times* hailed the young American as an overnight sensation. Gate directors Hilton Edwards and Micheal MacLiammoir retained Orson's services for the

remainder of the season. MacLiammoir later insisted that he had known immediately that Orson was only sixteen and an amateur. Welles however recalled that MacLiammoir was not even present at the theater on the occasion in question!

Returning to America, Welles rejoined the Todd School as drama coach, writing his first play, *Marching Song*. Although unproduced, this drama is significant for its subject matter and structure — an investigation into the life of a public figure (John Brown) from a number of different viewpoints.

A book followed: *Everybody's Shakespeare*, co-written with Roger Hill, became a standard reference for use in schools and colleges. Acting jobs, though, were harder to find until a chance encounter with playwright Thornton Wilder who recognized the "actor from Ireland." Wilder sent Orson to see Alexander Woollcott who in turn recommended him to Guthrie McClintic and Katharine Cornell. Such was the power of a recommmendation from Woollcott that Welles was engaged without an audition.

RKO star/director/producer/writer at the age of twenty-four.

In Rio shooting the ill-fated *It's All True* in 1942.

Dolores Del Rio, glamorous star of *Journey Into Fear* and Orson's companion during the early forties.

Nightlife in Rio.

A five-month tour with the Cornell company saw Orson receive fine notices — most notably for his Mercutio in *Romeo and Juliet*. Another spell at Todd followed, running a summer theater school during which he met the nineteen-year-old Virginia Nicolson, a Chicago debutante who was to appear in several of the group's productions as well as the four-minute home movie, *Hearts of Age*, shot one Sunday afternoon in 1934.

In November of that year, Welles married Virginia Nicolson, immediately rejoining the Cornell company for his New York debut, although losing his role of Mercutio to Brian Aherne. Instead, Orson took the lesser part of Tybalt, replacing Tyrone Power.

A second unproduced play — *Bright Lucifer* — was written about this time, though perhaps more important was Orson's meeting with John Houseman who, in mid-1935, was involved in the government's new Federal Theater Project, designed to give work to the countless unem-

Directing *The Stranger* in Hollywood.

ployed actors and theater people in New York. Highly impressed by Welles' performance in *Romeo and Juliet*, Houseman approached Orson backstage and shortly afterward asked him to become his partner under the Federal banner.

With a limited budget, the first Federal Theater production was to be *Macbeth* featuring an all-black cast. This "voodoo" production, complete with apparently authentic African witch doctors and drummers, caused a sensation, with traffic jams around the Harlem Theatre every night ensuring that the new company was a smash hit. As a reward, the company was moved to a new, larger theater — the Maxine Elliott — changing its name to *Project 891*.

The 891 group — attracting new, mainly

Columbia's top box-office star, lovely Rita Hayworth, at the time of her marriage to Orson Welles.

unknown actors — featured Arlene Francis and Joseph Cotten in its next play, *Horse Eats Hat*, a farce which ran into some minor censorship problems with the project's sponsors — the government — which found some scenes too suggestive.

Around this time, Welles was to be heard frequently on radio, although anonymously, playing anything from German politicians to newly born quintuplets! Orson quickly became one of the highest paid radio performers in New York, using much of his salary to finance his increasingly adventurous 891 productions, much to the Federal Theater's dismay as it saw its control over the group disappearing.

The Federal/891 partnership ended with a highly political piece by Marc Blitzstein, *The Cradle Will Rock*. Coming at a time when striking steel workers had been shot dead in Chicago, the play was strongly pro-union and was condemned by the government, which locked the company out of the theater on opening night. Welles and Houseman were sufficiently incensed by this action to lead their audience through the streets to another theater where, because of another ban by the Actors Union forbidding its members to appear on stage, the cast performed from among

Promoting *The Lady From Shanghai* with Rita.

the audience with writer Blitzstein — not an Equity member — explaining the story from the stage.

This signaled the end of the Federal involvement and, financed largely by Welles' continuing radio work which now included a starring role in a thriller series as "The Shadow," the Mercury Theatre was born in August 1937 with a stunning modern dress version of *Julius Caesar* subtitled *The Death of a Dictator* and clearly meant as a warning on the growing dangers of fascism in Europe.

This first billed "Production by Orson Welles" ensured that there was no doubt just who was responsible for the audacious adaptation of Shakespeare's play, which used military uniforms, fascist salutes and a lighting design modeled on the Nuremberg rallies. A press release prepared by Welles outlined the moral of their play: ". . . not assassination, but education of the masses, permanently removes dictatorships." The production was a huge commercial and critical success, with Brooks Atkinson of *The New York Times* hailing Orson Welles as ". . . theatrically brilliant and . . . an actor of remarkable cogency."

By the end of the first Mercury season, Orson

At one point in the mid forties, Orson considered giving up his screen career in favor of politics and public speaking.

In England in 1948 to discuss projects with Alexander Korda.

With Herbert Yates, head of Republic Pictures, who produced Orson's *Macbeth* in 1948.

Welles was the most talked about new star of the New York stage; his celebrity confirmed on the cover of *Time* magazine in May 1938, just a few days after his twenty-third birthday.

The fame of the Mercury Theatre, together with the continuing success of Orson's "Shadow" radio broadcasts, led to CBS offering the company a weekly radio slot under the title *First Person Singular*, with the proviso that Welles should write, direct, introduce and star in each program. The ten-week season opened on July 11 with *Dracula* and included *Treasure Island, The Thirty-Nine Steps* and *The Count of Monte Cristo*. A second season followed, renamed *The Mercury Theatre on the Air* and contracted for thirteen weeks, enthusiastically introduced each week as ". . . the unique series which signalizes radio's first presentation of a complete theatrical producing company."

The radio company included several non-Mercury players, including Agnes Moorehead, Ray Collins, and Orson's wife Virginia, billed as "Anna Stafford." With the busy theater season also running, it was impossible for Welles to perform all of the roles which CBS suggested, so John Houseman and Howard Koch became involved in the preparation of the broadcasts, which were then rewritten and directed by Welles. An important addition to the group was the brilliant composer/conductor Bernard Herrmann, head of the CBS Music Workshop, who contributed highly effective musical backgrounds to the shows, which included versions of *Jane Eyre, Sherlock Holmes, Oliver Twist* and, as a Halloween special on October 30, 1938, H.G. Wells' *The War of the Worlds*.

Destined to become perhaps the most famous — or infamous — broadcast of all time, *The War of the Worlds* had an effect on its listeners that is legendary. At this distance in time, there are many who consider that the reports were greatly exaggerated, but whatever the truth may have been, there is no doubt that CBS was bombarded with callers, and that the story hit the front page of *The New York Times* the following morning. Welles was even brought before the newsreel cameras to publicly apologize for his broadcast's success in scaring its audience out of their collective wits.

Suddenly big news, the Mercury show won itself a sponsor — Campbell Soups — and a new CBS contract, but more significantly, offers began to arrive from Hollywood for the young Orson Welles — still only twenty-three — to come out and make movies.

Welles had, in fact, already been approached by both Warner Bros. and MGM in 1937, making a screen test for Metro, but eventually turned both studios down. Fully occupied with his theater company, together with his radio work, Welles genuinely had no interest in making motion pictures. Now, though, the second Mercury theater season was in trouble. Two successive productions had failed badly, throwing the company into considerable debt. Undaunted, Welles chose to mount his most ambitious show yet — a joint venture with the Theatre Guild but produced by Welles, called *Five Kings*.

Adapted from five of Shakespeare's History plays, *Five Kings* was a huge production which inevitably ran into problems almost immediately. Once again the show closed sharply in debt, the Theatre Guild having withdrawn from the project during the run in Philadelphia.

At such a time, RKO-Radio Pictures held out an extraordinary offer. Convinced that the only way to work in movies would be as his own boss, Welles asked for "impossible" conditions in his contract with the studio to which, incredibly, it agreed. It was stated that Orson Welles would make two films as actor, director, producer, writer and star. RKO was to initially approve the subject matter whereupon a limited budget was to be made available to the unit, but from then on Welles would have complete and unlimited artistic freedom; even the RKO heads would not be allowed to view a single frame of film until being invited by Welles. Such things were unheard of in Hollywood.

Up until this point, one might say that Welles had led something of a charmed life. His childhood had been spent with a doting mother constantly encouraging her young son; there then followed the flattering if not entirely wholesome prospect of Dr. Bernstein and Dick Welles battling for control of the boy; the successful years at Todd were followed by his triumph in Dublin; making a name for himself in New York; his own theater company at twenty-two; Mercury's astonishing radio series; and now the most powerful contract ever awarded by a major Hollywood film studio.

All of these triumphs were achieved largely — as Welles later noted — by a form of innocence. If he could present himself at the Gate Theatre as a famous New York actor and be believed; if he could stage *The Cradle Will Rock* in defiance of the U.S. government; if he could improvise a performance from the stalls of a theater; if he could produce *Macbeth* with a cast of unknown black actors who had never even read Shakespeare before; if he could terrify a large section of the country with a single radio show — well then, why shouldn't Orson Welles demand the impossible from Hollywood and receive it? RKO was only too happy to allow him to make his movie exactly as he wanted.

Such a contract inevitably led to resentment from some Hollywood residents, most demonstrative of whom seemed to be the numerous supporting players. One — Guinn "Big Boy" Williams, a Warner Bros. character player featured in many Errol Flynn movies — cut off Welles' tie in the middle of Chasen's Restaurant. Just why this group should take such exception to Welles' presence is not entirely clear, but it is worth noting that many leading directors, including John Ford and King Vidor, were both helpful and genuinely encouraging toward the newcomer.

By now the Mercury radio series — renamed *Campbell Playhouse with Orson Welles* in honor of its sponsor — had ended. So, too, had Welles' marriage; a separation agreement in November 1939 gave Virginia custody of the couple's eighteen-month-old daughter Christopher, whose birth had prompted the memorable telegram from Welles to "Skipper" Hill: "Christopher, she is born."

With only his first movie to demand his attention, Orson began work on a screenplay of Joseph Conrad's *Heart of Darkness*, a story already performed as a Mercury radio play. With total control, Welles hired almost his entire Mercury staff to appear with him in the film. This would ensure that the unfriendly atmosphere in Hollywood did not interfere with filming, and in any case, the company worked genuinely well together. Hostility was still evident though, when RKO head George Schafer announced substantial pay cuts for studio staff but did not apply these to the Mercury unit.

Schafer was to be Welles' champion during his stay at RKO, often coming under fire from his own board for his ceaseless support of the as-yet untried director/star, whose initial comment on seeing the RKO lot was reportedly, "This is the most expensive train set a boy ever had." Such flippancy went down badly with businessmen who expected a more responsible approach from their employees.

After several false starts, however, *Heart of Darkness* was reluctantly abandoned, either because the budget could not be reduced by $50,000 as Welles later claimed, or due to the outbreak of the Second World War, which greatly

On set with a favorite director: Carol Reed and *The Third Man.*

restricted the European market for movies, particularly one dealing with a fanatical dictator-style leader controlling his own diabolical empire.

A short-lived second project, *The Smiler With a Knife*, based on a C. Day Lewis story, went the same way as *Heart of Darkness* following difficulties over casting, which provided yet further ammunition for Welles' critics and enemies in Hollywood. An article in *The Hollywood Reporter* snidely suggested that ". . . the Orson Welles deal will end up without Orson ever doing a picture there [RKO]."

A new project was raised — an original screenplay by Herman Mankiewicz and Orson Welles called *American*. Later renamed *Citizen Kane*, the story bore great similarities in construction to Orson's unproduced play *Marching Song*, examining the main character's life in flashback, drawing from several different viewpoints.

Despite the secrecy surrounding the set, news leaked out that *Citizen Kane* was little more than a thinly veiled attack on newspaper tycoon William Randolph Hearst, one of the most powerful men in America. Led by gossip columnist Louella Parsons, the Hearst press launched a fearsome assault on Welles, the Mercury company and RKO, with at one stage all studio advertising being banned by Hearst-owned newspapers. This was later relaxed, although ads for *Citizen Kane* were still refused. In addition, the film would never be mentioned, nor any of its stars by name. This even applied for several years afterward whenever any of *Kane*'s actors appeared in other movies.

In such an atmosphere, and with the other studios suggesting the film be scrapped, *Kane* received a limited release which inevitably made a loss for the studio of over $100,000, despite some excellent reviews hailing the film as ". . . the birth of a new art form," and ". . . among the screen's great achievements."

Given the reputation of *Citizen Kane* today, it may come as a shock to recall that the climate of the time led to the film, nominated in nine categories, winning only one Academy Award — for Best Original Screenplay shared between Orson Welles and Herman Mankiewicz.

To follow *Citizen Kane*, Welles considered Charles Dickens' *Pickwick Papers*, starring W.C. Fields, but when the star was unavailable turned instead to *The Magnificent Ambersons* from the Booth Tarkington novel.

The Mercury players had already performed the story on radio, but as another point of reference, Booth Tarkington was thought to have based the character of Eugene Morgan on his friend Dick Welles, Orson's father.

The Magnificent Ambersons was filmed under a new contract between Welles and RKO. The delays over the completion of the first Mercury film had effectively broken the remarkable agreement, so the new document again offered a limited budget, but Welles as director was no longer guaranteed the final cut of his film. At the time, this must have seemed a small concession to make, but as his first loss of authority in Hollywood, this was to cost Welles dearly in the coming months.

Shooting progressed at a painfully slow pace, further aggravated when several of the cast fell ill, causing further delays and taking the movie over its agreed budget, all of which again stacked up against Welles and his crew.

Even before *Ambersons* was completed, a third Mercury film went into production: *Journey Into Fear*, based on an Eric Ambler novel, with a screenplay by Welles and Joseph Cotten, who both acted in the film alongside the exotic star Dolores Del Rio. Orson's constant companion for the past year, Miss Del Rio, it was claimed, would marry Welles as soon as the film was completed. Norman Foster was to direct.

With two films in various stages of completion, Welles was approached by the government to fly to South America on a goodwill tour similar to those already undertaken by both Douglas Fairbanks, Jr., and Walt Disney. Welles was told to take a film crew and produce a movie as a gesture to consolidate relations between South America and the U.S., fearful of a rise in fascism at a critical point of the war.

Improvising a portmanteau film, to be called *It's All True*, Orson was away from Hollywood at what proved a crucial moment. RKO insisted that *The Magnificent Ambersons* should be released without waiting for Welles' return. A disastrous preview in Pomona, California, sealed its fate when George Schafer attended what he called "the worst night of my life."

Welles in South America eventually learned what was happening and frantically suggested cuts by a series of lengthy telegrams, but in the end, film editor Robert Wise was ordered to cut the film himself, also inserting several new scenes to alter the tone and ending of the movie, considered too "downbeat." Powerless and stranded in Rio, Welles could do nothing as even this new version was a flop with audiences.

Journey Into Fear also ran into trouble and was recut "by the studio janitor" according to Welles. The cool reception to both releases led to George Schafer's resignation from RKO with his replacement, Charles Koerner, recalling Welles from South America, canceling *It's All True*, and evicting the Mercury unit from the lot. The South American footage, largely consisting of color shots of the Rio carnival, was consigned to the vaults. Although Welles would attempt to resurrect the project over the next few years, the film was to be rediscovered forty years later in the studio vaults labeled "test footage."

It may not be entirely fanciful to speculate that Welles' downfall at RKO was partially engineered by those same figures who had resented his presence in Hollywood and his dazzling performance in *Citizen Kane*. Is it possible that *The Magnificent Ambersons* — even given Welles' original screenplay with its relentless disintegration of the Great American Family — could have provoked such open hostility merely on its own merits?

Ironically, the central theme of *Ambersons* — the young spoiled Georgie receiving his long overdue "comeuppance" — may well have found its equivalent in Hollywood's attitude toward the Mercury production. There were still many who considered Orson Welles an upstart and would have been delighted at him receiving his own "comeuppance" from the new regime at RKO.

Meanwhile, Orson's romance with Dolores Del Rio had ended — some said as a result of the reception given to *Journey Into Fear* — and the new woman in his life was the beautiful Rita Hayworth, then beginning to take steps toward major stardom. In mid-1942, she took a few hours off from filming *Cover Girl* at Columbia with Gene Kelly to become the second Mrs. Orson Welles, with Joseph Cotten as best man. This marriage produced another daughter, Rebecca, born in 1944.

The newlyweds toured Army bases with Orson's magic act, billed as "Orson the Magnificent," with "JoJo the Great" (Joseph Cotten) and "Calliope Aggie" (Agnes Moorehead). Rita also performed a mind-reading act and the highlight of the show was Orson's sawing Marlene Dietrich in half, as seen in a brief filmed sequence for Universal's *Follow the Boys*, an all-star morale booster of 1943.

Without a home studio and with the Mercury unit broken up, Orson accepted an offer from David O. Selznick to appear in *Jane Eyre* with Joan Fontaine. The film was to be directed by Robert Stevenson, although some claimed — not for the last time — that Welles took rather more than a mere acting role in the film.

Jane Eyre as a project was sold by Selznick to Twentieth Century-Fox and released in 1944 to fine reviews, reestablishing Welles as a star actor, which he consolidated with a part in a 1946 weepie, *Tomorrow Is Forever*.

Unable to find work as a director in Hollywood, Welles actually considered giving up filmmaking in favor of politics, having been an active campaigner for Roosevelt and giving a number of well received speeches, as well as writing a regular political column in the *New York Post*. Although it was suggested he should run for the Senate in his home state of Wisconsin, Welles finally pulled out, leaving the way clear for Joseph McCarthy to launch his own career — something on which Orson reflected many years later after McCarthy had instigated the notorious "witch trials" of the next decade.

Tomorrow Is Forever was however a box-office success, and Orson won a contract with International Pictures to direct a movie again. The result was *The Stranger*, a timely reminder of the latent threat of fascism even in peacetime. The film starred Loretta Young and Edward G. Robinson together with Welles himself. The director later claimed that *The Stranger* was merely an exercise in making as uncomplicated a picture as possible, and to prove that he "didn't glow in the dark."

A modest success, *The Stranger* was followed by a return to the theater for an impossibly extravagant musical production of Jules Verne's *Around the World in Eighty Days*, originally a co-production with Mike Todd who pulled out of the show at an early stage. Despite a score by Cole Porter, the show closed after only seventy-five performances, a financial disaster which would have far-reaching consequences over the next decade.

Back in 1946 however, and in return for desperately needed financial backing on *Around the World*, Welles reported to the Columbia lot to write and direct what had originally been envisaged as a quick, inexpensive picture in order to repay a debt to studio boss Harry Cohn.

At a 1946 rally to save Price Control.

The budget and status of the film grew considerably though when Rita Hayworth asked to costar with her husband in the picture, *The Lady From Shanghai*. Cohn was reportedly outraged when Rita's famous auburn hair was cropped short and dyed blonde for her role as *femme fatale* Elsa Bannister, and when the movie was finished, he declared it incomprehensible. Once again, the film was recut after Welles had left the studio. The Orson Welles-Rita Hayworth marriage broke up soon afterward.

With *Lady From Shanghai* another commercial failure — not helped by Columbia and Harry Cohn's attitude toward the film — Welles' reputation as a director was becoming more tarnished. Determined to prove that he could produce a movie quickly and cheaply, Welles' newly formed Mercury Theatre Company completed shooting a screen version of *Macbeth* in an astonishing twenty-one days. The film was financed by Republic studios, a "Poverty Row" outfit known chiefly for its stream of "B" westerns despite an

Harry Lime.

occasional major release directed by the likes of John Ford.

Meanwhile, Orson Welles filed his tax return for the year, claiming substantial financial losses for the failure of *Around the World in Eighty Days* which were unaccountably denied by the government. Faced with a huge tax bill and with the experimental *Macbeth* completed, Welles set off for Europe where several projects were discussed with Alexander Korda, though none ever materialized. Instead, Welles went to Rome and a film called *Black Magic* which he also codirected, though uncredited.

The association with Korda eventually proved fruitful with *The Third Man*, coproduced with David O. Selznick with a screenplay by Graham Greene and shot in Vienna with Joseph Cotten, Trevor Howard and Selznick's latest discovery, Alida Valli. Welles' performance in this picture — limited as it is to a mere ten minutes of screen time — is probably his most famous, more so even than Citizen Kane. A few years later, Welles recorded a BBC radio series *The Adventures of Harry Lime*, although the stories had no connection with *The Third Man*.

Most of his salary from *The Third Man* went toward his second Shakespeare film, *Othello*. Deciding that his only hope of retaining control over his films would be by financing them himself, Welles appeared in a variety of roles in other people's productions in order to raise the money to complete *Othello* in several locations across Europe. At that time, of course, he could not possibly have known that it would be a full three years before the film would be completed and released.

When *Othello* finally appeared, it was enthusiastically received, and awarded the Grand Prize at the 1952 Cannes Film Festival; this was in sharp contrast to the 1948 Festival when Welles had voluntarily withdrawn *Macbeth* from the competition, unwilling for it to be compared with Laurence Olivier's lavish and better financed *Hamlet*.

The success of *Othello* nevertheless failed to generate any new offers from Hollywood where Welles' insistence on providing his own finance was, perversely, considered something of an insult to the studio system. Instead, the next few years saw Orson lead a nomadic existence, filming in France, Yugoslavia and England, where he made his West End debut in a well-received stage production of *Othello*. On his brief return to

America, an acclaimed television performance in New York as King Lear again brought no further offers from Hollywood.

By 1955, Orson Welles had published two novels — *La Grosse Legume* and what was to be his next movie, *Mr. Arkadin*. It was shot in Spain, France and Germany, with leading roles going to the relatively unknown Robert Arden, who had worked on the *Harry Lime* radio series, Patricia Medina (Mrs. Joseph Cotten), and the Italian Countess di Girfalco who, making her film debut under the name of Paola Mori, appeared as Arkadin's daughter. The cast was filled out by stars Michael Redgrave, Gregoire Aslan, Katina Paxinou, Mischa Auer, Akim Tamiroff and Welles himself in the title role.

Such an exceptional cast, many making only cameo appearances, was compelling proof of the esteem in which Welles was held by his fellow performers. Such feeling was certainly mutual, as Robert Arden confirms: "He treated his actors with the greatest respect and consideration, at least as far as I was able to see during the few years in which we worked together."

Perhaps it was Orson's approach to the non-acting members of his crew which summed up his opinions of the filmmaking process. Since Gregg Toland had apparently told Welles during the early days of *Citizen Kane* that there was nothing about movies which he (Toland) could not teach him in three hours, Welles not surprisingly demanded the best from his technicians, often with the most remarkable results.

"I never saw him behave badly to any actor," says Robert Arden, "although he had little tolerance of technicians. He claimed that those that worked with machines [sound, camera, lights, etc.] created a mystique to cover the fact that the work was simple enough to those who gave it their total concentration. With actors, however, he felt that the creative process was a subtle thing, and it was a director's job to build an atmosphere in which an actor could function to his or her optimum."

Mr. Arkadin was, according to Welles, savagely cut by producers — more so than *The Magnificent Ambersons* — before release, and was not a commercial success. Known as *Confidential Report* in Britain, it was not handled well by its distributors and remains one of the least seen of all of Welles' movies.

Now resident in England, Welles opened a London stage production of *Moby Dick* with himself

as Captain Ahab among an otherwise British cast. Once again the production confirmed that Welles' imagination and creative energy were undiminished.

Gordon Jackson, Ishmael in the production, recalled: "He was very exciting to work with in the theater. His whole concept of the stage version of *Moby Dick* was quite breathtaking! Curtains of ropes unfurled from the flies, swaying around to give the impression of a ship at sea — with a ramp running out into the center of the audience, to represent the small boat we all clambered into, to get near and to harpoon Moby!"

As for Welles' performance as actor in the production, Michael Powell was among the audience, and wrote, "I saw him play Captain Ahab on the stage, and shall never forget how he grew before us, inch by inch, from an ordinary man into a monster, preparing to fight with another monster, Moby Dick."

Reviews were predictably mixed, as Gordon Jackson conceded: "Some nights he was *dreadful* — other nights he *soared* and was absolutely *bril-*

Gregory Arkadin.

liant! That to me is the hallmark of a *great* actor! Orson's definition of a 'ham actor' was an actor who gave the same performance every night!"

A planned film of the production was abandoned, at least partly due to John Huston's movie version then in preparation, for which Welles provided a memorable cameo performance as Father Mapple.

Welles married his screen "daughter" Paola Mori shortly after completing *Mr. Arkadin*, and Beatrice Welles, Orson's third daughter, was born in New York in November 1955, where a new stage production of *King Lear* proved an extraordinary experience. Welles managed to break both ankles in separate accidents on opening night, completing the run in a wheelchair. Reviews, though, were generally poor and the show closed quickly.

More appearances on American television, in a live production of Hecht-MacArthur's *Twentieth Century* and guesting on *I Love Lucy*, led to a promising arrangement with Desilu to direct a series of half-hour dramas. The pilot show, *Fountain of Youth*, was considered "too sophisticated and complicated" (!) for viewers and shelved until 1958 when, ironically, it won the George Foster Peabody Award for excellence.

After a seven-year absence, Orson Welles reached agreement with the Internal Revenue Service and finally returned to Hollywood moviemaking in 1957, appearing for producer Albert Zugsmith in *Man in the Shadow* (in Great Britain, *Pay the Devil*), with an offer of a featured role in Zugsmith's next picture, *Badge of Evil*.

Charlton Heston, fresh from completing *The Ten Commandments* for Cecil B. DeMille, was to be the star of *Badge of Evil*. When told that the film did not yet have a director, he successfully campaigned for Orson Welles to be assigned to the job with the result that the movie was virtually rewritten by Welles from its original source novel by Whit Masterson, becoming something more than the routine police thriller it had promised to be.

Universal, however, was cautious about allowing Welles too much freedom, though delighted at the speed with which Welles raced through the first few days of shooting. Upon the film's completion, though, the studio had cold feet about its tone, and set about recutting it, without reference to Welles, or to the pleas of stars Charlton Heston and Janet Leigh. The truncated version, renamed *Touch of Evil*, was not a success, marred by Universal's hesitant attitude toward its release.

With tales in Hollywood suggesting that Welles had again been unable to complete his picture, the next five years saw him appearing in largely indifferent movies, with a few notable exceptions – chiefly his towering performance as a Clarence Darrow figure in Darryl F. Zanuck's production of *Compulsion* in 1959.

At last a new Orson Welles movie was begun in 1962 when Alexander and Michael Salkind backed a production of Franz Kafka's *The Trial*. Shot in Yugoslavia and Paris, Welles' version of this enigmatic story starred Anthony Perkins as Josef K, and Orson himself, Jeanne Moreau and, inevitably, Akim Tamiroff.

A reworked stage version of the old Mercury play *Five Kings* opened in Belfast under the title of *Chimes at Midnight*, later moving to Dublin but closing before it crossed to the West End. Instead Orson found himself in London for what proved to be his final theatrical venture, directing Laurence Olivier in Ionesco's *Rhinoceros*, though this was evidently not a very happy experience.

More brief appearances in largely unremarkable screen fare were followed by a film version of *Chimes at Midnight*, a Spanish-Swiss coproduction filmed in Spain with a typically illustrious cast – Jeanne Moreau again, Fernando Rey, Margaret Rutherford and Sir John Gielgud, with Welles in perhaps his finest role as Sir John Falstaff.

Let down by financiers yet again, Welles finally completed *Chimes at Midnight* with his own money. The fulfillment of his *Five Kings* project, which had taken some twenty-five years to come to fruition, was to rightly remain a personal favorite among Welles' films.

Among the cast of *Chimes at Midnight* was British actor Andrew Faulds — today a successful Member of Parliament — who recalled one evening when he, Welles and three or four others retired to the hotel bar for a quick tequila, which developed as the evening progressed and broke up at midnight. Orson, "his cloak trailing from one shoulder on the floor, walked with great dignity towards the door," where he signed autographs for two members of the hotel staff, before leaving for his villa.

"We learned later that two or three miles up the road, he had to stop the car and was violently sick. The next morning, we all turned up with terrible hangovers. He was there on the set at 7:30 with absolutely no sign of that heavy, heavy night, and went straight into work. The physical strength . . . and strength of will, of the man."

Paola Mori as she appeared in *Mr. Arkadin*. The Countess di Girfalco became the third Mrs. Orson Welles soon afterward.

It was this determination which saw *Chimes at Midnight* through to completion. "I think that he was always very aware that he had to bring the film in somehow, as near within budget as he could," said Andrew Faulds, who experienced an example of Welles' single-mindedness on set one day: "A couple of Spanish girls made this phenomenally decorated cloak for John Gielgud, with the most marvellous needlework — a superb piece of craftsmanship, and they complained one day that they weren't getting paid."

"Rather foolishly" approaching Welles, Faulds recalled, "I mentioned that these poor women hadn't received a farthing in pay yet. Orson just said, 'Absolutely nothing to do with me. Raise it with the business manager.' He didn't want to know. I don't think it endeared me to him; I was bothering him with trivialities."

A distinguished role as Cardinal Wolsey in Fred Zinnemann's *A Man for All Seasons* again confirmed Welles' reputation as a formidable screen actor, only to be followed by the dismal *Casino Royale*.

Now living in Spain, Orson received an offer from French television to make a modest fifty-minute version of the Karen Blixen tale *The Immortal Story* starring Jeanne Moreau, who was to star in Welles' next project *The Deep/Dead*

Back in Hollywood for the first time in seven years to film *Man in the Shadow* at Universal, Orson meets James Stewart (filming *Night Passage*) and James Cagney (as Lon Chaney in *Man of a Thousand Faces*). All three were to be future recipients of the AFI Life Achievement Award.

Calm. The latter was shot in Yugoslavia entirely at Welles' own expense. The director also acted as cameraman, recruiting his old Todd mentor "Skipper" Hill to help out when Orson was acting in a scene. At the time of writing (1990), the film remains unreleased.

A 1970 book by Charles Higham, followed two years later by an extensive article by critic Pauline Kael, succeeded in giving rise to the unfounded and damaging theory that Welles was somehow afraid to finish his own movies and deliberately sabotaged them before release. This was supposedly due to some deep-rooted psychological fear of having his work compared to the stunning early success of *Citizen Kane*.

Such articles hurt Welles deeply, particularly as the available evidence makes clear the extraordinary efforts over the years to complete projects, beginning with *It's All True* in 1942. The non-completion of *The Deep*, and a version of *Don Quixote* — begun in the mid-1950s and continuing in fits and starts — was due entirely to difficulties in attracting backers rather than any conscious decision on Welles' part.

Those films which had been completed — *Othello, Mr. Arkadin* and *Chimes at Midnight* — owed their existence to Welles' unrelenting efforts against what must have often seemed impossible odds. Yet there had to be a limit to what even Orson Welles could achieve in such adverse circumstances.

More satisfying, though probably equally frustrating, a 1962 critics' poll in the influential *Sight and Sound* magazine had named *Citizen Kane* the Best Movie of All Time, where it was again to be found in its next vote a decade later.

Even in Hollywood, Orson Welles received an Honorary Academy Award in 1970 *"for superlative artistry and versatility in the creation of motion pictures."* This belated recognition from the American film colony may have given Welles cause for optimism, but perhaps wary of the situation, he did not attend the award ceremony, John Huston accepting the statuette on his behalf.

Another unreleased project followed: *The Other Side of the Wind*, starring Lilli Palmer and John Huston as an eminent film director unable to find the money to complete his latest movie! Welles insisted that the film was in no way autobiographical — one reason why he chose not to appear in it himself.

In reality, the situation was sadly similar, with finance drying up constantly. Back in Hollywood once again in 1975 — this time to receive the American Film Institute's third Life Achievement Award — Orson used the occasion to make an urgent plea to the community to put forward the cash to complete *The Other Side of the Wind*, showing two brief clips from the unfinished picture which ought to have achieved the required response. Despite some half-promises to help out, the project floundered, with further complications to follow. The existing print was confiscated by Iranian business interests, who claimed ownership after supplying some of the cash. Even with later developments, the film again remains unseen as of 1991.

What was to be the final completed Orson Welles movie had been released in 1973. *F for Fake* was a curio grown from television material on the art forger Elmyr de Hory and — by sublime coincidence — Clifford Irving, later revealed as the hoax author of Howard Hughes' "autobiography." An entertaining and brilliantly edited piece, *F for Fake* could never have been a commercial success, though Welles seemed genuinely surprised by its failure at the box office. According to Henry Jaglom, *F for Fake* was Orson's personal favorite among his films.

Much television work followed, including several guest spots on *The Dean Martin Show*, as well as numerous commercials which somehow had the effect of damaging his reputation, particularly outside the U.S., although Welles himself insisted that he saw nothing wrong in accepting work of this type, it being merely another acting job. Both Laurence Olivier and John Gielgud had made commercials for American television without attracting adverse comment.

Orson did however admit that he had not liked most of his films, although insisting that he had never accepted a role to which he objected on either moral or political grounds.

The 1980s began promisingly, with an extensive interview for BBC Television during which Welles revealed that he was hoping to start work on at least two new movies. He also planned to complete *Don Quixote*, despite the deaths some years earlier of its two stars. Weary of being questioned on its progress, he had now retitled his movie *When Are You Going to Finish Don Quixote*!

Alexander Salkind popped up again, offering Welles the chance to film a low-budget version of *King Lear* only for the deal to eventually fall through. A French TV offer to finance the film also floundered, despite the government's award to Orson of its highest civilian honor, the *Legion*

Marlene Dietrich and Orson Welles between takes of *Touch of Evil.* Both stars looked somewhat different in the film!

d'Honneur. More awards followed, including a Fellowship of the British Film Institute in 1984, but cut off from finance to make new movies, Welles sadly described himself as "an old Christmas tree whose roots have died."

Efforts to raise the $4 – 5 million to film *King Lear* from a number of Hollywood's top producers and filmmakers — many of them self-confessed admirers of Welles' work — proved fruitless, even at a time when an average movie budget was approaching the $20 million mark. A new original screenplay, *The Big Brass Ring*, to be the first venture of Weljag, the production partnership of Welles and Henry Jaglom, failed for want of a leading actor.

An intriguing project raised by an independent producer that Orson should direct a movie version of the events surrounding the Mercury's 1937 production of *The Cradle Will Rock* was considered a strong possibility, even to the extent of casting young English actor Rupert Everett in the role of the young Orson Welles.

Meanwhile, passing his seventieth birthday in May 1985, the real Orson Welles released a record called "I Know What It's Like to Be Young But You Don't Know What It's Like to Be Old" and

Orson directing *Touch of Evil*, his first American film in almost ten years.

made further appearances on television as himself — on shows like *The Merv Griffin Show* or introducing a special 1940s style episode of *Moonlighting*.

Possibly more active than for several years, with a number of projects including a television special in preparation, and still hopeful of finding a backer for his *King Lear*, Orson Welles died of a massive heart attack on October 9, 1985.

Much was written immediately of the so-called waste of his enormous talent, many writers crediting Welles with his own downfall. Old myths were repeated: Welles was extravagant, difficult, undisciplined, unreliable, temperamental, unable to finish his pictures. *The Times* of London wrote ". . . of his acting roles outside his own films, the less said the better," while of his thwarted plans to film *King Lear* it dismissively assumed ". . . as so often with Welles, the promise was unfulfilled."

Even in death, Orson Welles was to be the subject of yet more legal complications. Fully nineteen months elapsed before his youngest daughter Rebecca was able to bury her father's ashes as he had wished beneath an oak tree at the ranch of Welles' friend Antonio Ordonez near Ronda in southern Spain. Both Rita Hayworth and Paola Mori had died in the intervening months.

Of the unreleased films, a portion of edited

At the British Film Institute in the late fifties.

A typically ebullient Orson Welles filming *The Sailor From Gibraltar*.

Filming *A Man for All Seasons* (1966).

footage from *It's All True* was screened at the Directors Guild of America tribute to Welles shortly after his death, a Paramount executive announcing that they hoped to "do something" with it. Although Welles had always refused to show any of *Don Quixote* in public, some forty-five minutes of edited material was screened at the Cannes Festival of 1986, again with a vague promise of more to follow. Both *The Other Side of the Wind* and *The Deep* remain either incomplete or the subject of legal argument; neither has yet been screened commercially.

In a screen career lasting forty-five years, Orson Welles had directed only twelve features. Yet the very first of those movies has dominated international critics' polls ever since its release, while French critic Andre Bazin said, "If Orson Welles had only made *Citizen Kane*, *The Magnificent Ambersons* and *The Lady From Shanghai*, he would still deserve a prominent position on any filmmaker's Arch of Triumph."

The scarcity of Welles' directorial output is on the surface baffling, yet given the circumstances — the resentment and hostility he faced in Holly-

Orson Welles in the late sixties.

wood, that same community's failure to support his projects, the obstacles in trying to finance his movies himself — the wonder is that he should have achieved as much as he did. Given his early success, Welles ironically stated in his last screen appearance — Henry Jaglom's *Someone to Love*, released posthumously — that "happy endings depend on stopping the story before it's finished."

As an actor, Orson Welles has scarcely been seriously appreciated despite such magnificent performances as Kane, Harry Lime, Edward Rochester, Falstaff, Cardinal Wolsey, Othello and Jonathan Wilk in Richard Fleischer's *Compulsion*.

Significantly, in films which featured Welles prominently such as *Jane Eyre*, *The Third Man* and *Journey Into Fear*, the star often was cited by reviewers as having taken a secret hand in direction, although Orson consistently denied this. More likely, Welles' appearance in a substantial role created an "Orson Welles feel" to a movie; this would confirm his own comment on his screen persona as what French theater calls a "King Actor" — not necessarily the best per-

The keen magician in Henry Jaglom's *A Safe Place*.

1973 Welles in *The Southern Star*.

former but the most authoritative. Such a personality could dominate a film by his mere presence, making a lasting impression on the audience. Certainly no one ever accused Orson of directing such minor (from a Welles point of view) projects as *The VIPs* or *Casino Royale*.

Orson Welles saw filmmaking as a collaborative process, and it was with like-minded directors that he was happiest working. Carol Reed, Gregory Ratoff, Michael Winner and Fred Zinnemann were comfortable enough in their relations with Orson to invite suggestions, while others including Henry Hathaway and Richard Fleischer reportedly considered Welles difficult to work with, perhaps feeling their own position threatened in view of Welles' own illustrious directorial record.

In an age when the independent filmmaker was a rarity, Orson Welles was perhaps the most independent of them all. Fellow independent, and arguably the greatest of all British film directors, Michael Powell has written:

> Orson was one of those artists, whose very existence is important for all the rest of us smaller people. When he died, a piece of independence and respect for talent and love for the theatre died in all of us.

Francisco Riguera and Akim Tamiroff as the Don and Sancho Panza in Welles' legendary and as yet unreleased *Don Quixote*.

Orson's final screen role: "Danny's Friend" in Henry Jaglom's *Someone to Love*.

CITIZEN KANE: An opening shot from "The Best Film of All Time."

CITIZEN KANE

1941. RKO-RADIO PICTURES.
A MERCURY PRODUCTION.

Produced and Directed by Orson Welles.
Executive Producer: George J. Schafer. Screenplay: Herman J. Mankiewicz and Orson Welles. Director of Photography: Gregg Toland. Art Direction: Perry Ferguson. Music Score: Bernard Herrmann. Film Editors: Robert Wise and Mark Robson. Special Effects: Linwood G. Dunn. Sound Recording: James G. Stewart.
Running Time: 119 minutes.

CAST:

Orson Welles (*Charles Foster Kane*); Joseph Cotten (*Jedediah Leland*); Everett Sloane (*Bernstein*); Dorothy Comingore (*Susan Alexander/Kane*); Ruth Warrick (*Emily Norton Kane*); Agnes Moorehead (*Mary Kane*); Ray Collins (*James W. Gettys*); George Coulouris (*Walter Parks Thatcher*); Erskine Sanford (*Herbert Carter*); William Alland (*Jerry Thompson*); Harry Shannon (*Jim Kane*); Philip van Zandt (*Rawlston*); Paul Stewart (*Raymond*); Gus Schilling (*Head Waiter*); Fortunio Bonanova (*Matisti*); Buddy Swan (*Kane, aged 8*); Sonny Bupp (*Kane Jr.*); Georgia Backus (*Miss Anderson*). ALSO FEATURED: Richard Barr, Joan Blair, Al Eben, Charles Bennett, Milt Kibbee, Irving Mitchell, Arthur Kay, Herbert Corthell, Frances Neal, Ellen Lowe, Robert Dudley, Tudor Williams, Tom Curran, Benny Rubin, Edmund Cobb, Alan Ladd, Gino Corrado, Louise Currie, Walter Sande, Richard Wilson, Eddie Coke, Arthur O'Connell, Katherine Trosper.

CITIZEN KANE: Orson Welles' film debut as the dynamic young Kane.

SYNOPSIS:

When one of America's wealthiest and most powerful men, Charles Foster Kane, dies alone at his castle Xanadu, a cinema newsreel director sets out to discover the real man by tracing the significance of Kane's last word: "Rosebud."

Assigned to contact as many of Kane's associates as possible, newsreel reporter Jerry Thompson (William Alland) interviews the tycoon's oldest friend, his business manager and his second wife, and researches through the diaries of Kane's legal guardian for information on his childhood and early years. Each interview gives a differing account of the Kane they knew, and in a series of flashbacks, we learn Kane's life story:

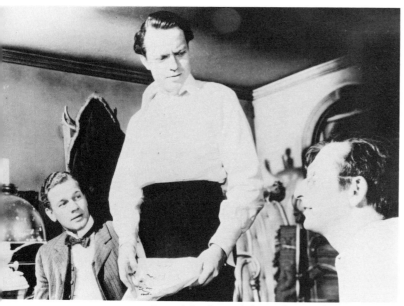

CITIZEN KANE: Stars of the classic: left to right, Joseph Cotten, Orson Welles and Everett Sloane.

Inheriting his fabulous wealth as a boy, Charles is taken away from his parents' run-down boarding house and raised in Chicago under the guidance of Mr. Thatcher (George Coulouris), a stern guardian who controls Charles until he reaches maturity and the full estate becomes his.

Coming of age, Kane (Orson Welles) decides — against the advice of Thatcher — to take control of a small Chicago newspaper from among his uncles' assets. With his college friends Bernstein (Everett Sloane) and Jedediah Leland (Joseph Cotten), he moves into the offices of the "Enquirer," evicting its aging editor and staff and attracting the top newsmen of the city by a combination of high ideals and top salaries. The "Enquirer" becomes the top selling newspaper in the city, with Kane a champion of the people and a much respected figure.

Kane's empire grows rapidly, with a network of radio stations and newspapers across the country. With power, though, comes corruption. A mar-

CITIZEN KANE: Kane rejects the advice of former guardian Thatcher (George Coulouris): "At this rate, I'll have to close this place in . . . sixty years."

riage to Emily Norton (Ruth Warrick), daughter of a senator and later president, disintegrates as Kane becomes more concerned with his own political ambitions. Seeking election as governor, he is thwarted when rival Jim Gettys (Ray Collins) exposes Kane's relationship with nightclub singer Susan Alexander (Dorothy Comingore).

Emily leaves Kane, taking their son with her, and shortly afterward, Susan becomes the second Mrs. Kane. Charles' attempts to promote Susan as an opera singer fail miserably when, presenting her at his own theater in a lavish production, the performance is a disaster. Finding a drunken Jedediah slumped over his typewriter, Kane fires his old friend, but completes the scathing review himself.

Retreating to his newly built mansion Xanadu, Kane becomes more isolated as his publishing network begins to diminish. Susan, frustrated and bored away from the lights of New York, attempts suicide before finally leaving Kane alone in his castle, surrounded by fawning servants and a vast collection of art treasures from across the globe, many still in their packing crates unopened.

So Kane dies unloved, a lonely old man, his money and power unable to halt his decline.

Preparing to leave Xanadu, Thompson tells his fellow reporters that he has been unable to discover who or what "Rosebud" was, but that in any case it probably would not have explained anything of Kane's life.

As the reporters leave, the job continues of clearing away the vast array of junk and articles accumulated by Kane over the years. In the basements beneath Xanadu, as the workmen plow through the mound of articles, the identity of "Rosebud" is finally revealed to the cinema audience, though not to the investigators.

CITIZEN KANE: Fledgling magnate Kane (Welles) flanked by Jedediah Leland (Joseph Cotten) and Bernstein (Everett Sloane).

NOTES:

There were many people in Hollywood secretly delighted when Orson Welles had still not begun his first movie after twelve months at RKO. Others were not so subdued in voicing their opinions that the boy wonder who had been given such a free hand by the studio was going to fall flat on his face.

Citizen Kane began life as *American*. Controversy was later to rage over who supplied the initial suggestion for the script. Efforts to discredit Welles claimed that the driving force behind the story was Herman Mankiewicz, who received screen credit as cowriter. Many years afterward, Welles told a French reporter that the full credit should also have included John Houseman and Joseph Cotten.

Whatever the actual detail over who-wrote-what, the format of *Kane* is highly similar to that used in Welles' own unproduced play *Marching Song*, written six years earlier. Both used the device of investigating a prominent figure through the testimony of his friends and associates. Originally this was to be of a far more clearly defined nature — more like *Rashomon*, Welles later said. Kane was to be either lovable or totally hateful, depending on how the speaker felt about him. This idea faded though as Kane himself took shape during filming.

Filming began in June 1941, with Welles and his Mercury players being guided through their first few days by the brilliant cameraman Gregg Toland. It had indeed been a happy day when Toland arrived at the RKO Studios and told Welles, "I want to make your movie."

A vital addition to the Mercury unit, Toland was the top cinematographer in Hollywood at that time, having just won an Academy Award for his work on Goldwyn's *Wuthering Heights*. Beginning his career at the age of twelve with the Fox company, he had quickly learned his craft as a cameraman, working almost exclusively for the Goldwyn company from 1926 onward. His work during the 1930s had gained him increasing recognition and admiration for its use of expressionistic lighting and deep-focus photography on films like *Mad Love*, *The Grapes of Wrath* and *The Long Voyage Home*.

Toland seized the opportunity to work with Orson Welles — an "innocent" with whom he could explore new techniques without the need to please his front office or to conform to estab-

CITIZEN KANE: Head of an empire: Charles Foster Kane.

40

CITIZEN KANE: Kane's first meeting with Susan Alexander (Dorothy Comingore).

CITIZEN KANE: Kane the middle-aged tycoon.

lished working methods. In spite of his success, Toland told Welles, he was becoming bored with most of the pictures he was making, and felt that the Mercury production would be something different.

Despite later work including *The Best Years of Our Lives*, it is for his remarkable effects on *Citizen Kane* that Toland is best remembered. He died in 1948 from heart disease at the tragically early age of forty-four.

Claiming that they were only shooting "tests," the group managed to steal a few extra days on the strictly limited shooting schedule, so that when RKO finally realized what was going on, a number of actual scenes had already been shot which appeared in the final version of the film.

Toland was as good as his word, and constantly delighted Welles and his players with remarkable effects and stunning lighting designs. Aided by the art direction of Perry Ferguson, the picture was indeed promising to be something quite out of the ordinary.

In other departments, too, the making of *Citizen Kane* was breaking new ground. In a lengthy article for *The New York Times*, composer Bernard Herrmann confessed his doubts about coming to Hollywood where he felt convinced that music would be sacrificed to the demands of dialogue and sound effects. Orson Welles, however, had carefully chosen Herrmann to produce exactly the type of score the film needed. Long discussions were held between the composer and director, with Herrmann writing his score reel by reel as the shooting progressed, each piece being performed precisely as written and intended. In fact, some sections of the film — most notably the breakfast table scene between Kane and his first wife — were edited to fit in with Herrmann's pre-written score — the reverse of the usual practice.

As a radio performer, Welles was keenly aware of the use of dialogue and effects, with constantly overlapping speeches and often half-sentences of a type unheard of in a motion picture. According to John Houseman, the RKO staff was somewhat bemused by the care with which Welles' sound crew set about recording the film, although this undoubtedly gave the picture something of a "radio feel." French critic and director François Truffaut was later to observe that ". . . Orson Welles' films also make marvelous radio broadcasts; I have verified this by recording all of them on cassettes which I listen to in my bathroom with ever renewed delight."

CITIZEN KANE: Well-composed scene showing the much discussed ceilinged sets for *Kane*: breakfast with first wife Emily (Ruth Warrick). *"Your only correspondent is* The Enquirer."

Dispensing with a conventional opening credit sequence, as a brilliantly original and personalized coda to the movie, Welles himself introduced his players to the cinema audience at the end of the movie in a superb closing credit sequence which again harked back to the Mercury's radio broadcasts.

An integral feature of the film also involved the principal casting: with a few exceptions, all were new faces to the cinema screen, being drawn largely from the Mercury radio and theater com-panies. The euphoria of an inexperienced (in screen terms) cast creating their first movie together seems to have allayed any doubts and fears over the group's ability to come up with a completed film.

Of the non-Mercury players, Dorothy Comingore was to play the key role of Susan Alexander, Kane's second wife. Although she was discovered by Charlie Chaplin, Miss Comingore's career had been in the doldrums, previous screen appearances being mainly walk-ons. Achieving the

CITIZEN KANE: Kane for governor.

CITIZEN KANE: After the campaign speech, Emily tells Kane she knows of his affair with Susan.

unique position of being "discovered" by TWO great directors, Miss Comingore met Orson Welles at a party and was immediately cast for the role.

Joseph Cotten later recalled in his autobiography *Vanity Will Get You Somewhere* the innocent approach adopted during shooting: "Orson and I decided we would wait until the end of the day to shoot the scene where I got drunk and told my old friend Kane just what I thought of him. He worked me the entire day on the other scenes and then, very late at night when fatigue had obviously set in, he said, 'Now get ready for your drunk scene.'

"Throughout the night, we shot that scene. It is my favorite scene in the picture, at least my favorite scene of which I was a part. It turned out that extreme fatigue and drunkenness are very similar in effect. Thank goodness the former is somewhat easier to control. The unintentional verbal slip of 'dramatic *crimitism*' for 'dramatic *criticism*' was left in the final version."

The problem over the similarities between the fictional Charles Foster Kane and the real-life tycoon William Randolph Hearst were much harder to control. As one of the wealthiest and

CITIZEN KANE: Kane's political ambition crumbles along with his marriage, with Ray Collins, Dorothy Comingore and Ruth Warrick.

CITIZEN KANE: Bernstein
(Everett Sloane) prepares the
election front page: "Fraud
At Polls."

46

most powerful men in America, Hearst was in a position to cause serious damage to anyone to whom he took an exception. For this reason, Welles and his team insisted that Hearst was not the target of *Citizen Kane*, though it is blatantly obvious that the similarities were too abundant to be mere coincidence.

Like Charles Foster Kane, Hearst had inherited enormous wealth at an early age, had taken control of a small newspaper, the *San Francisco Examiner*, from his father's estate, and then built up a huge publishing empire across the country. His methods were open to question: allegedly his newspapers employed men to "persuade" stands to take Hearst papers over other titles. Hearst it was who, in a ratings war with a rival sheet, introduced a comic strip called "The Yellow Kid." Thus was born "the yellow press" — a byword for scare headlines and sensationalized articles. Hearst evidently boasted that he had sold more papers with his scandalous and prejudiced reporting of the Roscoe "Fatty" Arbuckle case in the early 1920s than since America entered the First World War.

Following Hearst's death in 1951, the *Manchester Guardian* commented that "No man has ever done so much to debase the standards of journalism." In 1898, artist Frederic Remington, dispatched to Havana following the sinking of a U.S. battleship, reported to Hearst that he was on his way home since there was no story to cover. The xenophobic Hearst immediately replied, "Please remain. You furnish the pictures and I'll furnish the war." Months later, during which time the Hearst press had carefully nurtured an open hostility toward Spain, a conflict was brought about between the two nations.

On another occasion, Hearst's mother was approached concerning her son's desperate struggle with a rival publisher, said to be costing him a million dollars a year. She coolly observed that he would only be able to continue "for another thirty years." Both of these incidents were included almost verbatim in *Citizen Kane*.

Hearst's retreat at San Simeon, high in the California hills, was clearly the model for Xanadu. Existing newsreels of the opulent palace, with its own private zoo and a vast collection of art treasures, is remarkably similar to the equivalent newsreel in *Kane*. Here he entertained the famous together with his mistress Marion Davies, a popular silent movie comedienne whose hits had included *Show People* for King Vidor. Hearst, however, began to press for more serious roles for Miss Davies, with the result that her career faltered badly and never fully recovered. Although still married, Hearst lived openly with Marion, though such was his influence that no reporter dared ever make mention of the fact.

Susan Alexander was a greatly exaggerated version of Marion Davies, and it is said that it was chiefly for her sake that Hearst took strong exception to the film. Many years later, Orson Welles would express some regret over their treatment of Miss Davies, finally admitting that Hearst had been the target of the picture.

Back in 1941, though, reaction was largely against RKO and Mercury, with Louella Parsons — a Hearst columnist — demanding the cancellation of the film. All RKO advertising was refused and none of its movies was to be mentioned in the pages of a Hearst publication. Only by claiming that Hearst was not the subject of the film could Welles hope to escape the wrath of Miss Parsons and her cohorts.

Hearst's own political ambitions had floundered, though in somewhat more dramatic style than Kane's. It was claimed that his rivals had stolen election boxes containing Hearst votes and dumped them in the river, thereby ensuring he would not be elected. An earlier version of the *Kane* script had used this same incident, which was later dropped, as were several other more blatant references which could only have derived from Hearst's story.

Amazingly, Welles did manage to convince the top executives from the other major studios in Hollywood — gathered to demand that RKO cancel the project in case it damaged their own interests — that the film depicted an amalgam of several public figures. So persuasive was he that they agreed that the film should be released as planned; this at a time when one columnist was dining out on the "joke" that "Orson Welles has signed for two more films — one NOT to be shown in 1941 and one NOT to be shown in 1942."

Welles had already contemplated legal action against RKO if it failed to release his film, but George Schafer was adamant that the release should go ahead. In any event, Radio City Music Hall, the studio's New York showcase for its "A" product, declined to show the film, which instead had its world premiere at RKO's Palace Theatre on Broadway — although, of course, New Yorkers who read only the local Hearst paper would never have known this.

Critical reaction was largely favorable, but with

CITIZEN KANE: Four faces of Orson Welles in his Oscar nominated performance as Charles Foster Kane.

48

many theater chains deciding not to screen the picture, it inevitably made a loss to the studio of over $100,000. Many theaters in fact bought the film as part of a "Block Booking" arrangement with the studio, but then declined to screen it.

Toward the end of 1941, the New York Film Critics and the National Board of Review voted *Kane* best picture of the year. Further honors seemed assured when the film received nine Academy Award nominations: as Best Film, Actor (Orson Welles), Director, Screenplay, Cinematography, Art Direction, Music Score, Editing and Sound Recording.

Ultimately, only the screenplay won the Oscar, shared between Welles and Mankiewicz. This in turn led to another attempted slur on Orson when it was suggested that the screenplay had been the work of Mankiewicz alone and that Welles was claiming the work as his own.

Variety reported that resentment by screen extras toward Welles had resulted in block voting against him both as Actor and Director, losing to Gary Cooper (*Sergeant York*) and John Ford (*How Green Was My Valley*) respectively, the Ford effort also scooping Best Picture.

Even the brilliant technical effects in the film were passed over, including the stunning work of Gregg Toland and the incisive editing of Robert Wise and Mark Robson (both later to become leading directors in their own right). The innovative score by Bernard Herrmann could perhaps claim a moral victory, since it was beaten into runner-up position by Herrmann's own score to another RKO picture, *All That Money Can Buy*.

With the initial release a financial flop, RKO dispatched the film to the vaults, where it remained largely forgotten until the mid-1950s when the RKO catalogue was sold to television. Art houses had been screening the movie from time to time, but its reputation was slight until it suddenly found a new audience on the small screen. This prompted a rerelease by the studio, with the critic for the London *Evening News* writing in 1952, "*Citizen Kane* turns up at the Everyman Hampstead next Monday . . . I inspected it again last week and came away marvelling."

Suddenly, the status of the film grew at an extraordinary rate, so that when the influential magazine *Sight and Sound* held its ten-yearly poll in 1962, *Citizen Kane* was voted Best Film of All Time by a group of international critics, although in the 1952 poll it had only squeezed in as one of the runners-up, outside the first ten. The 1972 poll reaffirmed *Kane's* position, as did the most recent to date (1982).

Today constantly exalted as "The Best Movie Ever Made," the debut feature of Orson Welles has far outstripped all of his later work in critical terms, and is allegedly the most written about and most studied film in American colleges and universities, where it has become a symbol of filmmaking *par excellence*.

All the more disturbing then that a November 1988 report should confirm that, despite massive protests, Ted Turner of Turner Entertainment had authorized the "colorization" of *Citizen Kane* for video and television release. Welles apparently had the last laugh on the matter when it was revealed sometime later that an obscure clause in his RKO contract precluded any future tampering with the film, making *Citizen Kane* effectively untouchable to Turner's colorizers.

In September 1989, *Citizen Kane* was included in the initial group of twenty-five American films chosen by the National Film Preservation Board of the Library of Congress to be placed on the newly created National Film Registry as "culturally, historically and esthetically significant."

As a footnote, in the early 1980s a television documentary took a rare look at the life style of William Randolph Hearst, with footage of the mass of art treasures accumulated by the tycoon during his lifetime. Entitled *Mr. Hearst and Mr. Kane*, the film was narrated by Orson Welles.

REVIEWS:

Citizen Kane is far and away the most surprising and cinematically exciting motion picture to have been seen here in many a moon. As a matter of fact, it comes close to being the most sensational film ever made in Hollywood . . . Mr. Welles has put upon the screen a motion picture that really moves . . . We would, indeed, like to say as many nice things as possible about everything else in this film — about the excellent direction of Mr. Welles, about the sure and penetrating performances of literally every member of the cast, and about the stunning manner in which the music of Bernard Herrmann has been used. Space, unfortunately, is short. All we can say, in conclusion, is that you shouldn't miss this film. It is cynical, ironic, sometimes oppressive and as realistic as a slap. But it has more vitality than fifteen other films we could name.

— Bosley Crowther, *The New York Times*

CITIZEN KANE: *Kane's* premiere at the RKO Palace in New York following Radio City Music Hall's Hearst-influenced refusal to exhibit the film.

The objection of Mr. Hearst, who founded a publishing empire on sensationalism, is ironic. For to most of the several hundred people who have seen the film at private screenings, *Citizen Kane* is the most sensational product of the U.S. movie industry. It has found important new techniques in picture-making and story telling. Artful and artfully artless, it is not afraid to say the same thing twice, if twice-telling reveals a fourfold truth . . . It is a work of art created by grown people for grown people . . . So sharply does *Citizen Kane* veer from cinema cliché, it hardly seems like a movie.
— *Time* Magazine

Probably the most exciting film that has come out of Hollywood for twenty-five years. I am not sure it isn't the most exciting film that has ever come out of anywhere.
— *C. A. Lejeune*

Orson Welles directs and takes the chief part, with the support of his own company, the Mercury Players of New York. He knows what he is up to with a vengeance. I urge everyone to see this brilliant, drastic, imaginative and rather terrifying film.
— *Evening Standard*

It is a tale, not a drama, a collection of greater and lesser character studies, vastly gilded, super-

50

splendid, amazingly devoid of glamour, embittered to poignancy with scepticism, empty of sympathy, sharp with sequences of interest — in total, a job of intensely graphic vivisection of a hypothesis. — *Motion Picture Herald*

A quite good film which tries to run the psychological essay in harness with the detective thriller, and doesn't quite succeed.

— *James Agate*

CITIZEN KANE: 1975 record release of Bernard Herrmann's superb score to the film.

THE MAGNIFICENT AMBERSONS

1942. RKO-RADIO PICTURES. A MERCURY PRODUCTION.

Produced and Directed by Orson Welles.
Executive Producer: George J. Schafer. Screenplay: Orson Welles from the novel by Booth Tarkington.

Director of Photography: Stanley Cortez. Art Director: Mark-Lee Kirk. Music Score: Bernard Herrmann (uncredited). Film Editor: Robert Wise. Running Time: 88 minutes (originally 131 minutes).

CAST:

Joseph Cotten (*Eugene Morgan*); Agnes Moorehead (*Fanny Minafer*); Dolores Costello (*Isabel Amberson Minafer*); Ray Collins (*Jack Amberson*); Tim Holt (*George Amberson Minafer*); Anne Baxter (*Lucy Morgan*); Richard Bennett (*Major Amberson*); Don Dillaway (*Wilbur Minafer*); Erskine Sanford (*Roger Bronson*); Gus Schilling (*Drugstore Attendant*); Charles Phipps (*Uncle John*); J. Louis Johnson (*Sam*); Orson Welles (*Narrator*). ALSO FEATURED: Dorothy Vaughan, Elmer Jerome, Anne O'Neal, Georgia Backus, Mel Ford, Lillian Nicholson, Bobby Cooper, Jack Baxley, Henry Roquemore, Bob Pittard, Kathryn Sheldon, Olive Ball, John Elliott, Hilda Plowright, Lew Kelly, Ed Howard, Jack Santoro, Heenan Elliott, Nina Guilbert, William Blees, Billy Elmer, Maynard Holmes, Drew Roddy, John Maguire, Nancy Gates, James Westerfield.

SYNOPSIS:

During the closing years of the nineteenth century, the young Eugene Morgan (Joseph Cotten) is thwarted in his love for the beautiful Isabel Amberson (Dolores Costello) when he disgraces himself one evening outside the Amberson mansion. The proud and powerful family disapprove of his college antics, and Isabel eventually marries the dependable but dull Wilbur Minafer (Donald Dillaway).

Many years later, Eugene returns to his hometown a successful inventor, manufacturing the new automobile bearing his name. Now a widower, he brings his daughter Lucy (Anne Baxter) to live in the place where he was born. At a grand ball at the Amberson house, Eugene renews his acquaintance with the Amberson family.

Isabel's spoiled young son George (Tim Holt) immediately takes a dislike to Eugene, who is paying a great deal of attention to his mother. Unaware of who this man is, George becomes interested in Lucy and arranges to see her again but continues to criticize Eugene when he is invited to dinner by the family.

When Wilbur Minafer dies, Eugene begins to spend more time with Isabel, and her spinster sister Fanny (Agnes Moorehead), much to the disapproval of George, who engineers to drive him away. When Major Amberson (Richard Bennett) dies, and Uncle Jack (Ray Collins) moves away, Isabel is herself struck down and, prevented from

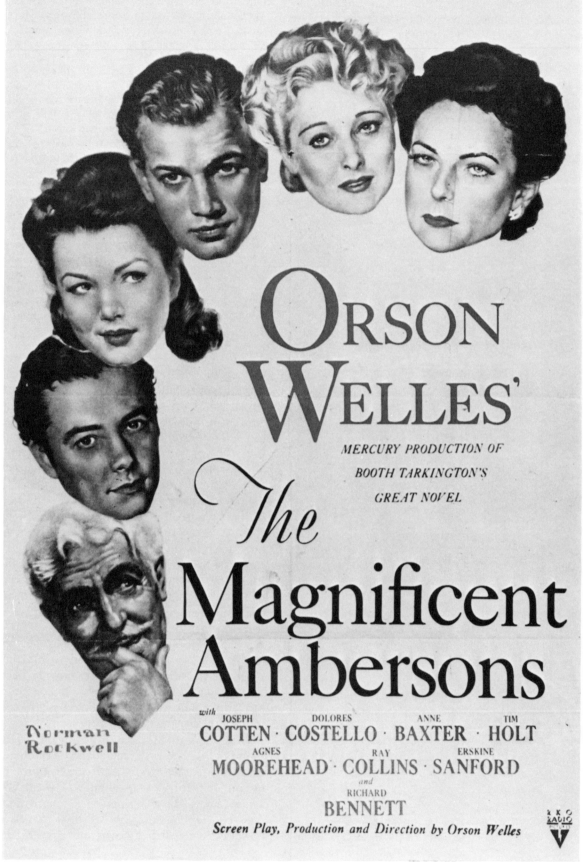

FROM THE MAN WHO MADE "THE BEST PICTURE OF 1941"

ORSON WELLES'

MERCURY PRODUCTION OF BOOTH TARKINGTON'S GREAT NOVEL

The Magnificent Ambersons

Norman Rockwell

with JOSEPH COTTEN · DOLORES COSTELLO · ANNE BAXTER · TIM HOLT

AGNES MOOREHEAD · RAY COLLINS · ERSKINE SANFORD

and RICHARD BENNETT

Screen Play, Production and Direction by Orson Welles

RKO RADIO

seeing Eugene by George's orders, she dies also.

George's life has been one of constant luxury and self-conceit; so much so that the whole town lives in hope of some day seeing him get his "comeuppance." With the death of his mother and the breaking up of the household, this finally happens, when it becomes clear that neither he nor Fanny has enough money to enable them to remain in the Amberson mansion.

The eagerly awaited fall of George Amberson Minafer passes almost unnoticed by the townsfolk, the once magnificent Ambersons now a fallen and forgotten family.

Moving to a cheap boarding house, George is forced to accept menial work in order to support his aunt and himself, but is seriously injured in a road accident — ironically knocked down by one of the very automobiles made by Eugene's company, and which George had labeled "a useless nuisance."

George and Eugene are finally reconciled, and during a hospital visit, Eugene confides to Fanny that he feels at last close to Isabel, his true love.

NOTES:

To follow up *Citizen Kane*, Orson Welles considered a number of projects; chiefly he had hoped to film Dickens' *Pickwick Papers* with W.C. Fields, but this idea fell through when Fields was unavailable. Various other stories were looked over, until Welles decided on Booth Tarkington's *The Magnificent Ambersons*.

Previously filmed in a silent version in 1925 under the title *Pampered Youth*, the story had already been performed by the Mercury radio company, with Walter Huston as Eugene Morgan and Welles himself in the role of George. An added attraction for Orson was that Tarkington had been a friend of his father and was said to have based the character of Eugene on Dick Welles, who also made a success of manufacturing for automobiles, though in a considerably smaller way.

By this time it was almost two years since he had first signed his contract with RKO, so Welles was obliged to negotiate a new deal, as the original document had called for two pictures within two years. The new conditions again gave the Mercury group a limited budget and artistic freedom, but RKO retained the right to the final cut of the movie.

Once again, Welles' cast was largely made of his Mercury group, though with some surprises:

Dolores Costello, silent star and former wife of John Barrymore, had not appeared on the screen in several years. More interestingly though were the two young leads: Anne Baxter, whose first major role this was, and Tim Holt in the pivotal role of George Minafer.

Having chosen not to appear in the film himself, Welles picked Holt after seeing him in John Ford's *Stagecoach*. The son of western star Jack Holt, Tim seemed to be following very much in the hoofprints left by his father, with a series of low-budget westerns already behind him. *The Magnificent Ambersons* was a complete departure for him, and he gave a fine performance in the picture. His later career would however see him revert to "B" westerns for RKO with one glorious exception in John Huston's 1948 *The Treasure of the Sierra Madre*.

Crucially, Gregg Toland was unable to work on the film, having been recalled by the Goldwyn studio, so Stanley Cortez — brother of the screen actor Ricardo Cortez — was selected to film *Ambersons*.

Cortez since 1937 had worked mainly on low-budget "B" pictures, and although he achieved some remarkable results on *Ambersons*, Welles felt that his work was slow — which, by comparison to the exceptional Toland, it probably was. Nevertheless, it was his work on this film that established Cortez' reputation and made him first choice when Charles Laughton directed his only feature — the remarkable *Night of the Hunter* in 1955.

Ambersons fell behind schedule. In addition, the cost of set construction was also soaring. Welles insisted on absolute perfection in the look of his movie and, possibly due to his years on radio where the sets were all in the minds of the listener, it is just conceivable that he did not realize just how expensive movie sets were to build.

Further problems arose when members of the cast began to fall ill. For authenticity, some scenes had been filmed in a huge icehouse where the opening sequences of Frank Capra's *Lost Horizon* had also been shot. In the sub-zero temperatures, Ray Collins contracted a case of pneumonia which seriously disrupted shooting, as did later illnesses which befell Anne Baxter and Agnes Moorehead. A final budget of the film was set at just over $800,000.

With shooting completed on *The Magnificent Ambersons*, Orson Welles was sent by the U.S. government to South America to make a movie as a gesture of goodwill and to cement relations between the Western Hemisphere neighbors against the rise of fascism. Welles set off for Rio, leaving his film to be cut and released on his return. RKO chiefs however grew impatient, and George Schafer was forced into previewing a rough 131-minute cut of the movie at Pomona in California, which he later described as the worst experience in all his twenty-eight years in the film industry.

Quite how serious was audience reaction seems to be divided. Schafer was appalled at the preview, as people left the theater throughout the screening. Robert Wise said that the audience laughed at some scenes, while one celebrated preview card claimed the film was like getting "one sock on the jaw after another for two hours." Peter Bogdanovich claims that the cards were far from all bad, with perhaps twenty favorable reactions including one suggesting that *The Magnificent Ambersons* was the greatest movie ever made.

It was decided that the original version of *Ambersons* was too "downbeat," with the disintegration of the family occurring quickly and relentlessly. Orson Welles had produced a highly disturbing film; a bleak look at human values and behavior, which its initial audience found unacceptable. A final scene between Eugene and Fanny in her room at a dilapidated boarding house, which Welles later claimed to be the very essence of the movie, was ordered removed.

Stranded in Rio, Welles sent detailed instructions by telegram for changes to the film, having learned of the preview reaction. At RKO, meanwhile, Schafer's position was seriously weakened when a new regime threatened to take over the studio. Plans for a copy of the film to be flown to Rio where Welles could cut it fell through due to the difficulties of wartime transport. Another print shipped to Rio went astray, and Robert Wise was ordered to edit the footage without waiting for Welles to return and, if necessary, shoot new scenes.

In all, some forty-three minutes were removed, with many scenes — originally long takes and sweeping camera movements around the Amberson mansion, particularly in the ball sequence — being shortened and some cut altogether. What Welles had intended to be the epic tale of the downfall of a great American family now lost a good deal of its intended poignancy, becoming, in Welles' later words, just "some rich people fighting in their house." New scenes were shot by

THE MAGNIFICENT AMBERSONS: The ball at the Ambersons mansion. Eugene (Joseph Cotten) and Isabel (Dolores Costello) share the last waltz.

THE MAGNIFICENT AMBERSONS: An awkward moment at dinner: Ray Collins, Joseph Cotten, Richard Bennett and Tim Holt.

Wise, by RKO production manager Freddie Fleck, and even by Jack Moss, Welles' business manager.

It was the final sequence which was perhaps the most glaringly obvious insert to the picture, bearing little relation to the remainder of the film. The use of a different cameraman and director is wholly apparent, as with another short scene some minutes earlier between Joseph Cotten and Anne Baxter. For this, as with other sequences, new music tracks were added, with the result that a justly outraged Bernard Herrmann insisted on his name being removed from the credits.

RKO finally pronounced itself satisfied with the new eighty-eight-minute version of the film, though the studio still had doubts as to its commercial potential. Pushed out uncertainly, it was even featured in some areas on a double bill with a Lupe Velez *Mexican Spitfire* "B" comedy.

THE MAGNIFICENT AMBERSONS: George Minafer (Tim Holt, right) takes an interest in Eugene's daughter Lucy (Anne Baxter).

THE MAGNIFICENT AMBER-
SONS: Eugene takes the
family for a drive on his
"horseless carriage." Left to
right: Dolores Costello,
Agnes Moorehead, Anne
Baxter, Joseph Cotten, Tim
Holt, Ray Collins.

Inevitably, with a budget finally topping $1 million, *Ambersons* was another loser for RKO, and a serious blow to George Schafer's position at the studio, where Welles and his group had always been considered a little too unconventional for their own — and RKO's — good. Still in South America, Orson Welles was unable to intervene, and in any case, the new contract with the studio meant that RKO had the absolute right to edit the movie in any way it saw fit.

In spite of all of this wholly unsettling experience, *The Magnificent Ambersons* was, incredibly, nominated for an Academy Award as Best Picture, losing to MGM's *Mrs. Miniver*.

Agnes Moorehead received an Oscar nomination as Best Supporting Actress and was named Best Actress by the National Board of Review. Tim Holt was also singled out for recognition by the Board, while Stanley Cortez was Oscar-nominated for his contribution.

The *Sight and Sound* poll of 1972 voted *The Magnificent Ambersons* into eighth position in its list of Best Films of All Time, and there are many commentators and critics today who genuinely prefer the film to *Citizen Kane*, even in its mutilated state.

As for the full-length version of the picture previewed in 1942, RKO's records indicate that no

THE MAGNIFICENT AMBERSONS: Fanny (Agnes Moorehead) tormented by George (Tim Holt) while Jack Amberson (Ray Collins) looks on.

THE MAGNIFICENT AMBERSONS: The famed Amberson staircase. It is featured in many later RKO productions including *Cat People*.

print survives, all footage being destroyed. Even David O. Selznick's suggestion at the time that the original negative be copied and stored in the Museum of Modern Art was rejected. The missing forty-odd minutes, which Welles insists tore the heart out of his picture, may be lost forever.

As with *Citizen Kane*, the credits are reserved until the close of the film, another entertaining sequence introduced by the off-screen Orson Welles.

Rumors in the mid-1960s that the missing reels of *The Magnificent Ambersons* had been recov-

ered were never substantiated. At around the same time, Welles fascinatingly proposed reshooting the lost sections with the original cast members twenty years on, but this was not considered a viable proposition.

We can only hope that somewhere a rogue copy of the original version exists and will eventually surface so that we may view *The Magnificent Ambersons* as Welles originally intended.

THE MAGNIFICENT AMBERSONS: Agnes Moorehead and Tim Holt, eavesdropping on the stairs, witness the beginnings of the Amberson troubles.

REVIEWS:

With only two pictures to his credit, last year's extraordinary *Citizen Kane* and now Booth Tarkington's *The Magnificent Ambersons*, Orson Welles has demonstrated beyond doubt that the screen is his medium. He has an eloquent, if at times grandiose, flair for the dramatic which only the camera can fully capture, and he has a truly wondrous knack for making his actors, even the passing bit player, behave like genuine human beings . . . All in all, *The Magnificent Ambersons* is an exceptionally well-made film, dealing with a subject scarcely worth the attention which has been lavished upon it.

— Thomas M. Pryor, *The New York Times*

The Magnificent Ambersons is going to drive the complacent filmgoer clean out of what wits he has, and will certainly influence film technique . . . for the next few seasons . . . One incontestable fact emerges from this film — Orson Welles

THE MAGNIFICENT AMBERSONS: George opposes his mother's meetings with Eugene.

THE MAGNIFICENT AMBERSONS: Fanny (Agnes Moorehead) confesses to George (Tim Holt) that she has no money to keep the mansion. The magnificence of the Ambersons is at an end.

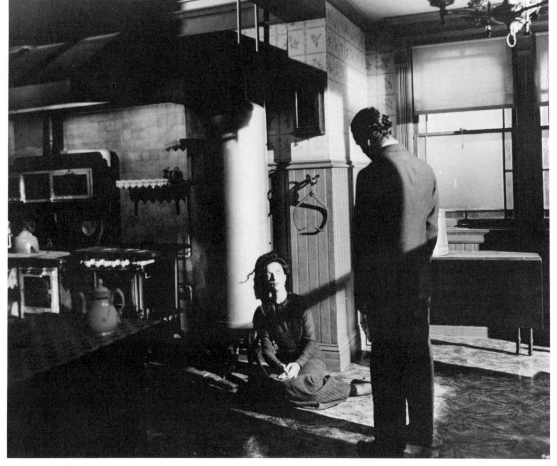

THE MAGNIFICENT AMBERSONS: Jack (Ray Collins) bids George farewell at the railway station as he heads back East.

THE MAGNIFICENT AMBER-SONS: Welles' "key scene," cut from the released film. Eugene (Joseph Cotten) visits a destitute Fanny (Agnes Moorehead) in a run-down boarding house.

THE MAGNIFICENT AMBERSONS: Between takes, Welles practices magic tricks for Joseph Cotten and Dolores Costello.

THE MAGNIFICENT AMBERSONS: Orson Welles with cameraman Stanley Cortez on the set.

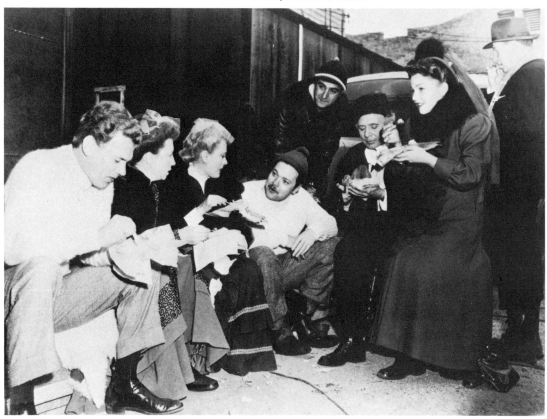

THE MAGNIFICENT AMBERSONS: Director and cast take a lunch break on location.

THE MAGNIFICENT AMBERSONS: The film's crew: Orson Welles (front) with Jim Daley, Robert Wise, Richard Wilson, Stanley Cortez and Jim Almond.

has style . . . As far as he is concerned, there might not have been half a century of cinema. For him, the film medium is now, and just beginning; a fresh page for him to cover with his bold, characteristic handwriting.

— C. A. Lejeune, *The Observer*

With a world in flames, nations shattered, populations in rags, with massacres and bombings, Welles devotes 9,000 feet of film to a spoiled brat who grows up as a spoiled, spiteful young man . . . it piles on a tale of woe, but without once striking at least a true chord of sentimentality. — *Life*

JOURNEY INTO FEAR

1943. RKO-RADIO PICTURES. A MERCURY PRODUCTION.

Directed by Norman Foster. Produced by Orson Welles. Executive Producer: George J. Schafer. Screenplay: Joseph Cotten and Orson Welles, from the novel by Eric Ambler. Director of Photography: Karl Struss. Art Directors: Albert S. D'Agostino, Mark Lee-Kirk. Music Score: Roy Webb. Special Effects: Vernon L. Walker. Film Editor: Mark Robson.
Running Time: 71 minutes.

CAST:

Joseph Cotten (*Howard Graham*); Dolores Del Rio (*Josette Martel*); Ruth Warrick (*Stephanie Graham*); Agnes Moorehead (*Mrs. Mathews*); Orson Welles (*Colonel Haki*); Everett Sloane (*Kopeikin*); Jack Moss (*Banat*); Edgar Barrier (*Kuvetli*); Jack Durant (*Gogo*); Eustace Wyatt (*Dr. Haller*); Frank Readick (*Mathews*); Hans Conreid (*Oo Lang Sang, the Magician*); Richard Bennett (*Ship's Captain*); Stefan Schnabel (*Purser*); Robert Meltzer (*Steward*); Shifra Haran (*Mrs. Haklet*).

SYNOPSIS:

Engineer Howard Graham (Joseph Cotten) is traveling through Turkey with his wife Stephanie (Ruth Warrick) when a trip to a nightclub ends with an apparent attempt being made on his life.

Interviewed by military officer Colonel Haki (Orson Welles), Graham is told that his life is in grave danger owing to information he holds which is vital to the Nazi war effort. Haki informs the bewildered Graham that he must leave Turkey immediately in secret, not even stopping to pick up his wife, whom Haki himself will escort to their rendezvous.

JOURNEY INTO FEAR: Orson Welles as the eccentric Inspector Haki.

JOURNEY INTO FEAR: Howard Graham (Joseph Cotten, second right) samples the delights of Turkish night-life with Everett Sloane and Dolores Del Rio . . .

Smuggled onto a tramp steamer, Graham becomes involved with a curious collection of fellow passengers, including the exotic Josette Martel (Dolores Del Rio) — the same dancer from the club where the murder attempt had taken place.

Kopeikin (Everett Sloane), another passenger, convinces the engineer that he ought to carry a gun, which is almost immediately stolen from the cabin. Meanwhile, Graham grows increasingly suspicious of a grotesque, silent passenger who is constantly observing his movements. The man, Banat (Jack Moss), is a Nazi assassin sent to kill him.

Despite several attempts on his life, Graham finally reaches land, only to be captured by Nazi agents. He escapes, however, and meets up with his wife, whom Haki has delivered as promised although he has made advances to her on the journey. Stephanie has been told nothing of her husband's predicament by Haki.

Banat again catches up with Graham and a chase ends with both men on the ledge of a hotel in torrential rain. The arrival of Haki saves Graham from Banat, whose vision is obscured by the downpour which leads to him falling from the ledge to his death.

JOURNEY INTO FEAR: . . . only to find himself and Kopeikin detained for questioning by Haki.

JOURNEY INTO FEAR: A curious set of expressions: Joseph Cotten, Everett Sloane and Ruth Warrick.

JOURNEY INTO FEAR: Graham is told his life is in grave danger. Haki is dumbfounded, "but then, I am dumbfounded every twenty minutes."

NOTES:

Joseph Cotten from his autobiography *Vanity Will Get You Somewhere:* "The minute *Ambersons* was finished, Orson invited me to join him in adapting *Journey Into Fear* from Eric Ambler's novel into a screenplay. When Eric saw the movie, he was delighted with it and said it bore so

JOURNEY INTO FEAR: Spirited out of the country, Howard Graham is smuggled aboard a run-down tramp steamer.

little resemblance to his book that he'd be able to sell it again."

Journey Into Fear had been suggested by George Schafer as a follow-up to *Citizen Kane*, but had been postponed by Orson Welles until work on *The Magnificent Ambersons* was virtually completed. This third Mercury production was a diversion from the two previous projects, being a more conventional and lightweight drama, rich in humor (attributed by Welles to Joseph Cotten). The tone of the screenplay is set early on when a bemused Colonel Haki (Welles) warns Graham (Cotten) of the danger he is in; declaring himself dumbfounded, Haki concedes, "But then, I am dumbfounded every twenty-five minutes."

Having decided not to appear in *Ambersons*, Welles chose not to direct *Journey Into Fear* and claims little personal involvement with the film other than as producer and his deliberately outrageous performance as the official Colonel Haki, the first of many roles in which Welles clearly set out to enjoy himself.

Although later reviewers and writers would insist that Welles had secretly directed much of the film himself, Orson was adamant that it had been the sole work of his friend Norman Foster, a former leading actor and singer whose directing

JOURNEY INTO FEAR: Graham meets dancer Josette (Dolores Del Rio) once again.

experience at that point consisted largely of episodes in the *Mr. Moto* series starring Peter Lorre. In early 1942, he had been assigned by Welles to direct a second unit in South America for one of the episodes of the government-backed *It's All True* which had taken Welles to Rio.

Recalled from South America, Foster was charged with taking control of *Journey Into Fear* instead, with once again a cast of virtually the entire Mercury company. Others included the glamorous Dolores Del Rio, Orson's current love, who rumor declared would soon be the next Mrs. Orson Welles. Also featured were Shifra Haran, Orson's personal secretary, in a minor role, and Jack Moss, his business manager, who had never acted before, but made a memorably grotesque villain, albeit a silent one. Missing though was Bernard Herrmann, the Mercury's resident composer, replaced by RKO in-house composer Roy Webb.

During the shooting, Welles flew to South America to work on *It's All True*, leaving his crew to complete the picture. RKO, however, was dissatisfied with the movie as previewed in June 1942 and immediately sent it back to be reedited by Mark Robson. The *Motion Picture Herald* had remarked on that screening ". . . previewed at a

JOURNEY INTO FEAR: Kopeikin (Everett Sloane) tries to reassure Stephanie Graham (Ruth Warrick) that things are relatively normal.

JOURNEY INTO FEAR: Odd characters at sea: Joseph Cotten, Agnes Moorehead, Jack Moss, Frank Readick and Dolores Del Rio.

JOURNEY INTO FEAR: Kidnapped by Nazi agents.

JOURNEY INTO FEAR: The climax on a hotel ledge high above the street. Joseph Cotten and Jack Moss (Orson Welles' business manager, making his only screen appearance).

customs' screening in New York. The inspector and an office boy were puzzled."

Welles was quick to defend the work of Norman Foster, complaining that the studio's cuts had damaged the film, but agreed to reshoot the ending himself before the film finally went on release in March 1943.

By this time, the regime at RKO had changed, Welles and his unit has been recalled from South America, *It's All True* canceled, Mercury's contract broken, and *Journey Into Fear*, following the disastrous reception met by *The Magnificent Ambersons*, became another financial loss to the studio.

An entertaining and modest thriller, *Journey Into Fear* marked the end of the Mercury company's association with RKO-Radio Pictures. By the time of its release, so too had ended the romance between Orson Welles and Dolores Del Rio; some claimed she was aghast at the effect the film would have on her career.

In 1976, *Journey Into Fear* was filmed again, this time with Vincent Price, Ian McShane, Zero Mostel, Shelley Winters and Stanley Holloway. (Sam Waterston and Yvette Mimieux had the Cotten-Warrick roles.) A limited release did not help its chances and it failed to excite audiences.

REVIEWS:

Out of Eric Ambler's thriller, *Journey Into Fear*, Orson Welles and his perennial Mercury Company have made an uneven but generally imaginative and exciting tale of terror. Less ambitious than any of the company's previous productions, [it] is nevertheless many notches above the garden variety regularly sent to Broadway. Although Norman Foster directed it, Mr. Welles, in collaboration with Joseph Cotten, has written the adaptation and either directly or indirectly it is Welles's fine flair for melodrama that is stamped on every scene . . . To select outstanding performances would be to name practically the entire cast — in which Mr. Welles's characterization of the Turkish police chief is the only one which is overdrawn.

— Theodore Strauss, *The New York Times*

As usual Welles casts his picture with exceedingly competent actors. Many of their scenes are excellent in vignette yet the effect is lost in whole . . . Everett Sloane as Kopeikin . . . Jack Moss as the killer and Richard Bennett . . . are memorable for the contribution to the weird mood . . . Nor-

man Foster directed the screenplay . . . Roy Webb's music is useful, but sometimes intrusive.
— *Motion Picture Herald*

Orson Welles, Hollywood's fiery rebel and scorner of film conventions, has come off his high horse and made a brilliant spy thriller.
— *Daily Express*

JANE EYRE

1943. TWENTIETH CENTURY-FOX.

Directed by Robert Stevenson. Produced by William Goetz.
Executive Producer: Darryl F. Zanuck. Screenplay: Aldous Huxley, Robert Stevenson and John Houseman, from the novel by Charlotte Brontë. Director of Photography: George Barnes. Art Directors: James Basevi and Wiard B. Ihnen. Music Score: Bernard Herrmann. Special Effects: Fred Sersen. Film Editor: Walter Thompson.
Running Time: 97 minutes.

CAST:

Orson Welles (*Edward Rochester*); Joan Fontaine (*Jane Eyre*); Margaret O'Brien (*Adele Varena*); Henry Daniell (*Mr. Brocklehurst*); Peggy Ann Garner (*Jane, as a child*); Agnes Moorehead (*Aunt Reed*); Sara Allgood (*Bessie*); Elizabeth Taylor (*Helen Burns*); John Sutton (*Dr. Rivers*); John Abbott (*Mason*). WITH: Aubrey Mather, Edith Barrett, Barbara Everest, Hilary Brooke, Ethel Griffies, Mae Marsh, Yorke Sherwood, Ronald Harris.

SYNOPSIS:

A young orphan, Jane Eyre (Peggy Ann Garner), lives with her Aunt Reed (Agnes Moorehead) who has no love for the child, neglecting and mistreating her, and finally sending her away to Lowood School, run by the tyrannical Mr. Brocklehurst (Henry Daniell).

At Lowood, the girls are taught to "rise above nature" by Brocklehurst, which means living in harsh conditions, poorly fed and suffering extreme punishments. Despite the attentions of local Dr. Rivers (John Sutton), Jane's only friend, Helen Burns (Elizabeth Taylor), dies after being forced to walk in the rain as a punishment for having curly hair.

JANE EYRE: Star of one of the great romantic films of the forties, Orson Welles as Edward Rochester.

69

JANE EYRE: The young Jane Eyre's future is decided by Aunt Reed (Agnes Moorehead, center) and tyrannical Squire Brocklehurst (Henry Daniell, right).

JANE EYRE: Rochester reassuring his guests over things that go bump in the night: "It's only the madwoman upstairs."

JANE EYRE: Rochester during his short-lived engagement to the glamorous Blanche Ingram (Hilary Brooke).

JANE EYRE: Mason (John Abbott) is treated after being attacked by the mystery woman at Thornfield.

Years pass, and Jane (Joan Fontaine) is offered a position as teacher at the school, but refuses, having already placed advertisements in the press offering herself as a governess. A response from Thornfield, a mansion house in Yorkshire, is accepted and she leaves to take up her appointment.

Arriving at Thornfield, Jane takes on the education of Adele, a young French orphan whose guardian, Edward Rochester (Orson Welles), spends little time at the house but returns unexpectedly one night shortly after Jane's arrival.

Rochester's manner is cold and imposing, but gradually he softens toward Jane, more so when she rescues him one evening from a fire which breaks out in his room while he is asleep. He confides to Jane that the fire is the work of a former servant — a madwoman kept under guard at all times.

Shortly afterward, Rochester announces that he is to be married to the beautiful Blanche Ingram (Hilary Brooke), but the engagement is quickly broken off. Meanwhile, the mysterious Mr. Mason (John Abbott) arrives from Jamaica, his presence plainly disturbing Rochester.

Rochester now asks Jane to marry him, but during the ceremony in church, Mason objects to the marriage, claiming that Rochester already has a wife still living. Returning to Thornfield, Edward reveals that the woman upstairs is, in fact, his wife, now an insane and vicious creature.

Unable to remain despite Rochester's pleading, Jane returns to her childhood home, finding Aunt Reed near death. Later, she begins to contemplate approaching Brocklehurst for a position at Lowood, but is seized by an overwhelming impulse which draws her back to Thornfield, only to find the house almost completely destroyed.

Jane learns that Rochester's wife had started another fire, which engulfed the entire house, during which she had fallen to her death from the roof. Edward, trying to rescue her, had been trapped by the flames and was now crippled and blind.

Despite his protests that she cannot love the wreckage of a man, Jane nurses Edward back to health and they are at last married, his sight finally being restored with the birth of their first son.

NOTES:

Sacked from RKO, Orson Welles' Mercury company disbanded, with Welles experiencing difficulty in finding a new directorial assignment following the *It's All True* episode.

David O. Selznick then approached Welles with an offer to star in *Jane Eyre*. The success of Samuel Goldwyn's version of Emily Brontë's *Wuthering Heights* had led to Selznick purchasing the screen rights to Charlotte's most popular novel as a vehicle for his contract star Joan Fontaine, fresh from successes in *Rebecca* and her Oscar-winning role in *Suspicion*.

Selznick evidently had great faith in Orson's ability as an actor, despite his screen appearances to date consisting of only two roles — the intense character study of Charles Kane and the eccentric Colonel Haki. Once again, though, Welles had already performed the role of Rochester on radio, and *Jane Eyre* had been considered briefly as a film project by the Mercury company during its short stay at RKO.

With a brilliantly literate screenplay the combined work of celebrated English novelist Aldous Huxley, Welles' old Mercury partner John Houseman, and the film's director Robert Stevenson, the entire project was then sold by Selznick to Twentieth Century-Fox, where Darryl F. Zanuck took control as executive producer.

At this point it was suggested that Welles should receive credit as either producer or associate producer, but — partly at the suggestion of Selznick in one of his legendary memos — this was dropped. While it is not entirely clear what the extent of Welles' influence on the making of the film might have been — Joan Fontaine's autobiography, *No Bed of Roses*, suggests that it was considerable — Welles himself was later to insist that it was solely the work of Robert Stevenson.

Stevenson had come to America with his wife, the actress Anna Lee, after a run of directing assignments in England during the thirties culminating in the beautiful romantic comedy *Return to Yesterday* costarring Miss Lee with Clive Brook. His later career would take him almost exclusively to the Walt Disney Studios where he directed, among others, *Mary Poppins*.

Comparing *Jane Eyre* with Stevenson's other work, though, it is not difficult to see what appears to be a Mercury/Welles style to the film, aided no doubt by the presence in the credits of Houseman, Agnes Moorehead and a stunning music score by Bernard Herrmann which included themes first heard during his work on the Mercury radio broadcasts five years earlier.

JANE EYRE: Rochester with his ward Adele (Margaret O'Brien) and Jane (Joan Fontaine).

JANE EYRE: A wedding is called to a halt by Mason's untimely interruption.

Jane Eyre once again established Orson Welles as a star actor, and he was extremely effective in the movie, conveying the troubled character with great conviction. In his scenes with Joan Fontaine, too, he was a remarkable, passionate and romantic figure.

As a faithful version of a classic novel, *Jane Eyre* is acknowledged by the Brontë Society of Haworth, Yorkshire, as the best film adaptation of any of the Brontë novels. Previously filmed in 1934 with Colin Clive and Virginia Bruce, a later television version was to follow with George C. Scott and Susannah York. Neither, however, compares with this definitive 1943 production, one of the great romantic films of the era.

REVIEWS:

With Orson Welles playing Rochester, the anguished hero of the book, [the producers] mainly gave way to the aspects of morbid horror to be revealed. They tossed Mr. Welles most of the story and let him play it in his hot, fuliginous style. As a consequence, the heroine of the classic, little Jane, played by Joan Fontaine, is strangely obscured behind the dark cloud of Rochester's personality . . . Mr. Welles's ferocious performance doesn't limn Miss Bronte's hero, but it does strike off a figure which is interesting to observe. His Rochester has the studied arrogance, the restless moods of a medieval king carrying his own soul to a halberd and demanding that everybody look at it. We only wish that he spoke more clearly; he so mumbles and macerates his words that half the time we are unable to tell what he was talking about.

— Bosley Crowther, *The New York Times*

Joan Fontaine appears as Jane . . . For "movie" magnates plain women do not exist, but they have chosen a player who can give a sensitive portrayal . . . Orson Welles is a strong, fantastic Rochester — the right vein exactly.

— *Manchester Guardian*

There's electricity enough in Orson Welles' looks and presence . . . He gives a fine performance as Rochester, the only fault of which is that it leaves to Joan Fontaine little more than the role of a spectator.

— *New Statesman*

FOLLOW THE BOYS

1944. UNIVERSAL.

Directed by Edward Sutherland. Produced by Charles K. Feldman.
Screenplay: Lou Breslow and Gertrude Purcell. Director of Photography: David Abel. Art Directors: John B. Goodman and Harold H. MacArthur. Music Director: Leigh Harline. Film Editor: Fred R. Feitshan, Jr.
Running Time: 114 minutes.

CAST:

George Raft (*Tony West*); Vera Zorina (*Gloria Vance*); Grace Macdonald (*Kitty West*); Charley Grapewin, (*Nick West*); Charles Butterworth (*Louie Fairweather*); George Macready (*Walter Bruce*); Elizabeth Patterson (*Annie*); Regis Toomey (*Dr. Henderson*). WITH: Orson Welles, Marlene Dietrich, The Andrews Sisters, Dinah Shore, Jeanette MacDonald, W. C. Fields, Donald O'Connor, Sophie Tucker, Ted Lewis, Artur Rubinstein, Peggy Ryan, others.

SYNOPSIS:

Following America's entry into the war in 1941, Nick West (Charley Grapewin), an old-time vaudeville performer, promises an Army pal that his son Tony (George Raft), now in Hollywood, will put together a show to entertain the troops.

Tony founds the Hollywood Victory Committee and persuades a number of top stars to appear in his show, including Orson Welles, Marlene Dietrich, The Andrews Sisters and W. C. Fields.

Tony is later killed while helping a member of his company escape as their ship is torpedoed en route to Australia.

NOTES:

Unfit for active service in the war due to asthma, Orson Welles put together "The Mercury Wonder Show," and visited American troops with a variety of performers.

Among the star attractions were Joseph Cotten as "Jo-Jo the Great," Agnes Moorehead (Calliope Aggie), Rita Hayworth and of course top of the bill Orson the Magnificent (Welles) with his magic act. The show climaxed with the conjurer sawing Marlene Dietrich in half, and was a great success.

When Universal decided to produce its own all-star revue, following similar morale-boosting efforts such as *Thank Your Lucky Stars* (Warner Bros.) and *Star Spangled Rhythm* (Paramount), Welles was approached to reprise his act on film.

In *Follow the Boys*, Orson is seen only briefly, first accepting a telephone invitation from the show's organizer (George Raft), and then in a

short magic act. Rita Hayworth was not seen in the film due to Harry Cohn's refusal to release her from Columbia.

Miss Dietrich was to strike up a permanent friendship with Welles which would achieve its professional peak some fifteen years later.

Welles' involvement with *Follow the Boys* was merely as one of several guest acts. The film itself was less successful than those produced by the other studios, and was among the last of the flag-waving propaganda pieces of the war years.

REVIEWS:

What do you get in this picture? You get Jeanette MacDonald singing two songs . . . you get Dinah Shore singing three others . . . Orson Welles in a magic act with Marlene Dietrich and W. C. Fields doing his delicious pool-table act. You get Sophie Tucker barrel-housing two numbers, Gautier's Bricklayer Dogs, Donald O'Connor and Peggy Ryan clowning and dancing and — oh, heaven only knows what else. All are jumbled together as acts presented to the troops by the Hollywood Victory Committee, with George Raft directing the works.

— Bosley Crowther, *The New York Times*

A couple of sketches come through very satisfactorily — a new version of W. C. Fields' billiards act, and a sketch in which Orson Welles, as a conjurer, saws Marlene Dietrich in half.

— *Observer*

FOLLOW THE BOYS: The Mercury Wonder Show as seen in the all-star musical. Orson Welles, assistant Marlene Dietrich, two men and a saw.

FOLLOW THE BOYS: Orson the Magnificent.

TOMORROW IS FOREVER

1946. INTERNATIONAL PICTURES. RELEASED BY RKO.

Directed by Irving Pichel. Produced by David Lewis. Screenplay: Lenore Coffee, from the novel by Gwen Bristow. Director of Photography: Joseph Valentine. Art Director: Wiard B. Ihnen. Music Score: Max Steiner. Editor: Ernest Nims.
Running Time: 105 minutes.

CAST:

Claudette Colbert (*Elizabeth Macdonald*); Orson Welles (*Erich Kesler/John Macdonald*); George Brent (*Larry Hamilton*); Richard Long (*Drew*); Lucile Watson (*Aunt Jessie*); Natalie Wood (*Margaret*); Sonny Howe (*Brian*); John Wengraf (*Dr. Ludwig*); Ian Wolfe (*Norton*); Douglas Wood (*Charles Hamilton*); Joyce MacKenzie (*Cherry*); Irving Pichel (*Commentator's Voice*); Milton Kibbee (*Postman*). WITH: Tom Wirick, Henry Hastings, Lane Watson, Michael Ward, Jesse Graves, Thomas Louden, Evan Thomas, Lane Chandler, Boyd Irwin, Marguerite Campbell.

SYNOPSIS:

In 1916 Baltimore, John and Elizabeth Macdonald (Orson Welles and Claudette Colbert) are separated when John is called away to the war. Shortly afterward, Elizabeth learns that he has been killed in action.

Twenty years later, during which time Elizabeth has married again, to local businessman Larry Hamilton (George Brent), a crippled Austrian scientist arrives in the town, and is hired by Hamilton as a chemist.

The Austrian, Erich Kesler, has left Europe on the eve of a Second World War, bringing with him a young foster daughter (Natalie Wood).

Elizabeth's son (Richard Long) intends to enter the war as soon as he can, against his mother's wishes. Kesler intervenes to resolve the conflict, while Elizabeth finally realizes that the Austrian is in fact her first husband, badly injured during the first war and now much changed.

Having settled the differences between mother and son, John/Erich suffers a heart attack and dies, leaving Elizabeth to resume her happy life with her "other" husband.

NOTES:

Offered a leading role in what was plainly a "woman's picture," Orson Welles accepted the opportunity to indulge in another serious piece of character playing, aided considerably by his talent with makeup.

Taken from a popular novel by Gwen Bristow, the story of *Tomorrow Is Forever* was far from new, having served as the subject matter of *Enoch Arden*, a poem by Alfred Lord Tennyson published in 1864. In Tennyson's version, itself drawn from a prose account by his friend Thomas Woolner, Arden is presumed drowned in a shipwreck but returns years later to find his wife remarried. Seeing their happiness, he keeps his identity a secret, revealing himself only to the local barmaid when he is close to death.

Seen first as a handsome young American, Welles appears throughout the remainder of the picture as a bearded, middle-aged Austrian paralyzed in one arm and with a crippled foot.

The film itself was largely dismissed by critics as improbable, but proved a commercial success with audiences. It is a typical example of the well-made, stylish dramas of the period, benefiting also from a notable and fitting romantic music score from Max Steiner.

Director Irving Pichel, a sometime actor himself, coaxed a praiseworthy performance from his leading players, and the film only added to Welles' reputation as a star actor of note. It also led to Welles being offered a directing assignment for International Pictures.

As the young foster daughter brought to America by Kesler, the six-year-old Natalie Wood had her first significant role in *Tomorrow Is Forever*.

REVIEWS:

The best way to take *Tomorrow Is Forever* . . . is as a straight piece of Hollywood taffy, slightly saline and gooey clear through. And the best way to view the performance of Orson Welles, who dominates the show, is as a studied display of overacting calculated to disguise an empty script . . . For a more overwrought and hackneyed telling of the Enoch Arden tale, with Mr. Welles playing Enoch, has not been thrown on the screen since the silent days.

— Bosley Crowther, *The New York Times*

Welles himself, posing as an Austrian scientist, does a far more skillful job of characterization than the creaky plot and prevailing platitudes warrant. — *Time*

. . . though we see through the disguises, Mr. Welles makes a figure to capture the eye. With one arm half-paralysed and one foot painfully turned in, dressed always in shabby black, awkwardly breaking into a smile, unapproachably kind, he keeps our uneasy sympathy; a considerable achievement . . . but what has been happening in the last eighteen months to Mr. Welles, the director? — *The Spectator*

TOMORROW IS FOREVER: Newlyweds John and Elizabeth Macdonald (Orson Welles and Claudette Colbert).

TOMORROW IS FOREVER: Later, Erich Kessler (Orson Welles) introduces his foster daughter (Natalie Wood) to Elizabeth and Larry Hamilton (Claudette Colbert and George Brent).

TOMORROW IS FOREVER: Orson Welles as the crippled Austrian scientist, Erich Kessler.

TOMORROW IS FOREVER: Kessler straightens out the Hamilton's son (Richard Long).

THE STRANGER: In this posed still, government agent Wilson (Edward G. Robinson) spies escaped Nazi Konrad Meinike (Konstantin Shayne) depositing his suitcase with local storekeeper Mr. Potter (Billy House).

THE STRANGER: Fresh from murdering Meinike, Rankin/Kindler (Orson Welles) increases his local standing by marrying Mary Longstreet (Loretta Young).

THE STRANGER: Welles with vaudeville star Billy House, an inexperienced screen performer who thought that his own stand-in was auditioning for his role! "I don't care! Give him the picture! Just let me know where I stand!"

THE STRANGER

1946. INTERNATIONAL
PICTURES. RELEASED BY RKO.

Directed by Orson Welles. Produced by S. P. Eagle. Executive Producer: William Goetz. Screenplay: Anthony Veiller (*and* John Huston, Orson Welles uncredited), from a story by Victor Trivas. Director of Photography: Russell Metty. Art Director: Perry Ferguson. Music Score: Bronislau Kaper. Film Editor: Ernest Nims.
Running Time: 95 minutes.

CAST:

Edward G. Robinson (*Wilson*); Loretta Young (*Mary Longstreet*); Orson Welles (*Charles Rankin/Franz Kindler*); Richard Long (*Noah Longstreet*); Philip Merivale (*Judge Longstreet*); Billy House (*Mr. Potter*); Konstantin Shayne (*Konrad Meinike*); Martha Wentworth (*Sara*); Byron Keith (*Dr. Jeff Lawrence*); Pietro Sosso (*Mr. Peabody*); Theodore Gottlieb (*Fairbright*); Isabel O'Madigan (*Mrs. Lawrence*).

SYNOPSIS:

Nazi war criminal Konrad Meinike (Konstantin Shayne) escapes from detention and heads for a small New England town where he is to contact a neo-Nazi leader for further instructions.

Franz Kindler, Meinike's contact, has been living as a college professor under the name of Charles Rankin (Orson Welles). On the day of his former comrade's arrival, he is preparing for his

THE MOST DECEITFUL MAN A WOMAN EVER LOVED!

Edward G. ROBINSON
Loretta YOUNG
Orson WELLES

IN The Stranger

WITH PHILIP MERIVALE
RICHARD LONG · BILLY HOUSE
DIRECTED BY Orson Welles

Produced by S.P. EAGLE Story by VICTOR TRIVAS and DECLA DUNNING Screenplay by ANTHONY VEILLER

marriage to Mary Longstreet (Loretta Young), daughter of the local judge; a calculating move designed to enhance his standing in the community while continuing to plot a new wave of Nazi actions.

Meinike is unaware that his escape was planned by the authorities, who hope that he will lead them to his superior; Kindler, however, immediately suspects the truth. Government agent Wilson (Edward G. Robinson) trails the fugitive to the town, but is knocked unconscious before he manages to learn the identity of the Nazi leader.

Kindler then murders Meinike and hides the body in the local woods before going ahead with his marriage to Mary. Recovering, Wilson stays on in the town under the guise of an insurance agent, quietly uncovering information on the townsfolk. He begins to suspect Rankin and enlists the help of Mary's brother Noah (Richard Long) in investigating the background of the "professor."

Rankin/Kindler is pressured into revealing his Nazi ideals, although Mary refuses to believe Wilson's allegations. Her husband, meanwhile, begins to undergo some changes of personality, killing Mary's dog when it threatens to uncover Meinike's body in the woods.

Mary finally confronts Rankin with Wilson's

THE STRANGER: With Loretta Young.

THE STRANGER: Wilson, invited to the Longstreet house, gets a close look at son-in-law Rankin.

suspicions, though she still does not believe him capable of the atrocities of which he is accused. Becoming unbalanced, Rankin arranges for her to meet him late at night at the clock tower, where he is working on repairing the mechanism. He intends to murder her there, sawing the rungs of the ladder through, but the attempt fails.

Wilson confronts Rankin at the tower, and in a shootout, the now insane Kindler is impaled on one of the giant figures of the clock movement — which he has, ironically, just repaired — and falls to his death in the street below.

NOTES:

William Goetz, producer of *Jane Eyre*, was now an executive producer at International Pictures, which had been responsible for Welles' most recent picture, *Tomorrow Is Forever*. Producer S. P. Eagle — later known as Sam Spiegel — was instrumental in offering Welles the chance to direct a movie again, though the studio insisted on certain conditions being written into the contract which would incur penalities if the film were either late or not completed.

Under these circumstances, Welles set out to make a conventional thriller in answer to those critics who accused him of being too extravagant or too complex. He later felt little for the picture, which because of these restrictions probably features less of Welles' own mark of individuality than do his other works.

For the first time in his movie career, Orson Welles found himself directing, appropriately enough, strangers. None of his Mercury players was featured in the cast, although Welles had particularly wanted Agnes Moorehead for the role of the government investigator eventually played by Edward G. Robinson. (Miss Moorehead was not considered a star attraction by the studio, a situation which also would lose her the starring role in the film version of *Sorry, Wrong Number* two years later. Despite the great personal success which Miss Moorehead had achieved in the radio play of the story, Paramount instead chose Barbara Stanwyck for the film.)

Although officially credited to Anthony Veiller, both Welles and John Huston also contributed to the script, originally including a lengthy opening sequence showing Kindler's escape from Germany at the end of the war and his flight to New England.

Evidently a 155-minute version was originally cut, but the final release version ran 95 minutes (85 in the U.S.). The completed movie is an effective thriller with at least something of a political message: that of the threat of a new rise in Nazism. (It is the 95-minute version — "colorized" — that today is seen on home video.)

Released through RKO in July 1946, *The Stranger* was a modest success, both critically and commercially, but failed to win Welles any long-term directorial contracts in Hollywood.

REVIEWS:

Orson Welles plainly gets much pleasure out of playing villainous roles, to judge by his choice and performances of bogey-men in the past. And now, in his new film, *The Stranger*, which he directed and in which he plays the title role, he is proving beyond any question that he loves to scare people to death . . . It is true that Mr. Welles

THE STRANGER: Loretta Young and Orson Welles.

THE STRANGER: Kindler at the clock tower.

THE STRANGER: Edward G. Robinson.

81

THE STRANGER: Cast and crew.

has directed his camera for some striking effects, with lighting and interesting angles much relied on in his technique. The fellow knows how to make a camera dynamic in telling a tale . . . But the whole film, produced by S. P. Eagle, comes off a bloodless, manufactured show.
— Bosley Crowther, *The New York Times*

This film will not entirely satisfy those (including myself) who raved over the early Orson Welles masterpieces — *Citizen Kane* and *The Magnificent Ambersons* . . . Welles, like many another bright spirit in Hollywood, has at last had to submit to the demands of the boys who handle the cash. — *Daily Sketch*

Both as actor and director, Mr. Welles is superb. The film has the sort of cosy intimacy of horror that Alfred Hitchcock can touch off so well in his better moods, with a bold grasp of form that is, as a rule, beyond Mr. Hitchcock's art. — *Observer*

. . . this time, Orson Welles, the very bright boy, has made a picture that is both current and choice . . . As a director, Welles seems to have found himself at last. He never lets up on you.
— *Daily Express*

THE LADY FROM SHANGHAI

1948. COLUMBIA.

Produced and Directed by Orson Welles.
Screenplay: Orson Welles, from the novel *If I Die Before I Wake* by Sherwood King. Director of Photography: Charles Lawton, Jr. Art Directors: Stephen Gooson, Sturges Carne. Music Score: Heinz Roemheld. Music Director: M. W. Stoloff. Sound Recording: Lodge Cunningham. Special Effects: Lawrence Butler. Film Editor: Viola Lawrence.
Running Time: 86 minutes.

CAST:

Rita Hayworth (*Elsa Bannister*); Orson Welles (*Michael O'Hara*); Everett Sloane (*Arthur Bannister*); Glenn Anders (*George Grisby*); Ted de Corsia (*Sidney Broome*); Erskine Sanford (*Judge*); Gus Schilling (*Goldie*); Carl Frank (*District Attorney*); Louis Merrill (*Jake*); Evelyn Ellis (*Bessie*); Harry Shannon (*Cab

THE LADY FROM SHANGHAI: First meeting between Michael O'Hara (Orson Welles) and Elsa Bannister (Rita Hayworth).

Driver); Wong Show Chong (*Li*); Sam Nelson (*Yacht Captain*). WITH: William Alland, Philip Morris, Tiny Jones, Edythe Elliott, Peter Cusanelli, Joseph Granby, Norman Thomson, Vernon Cansino, Doris Chan, Preston Lee, Heenan Elliott, Milt Kibbee, Billy Louie, Joseph Palma, Joe Recht, John Elliott, Alvin Hammer, Gerald Pierce, Al Eben, Edward Coke, Harry Strang, Jack Baxley, Byron Kane, Jessie Arnold, Mabel Smaney, George Charello, Maynard Holmes, Ed Peil, Dorothy Vaughn, Steve Benton, Mary Newton, Robert Gray.

SYNOPSIS:

When Michael O'Hara (Orson Welles), an out-of-work Irish seaman, rescues a beautiful woman, Elsa Bannister (Rita Hayworth), from muggers in Central Park, he is offered work the following day by her husband, wealthy lawyer Arthur Bannister (Everett Sloane).

Accepting the job of seaman on the Bannisters' yacht, Michael and the party set off on a pleasure cruise to South America. During the cruise, Elsa flirts relentlessly with Michael, making it plain that she loathes her husband, who is severely crippled. While he finds the situation bewildering, Michael's position is further complicated when Bannister's business partner, George Grisby (Glenn Anders), joins the cruise and offers the Irishman $5,000 to help him fake his own suicide.

THE LADY FROM SHANGHAI: Michael is offered a job with Bannister (Everett Sloane, second left). Others pictured are Gus Schilling (left) and Louis Merrill.

THE LADY FROM SHANGHAI: Elsa visits Michael in jail, not exactly reassuringly.

THE LADY FROM SHANGHAI: The repellent George Grisby (a marvelous performance by Glenn Anders) propositions Michael: "I want you to kill me, fellah."

THE LADY FROM SHANGHAI: Court room scene: Michael fakes an overdose.

84

A private detective, Broome (Ted de Corsia), hired by Bannister to tail Elsa, is murdered by Grisby, who then plans to kill Bannister and frame Michael. When Michael learns of the elaborate scheme, he rushes to Bannister's office, only to find that Grisby has been shot dead.

Incriminated by a false confession concocted by Grisby, Michael is arrested and sent to trial, to be defended by Elsa's jealous husband who, despite never having lost a case, is intent on seeing Michael found guilty.

Faking an overdose in the courtroom, Michael escapes in the confusion and hides out in a local Chinese theater. Elsa leads him to a deserted amusement arcade where, in a hall of mirrors, she admits to killing Grisby with whom she had planned the whole affair. Michael realizes she is insane, but they are interrupted by the arrival of Bannister, intent on bringing an end to their life of deceit.

In a bizarre shootout, Bannister is killed. Both Michael and Elsa are also wounded, but it is clear that she will not survive. Despite her pleading, Michael walks away, leaving her to die alone, reflecting that he might one day be able to forget her, but will more likely "die trying."

NOTES:

The story of the origins of *The Lady From Shanghai* has been told before, but is certainly worth repeating here, albeit briefly.

In Boston in mid-1946 for the opening of his mammoth stage extravaganza *Around the World in Eighty Days*, Welles found the show's costumes were being held at the railway station with $50,000 needed to secure their release. Frantically searching for someone who would loan him the money, Welles finally settled on Harry Cohn, universally loathed head of Columbia Pictures.

Orson managed to convince the studio boss that he should make a movie of a book called *If I Die Before I Wake* by Sherwood King — a paperback copy of which just happened to be in front of Welles at the time he was making the call from Chicago. Orson had not even read the book, but offered to make the film for Cohn in return for him sending him $50,000 straight away.

So persuasive was Welles that the money was wired to him immediately, and soon afterward Orson appeared at Columbia with a plan to make a quick, inexpensive movie — which bore little resemblance to the book on which it was supposedly based — as a means of fulfilling his obligation to the studio and to Cohn in particular.

At this time, Orson Welles and Rita Hayworth had been married for four years but were beginning to drift apart. Rita was, of course, Columbia's top box-office star and a particular favorite of Harry Cohn's, so that when she approached her boss and asked to work with Orson on his new movie, Cohn readily agreed and the budget of the

THE LADY FROM SHANGHAI: Orson Welles in the Chinatown Crazy House.

THE LADY FROM SHANGHAI: The famed shoot-out in the Hall of Mirrors. Left to right: Everett Sloane, Rita Hayworth, Orson Welles, Everett Sloane, Rita Hayworth, Orson Welles, Everett . . .

THE LADY FROM SHANGHAI: Farewell to a Wicked Lady: Elsa is left to die alone.

dresser's where Rita's famed auburn hair (actually dyed, she was not a natural redhead) was cropped short and dyed blond. The result was a no less beautiful but strikingly different Rita, but Harry Cohn was reportedly outraged. "What has he done to her?" he moaned. "Everyone knows that her hair is her most beautiful feature."

From then on, relations between Cohn and Welles cooled rapidly. Shooting, however, progressed smoothly. For location shooting, Errol Flynn's yacht, *The Zaca*, was chartered, with Errol himself acting as captain. Both he and his then-wife Nora Eddington can be glimpsed very briefly in one scene in the film.

Other roles went to several of Orson's old colleagues: Everett Sloane was superb as the crippled husband of Rita, while in minor roles were to be seen Gus Schilling, Erskine Sanford, William Alland and Harry Shannon from *Citizen Kane*. George "Shorty" Charello, Welles' real-life driver, also found a bit part in the movie, as did Rita's brother Vernon Cansino.

THE LADY FROM SHANGHAI: The stunningly beautiful Rita Hayworth that the public and Harry Cohn could not accept.

project was increased accordingly to transform the "B" movie Orson had envisaged into a star vehicle.

What Rita had in mind when she approached Cohn seems to have been two things: first, she appears genuinely to have wanted to patch up her marriage to Orson, and second, although a major star, she probably felt the need to "prove" herself as an actress. Her successes had first occurred in musicals like *You'll Never Get Rich* and *You Were Never Lovelier*, both with Fred Astaire, and *Cover Girl* with Gene Kelly. A fine dramatic performance in *Gilda* had elevated her to the position of "sex goddess" — a heavy burden for an actress as seemingly unsure of herself as Rita was. A leading role in a hit movie with Orson Welles would certainly enhance her reputation as a serious and capable actress.

The first thing to do was to change her image, achieved by a much-photographed trip to the hair-

THE LADY FROM SHANGHAI: In this publicity shot, Rita models the latest in seafaring fashions.

Those who constantly strive to find deep *significance* in Welles' movements were delighted that his opening narration to the movie stated "When I set out to make a fool of myself, nothing can stop me." Seized upon as a signal of the confusion to come, this innocent remark (spoken *in character*) was given added meaning, as was the transformation of Rita Hayworth from Cover Girl to *Femme Fatale*.

With the breakup of the Welles' marriage before the film was released, gossips claimed that Orson was taking some bizarre and unexplained "revenge" on his wife by supposedly spoiling her looks, presenting her in an unsympathetic role, and even letting her die at the end of the movie. "I was there the day Welles wiped up the floor with his wife," wrote columnist Hedda Hopper after watching the film's closing scene being shot. She was not alone in claiming that Orson was attempting to sabotage Rita's career.

With the passing years however, the reputation of *The Lady From Shanghai* has increased sharply, and rightly so. What seemed unfathom-

Glenn Anders, a stage actor with occasional screen experience, gave an astonishing performance as the repellently sinister George Grisby, while of the two leading parts, Welles took a surprisingly passive role in the drama. Rita Hayworth, though, was a revelation. Her performance in *The Lady From Shanghai* is surely her best in any movie, though at the time of the film's release this seems to have been overlooked.

On the film's completion, Harry Cohn labeled the plot "incomprehensible," allegedly offering $1,000 to anyone in the room who could explain it to him. Much was made of Orson Welles' failure to take Cohn up on the offer, but surely he did not feel the need to justify his film at such a loss of dignity.

This did little to enhance the picture's release, which suffered lengthy delays while Columbia insisted on retakes and reediting in attempts at making the story simpler for its audience. Some cuts were inevitably made, though it appears that no scenes were included in the film other than those shot by Welles. There are, however, a couple of small continuity errors which result from this reediting.

THE LADY FROM SHANGHAI: Candid shot on-set: Orson and Rita watch a "take."

able to Harry Cohn back in 1947 now seems complex but compelling, while much of the footage can almost be viewed as a homage to Miss Hayworth's beauty by her husband and director. Huge, glowing close-ups are a constant feature of the film, which has taken its place among the most respected of the *film noir* catalogue.

Most celebrated sequence in the film is inevitably the climax in the Hall of Mirrors between Michael, Elsa and her husband. Anyone today seeing this sequence for the first time has a rare treat in store.

REVIEWS:

There ought to be a law against the kind of murder and mayhem Orson Welles, genius at large, committed in making a picture called *The Lady From Shanghai*. I rather imagine Harry Cohn, Mr. Boss of Columbia, feels the same way, for in eighty-six minutes Willie Wonder Welles completely destroyed the beauty, glamour and feminine appeal of Rita Hayworth (to say nothing of the illusion of being an actress) which Mr. Cohn had spent expensive and careful years in building.
— *Los Angeles Examiner*

It can hardly be said that this infinitely detailed study of the multiple double-cross will please audiences looking for innocuous, relaxing entertainment. But there is no doubt that the film will have occasional fascination for some moviegoers who are more interested in the technique than the substance. For, as always, Welles has produced a flashy, bold, moody, uneven, unconventional show. Even if there is nothing at all here of lasting interest, it is often an intriguing show to watch.
— *Fortnight*

Welles has done nothing better since the electioneering passages of *Citizen Kane* . . . Here is the old insolent authority in the handling of the camera . . . But, once more, as with *The Magnificent Ambersons*, a gigantic narrative style is squandered on a trivial theme, and once more, in this confident, grandiose new world, cinema technique towers over its subject, the human being.
— *Sunday Times*

. . . this, aside from the exciting but frequently illogical story that spins so dizzily, it's almost impossible to follow, is the entertainment essence of Welles' film. The star's performance is in the bravura tradition, marred from time to time by an exaggerated sing-song brogue so fragrant you can almost smell the peat bogs of Ire-

land in it. Rita Hayworth . . . is glamorous and inscrutable in the fashion of movie ladies of mystery. Everett Sloane and Glenn Anders . . . are thoroughly and satisfactorily repulsive . . .
— *Cue*

MACBETH

1948. REPUBLIC PICTURES.
A MERCURY PRODUCTION.

Produced and Directed by Orson Welles.
Executive Producer: Charles K. Feldman. Screenplay: Orson Welles, adapted from the play by William Shakespeare. Director of Photography: John L. Russell. Art Director: Fred Ritter. Music Score: Jacques Ibert. Film Editor: Louis Lindsay.
Running Time: 89 minutes.

CAST:

Orson Welles (*Macbeth*); Jeanette Nolan (*Lady Macbeth*); Dan O'Herlihy (*Macduff*); Edgar Barrier (*Banquo*); Roddy McDowall (*Malcolm*); Erskine Sanford (*Duncan*); Alan Napier (*Holy Father*); Lionel Braham (*Siward*); Archie Heugly (*Young Siward*); John Dierkes (*Ross*); Peggy Webber (*Lady Macduff/Witch*); William Alland (*2nd Murderer*); Gus Schilling (*Porter*); George Chirello (*Seyton*); Christopher Welles (*Macduff Child*); Brainerd Duffield (*1st Murderer*); Jerry Farber (*Fleance*); Lurene Tuttle (*Gentlewoman/Witch*); Robert Alan (*3rd Murderer*); Morgan Farley (*Doctor*); Charles Lederer (*Witch*).

SYNOPSIS:

Victorious in battle against the rebels, Macbeth (Orson Welles) and Banquo (Edgar Barrier) are met on the heath by three witches who, addressing him as Thane of Cawdor, prophesy that Macbeth shall soon be king.

Reaching his castle, Macbeth learns that he has indeed been named Thane of Cawdor and now sentenced to death as a traitor. Lady Macbeth (Jeanette Nolan) becomes convinced that the witches' predictions are to come true, despite both Duncan the King (Erskine Sanford) and his heir Malcolm (Roddy McDowall) still being alive.

Duncan is shortly received as a guest at the castle, when Lady Macbeth goads her husband into murdering the king, having drugged the

90

MACBETH: (*Opposite page*) Grim opening image—the three witches on the heath.

guards. When Macbeth's nerve fails him, Lady Macbeth smears blood onto the guards to incriminate them. Macbeth then kills them, supposedly in anger at their crime against the king.

Macduff (Dan O'Herlihy), who discovers the murdered king, is suspicious of Macbeth's actions, more so when Macbeth claims the crown, the king's son Malcolm having escaped to England.

Macbeth next murders Banquo, who the witches foresaw would father a future king, but then learns that Macduff has formed an army

MACBETH: Striking portrait of Jeanette Nolan as Lady Macbeth.

with Malcolm in England in preparation for their advance into Scotland. The witches return to warn Macbeth to beware Macduff, although they say he will not be defeated until Birnam Wood moves against him. Ordering the death of Lady Macduff and her children, Macbeth prepares for battle.

Lady Macbeth, meanwhile, becomes insane, walking in her sleep and raving wildly. As the Macduff army approaches Dunsinane Castle, she dies, while the advancing forces camouflage themselves with branches and leaves — Birnam Wood is indeed marching against Macbeth, who is killed in a duel with Macduff. Malcolm finally takes his rightful place on the throne.

NOTES:

Jean Cocteau: "Orson Welles' *Macbeth* leaves the spectator deaf and blind and I can well believe that the people who like it (and I am proud to be one) are few and far between . . ."

Following the experience at Columbia over *The Lady From Shanghai* and the consequent delays in the film's release, Orson Welles was being spoken of in Hollywood as unable to complete a movie on schedule and within the agreed budget.

Responding to the criticism, Welles demonstrated how quickly he could work, given the freedom to do so. He proposed to make a film version of Shakespeare's *Macbeth* in only twenty-one days' shooting time, compared to an average schedule of five to six weeks.

Of the studios approached to finance this experiment, most refused to be drawn, partly due to Welles' unwarranted reputation, but also because Shakespeare was far from a commercial box-office proposition in American movies. Of previous attempts to film the Bard, the most successful in artistic terms had been Max Reinhardt's 1935 Warner Bros. version of *A Midsummer Night's Dream* (even this delightful film, though, had been a flop with audiences) and perhaps George Cukor's 1936 *Romeo and Juliet* at MGM.

Macbeth, with its legendary status as an unlucky play, had been filmed only once before, as a 1916 silent with Sir Herbert Beerbohm Tree. Orson Welles, however, had no qualms about preparing his version for the screen.

The play had been the Mercury's first theater success at Harlem in 1936, in a celebrated "voodoo" version, and was now being performed by a new Mercury company at the Utah Centennial Summer Festival with great success.

Welles finally reached agreement with Herbert Yates, president of Republic Pictures, to finance the low-budget movie. There were those in Hollywood who found this arrangement incredible. Republic was one of the "Poverty Row" studios, known largely as the home of a series of "B" westerns staring Roy Rogers, although occasionally a major production would appear starring John Wayne.

Nevertheless, Welles set to work, constructing a number of sets remarkably cheaply, mostly designed by himself and Dan O'Herlihy. With many of the players from the Utah production, the company was in need of little rehearsal, though at one point it had been hoped that Agnes Moorehead would be available for the role of Lady Macbeth. Similarly, Bernard Herrmann was approached to provide the music score but was contracted elsewhere.

Other casting included Mercury stalwarts Gus Schilling, Erskine Sanford, and William Alland, but perhaps more interesting was the inclusion of Welles' daughter Christopher from his first marriage in the role of Macduff's young son. Also, as

MACBETH: With Jeanette Nolan.

MACBETH: The deed is done: Lady Macbeth urges Macbeth to murder the king.

MACBETH: Christopher Welles, Orson's daughter in her only film, as Macduff's child.

MACBETH: Macbeth shares a noggin with the local gentry.

MACBETH: Dan O'Herlihy (left) and Orson Welles (center) admire their work as set designers.

one of the three witches, Welles gave a part to Charles Lederer, a screenwriter now married to Virginia Nicolson Welles, and Christopher's stepfather.

The filming was completed, amazingly, under schedule and under budget, much to the admiration of Herbert Yates, who announced that it was the most remarkable piece of filmmaking he had ever seen. The released film was, however, roundly dismissed by critics who complained of the poor sound quality and the visual style of the movie. Welles had shot much of the film in a mist, partly to obscure the cheapness of the sets, but also as an attempt to convey a strong theatrical atmosphere. Welles' decision to adopt Scottish accents for his players was also heavily criticized by reviewers who declared it "unintelligible." As a means of reducing costs, he had also dubbed a number of the roles himself, making it unnecessary to retain services of expensive performers during editing.

On this point, Jean Cocteau later wrote: "In the role of Macbeth, Orson Welles proves himself to be a remarkable tragedian, and if the Scottish accent imitated by Americans may be unbearable to English ears, I confess that it did not disturb me and that it would not have disturbed me even if I had a perfect command of English, since we have no reason not to expect that strange monsters express themselves in a monstrous language in which the words of Shakespeare nevertheless remain his words."

Life magazine, however, commented that Welles "doth foully slaughter Shakespeare," and was not alone in being critical of the film's treatment of the play, complaints being voiced over Welles' creation of a new figure, the Holy Father (Alan Napier), who served as an amalgam of several of the play's characters.

Nevertheless, the film can be viewed, in Welles' words, as a "violent charcoal sketch of a

great play." There is no doubt that the film retains a certain power, helped enormously by Orson Welles' own performance as Macbeth.

Originally screened at the Cannes Film Festival in 1948, the film was withdrawn by Welles from the competition, evidently to avoid comparison with Laurence Olivier's lavish production of *Hamlet*, the first real critical and commercially successful Shakespeare film.

REVIEWS:

Orson Welles's protean film production of William Shakespeare's *Macbeth* . . . turned out to be less of a vagary than its history might lead one to expect. As a matter of fact, the final rendering, which Mr. Welles directed and in which he stars, may not possess the searching insight and the dramatic clarity that one might desire but it has a great deal in its favor in the way of feudal spectacle and nightmare mood. In the established Welles tradition, which has been building for a number of years, the theatrical mechanics of the medium are permitted to dominate the play and Shakespeare is forced to lower billing than either the director, the star or the cameraman . . . Mr.

Welles deploys himself and his actors so that they move and strike the attitudes of tortured grotesques and half-mad zealots in a Black Mass or an ancient ritual.

> — Bosley Crowther, *The New York Times*
> (on the film's belated New York release
> in December 1950)

There is no doubt that Orson Welles is gifted with colossal ingenuity and imagination. It would take colossal ingenuity to make so great a bore of Shakespeare as he has done in this outrageously poor production of *Macbeth* . . . Welles is said to have thrown this film together in twenty-one days of shooting, at a cost of only $300,000. Even so, it was a waste of time and money and an insult to artistry.   — *Fortnight*

. . . happily, Shakespeare will continue to be a vivid element in theatrical culture long after the Orson Welles version of *Macbeth* is forgotten as one of the most disastrous of motion picture enterprises . . . It is photographed against a background of smoky haze. The characters appear from nowhere, speak their lines, and then depart into the mist. One is barely distinguishable from the other, thanks to their hideous makeups and

BLACK MAGIC: Cagliostro (Orson Welles) with Zoraida (Valentina Cortese)

BLACK MAGIC: Jiggery pokery with Cagliostro. Akim Tamiroff is on the left.

the aborted text . . . Welles' performance . . . is completely devoid of thoughtfulness or intelligence. It is big, broad and blustering—a booming elocutionary display that taxes the ear drums and never touches the heart. — *Hollywood Reporter*

BLACK MAGIC

1949. UNITED ARTISTS. EDWARD SMALL PRODUCTIONS.

Produced and Directed by Gregory Ratoff.
Executive Producer: Edward Small. Screenplay: Charles Bennett, based on Alexandre Dumas' account of Cagliostro from *Memoirs of a Physician*. Director of Photography: Ubaldo Arata, Anchise Brizzi. Music Score: Paul Sawtell. Film Editors: James McKay, Fred Feitshans.
Running Time: 105 minutes.

CAST:

Orson Welles (*Cagliostro*); Nancy Guild (*Marie Antoinette/Lorenza*); Akim Tamiroff (*Gitano*); Valentina Cortese (*Zoraida*); Charles Goldner (*Dr. Mesmer*); Berry Kroeger (*Alexandre Dumas*); Raymond Burr (*Alexandre Dumas, Jr.*); Margot Grahame (*Mme. Du Barry*); Frank Latimore (*Gilbert*); Stephen Bekassy (*de Montagne*); Robert Atkins (*King Louis XV*); Lee Kresel (*King Louis XVI*); Nicholas Bruce (*De Remy*); Gregory Gay (*Chambord*). WITH: Aniello Mele, Bruce Belfrage, Alexander Danaroff, Tatiana Pavlowa, Giuseppe Varni, Ronald Adam, Franco Corsaro, Lee Lenoir, Tamara Shayne, Giovanni Van Hulzen.

SYNOPSIS:

Novelist Alexandre Dumas (Berry Kroeger) tells his son (Raymond Burr) the story of Cagliostro, conjurer, hypnotist and master showman of the eighteenth century.

In flashback we learn that young Josef Balsamo, a gypsy in Southern France, grows up longing for revenge against the Viscomte de Montagne (Stephen Bekassy) who had tortured the boy and hanged both of the youngster's innocent parents.

Now a carnival magician, the grown Balsamo (Orson Welles) is approached by the famed hypnotist Dr. Mesmer (Charles Goldner), who suggests that he use his mystical power for healing the sick. Still bitter, Balsamo realizes for the first time that his abilities are genuine and decides to use them to gain wealth and power for himself.

Taking the name of Count Cagliostro, the showman travels throughout Europe, where he encounters Lorenza (Nancy Guild), a young girl who bears a striking resemblance to Marie Antoinette, Louis XVI's wife. Lorenza is being held by de Montagne, who plots to use her to impersonate Marie Antoinette and so cause a scandal. Cagliostro agrees to help de Montagne in this scheme, together with Madame Du Barry (Margot Grahame).

Using his hypnotic power, Cagliostro takes his long-sought revenge on de Montagne, forcing him to commit suicide. The magician then takes Lorenza as his bride, but cannot make her love him, because her heart belongs to the Queen's guard, Gilbert (Frank Latimore).

Dr. Mesmer intervenes during a court scene, turning Cagliostro's power against him. The self-styled count is exposed and then killed in a roof-top duel with the captain of the guard.

NOTES:

With no other commitments in America following the completion of *Macbeth*, Welles accepted an offer to travel to Italy to appear in Gregory Ratoff's production of *Cagliostro*, with a screenplay by Charles Bennett, whose earlier screen credits included such Hitchcock classics as *Blackmail*, *Young and Innocent*, *The Thirty-Nine Steps* and *Foreign Correspondent*.

Ratoff, a Russian-born actor/director, was a great admirer of Orson Welles and the two evidently enjoyed themselves enormously on the making of the film, eventually retitled *Black Magic*. Though often accused of influencing directors during his career, Orson certainly did direct large sections of *Black Magic*, with Ratoff's complete agreement.

Perhaps the most significant long-term effect of the shooting of *Black Magic* was that it introduced Welles to Akim Tamiroff, as one of Cagliostro's faithful gypsy friends. In reality, Tamiroff would become one of Welles' most faithful friends over the years, appearing for him in many of Orson's later movies.

REVIEWS:

Black Magic is quite a bundle of intrigue with plush, sprawling and lavishly appointed sets reflecting the splendor of the court of Louis XV

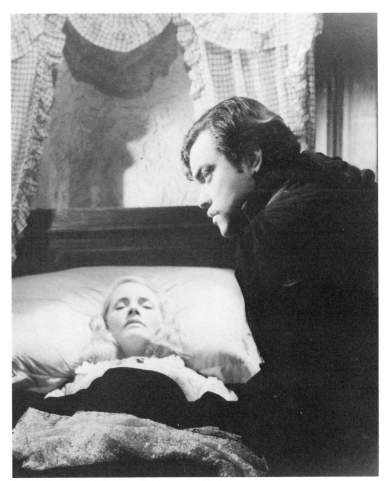

BLACK MAGIC: Cagliostro attempts to revive Lorenza.

BLACK MAGIC: Dr. Mesmer (Charles Goldner) unmasks Cagliostro in court.

BLACK MAGIC: Attempting to escape over the rooftops of Paris, Cagliostro fails to see Gilbert (Frank Latimore) creeping up behind him. Tsk!

. . . As a great charlatan who sweeps across eighteenth century Europe . . . Mr. Welles indulges to the full his penchant for flamboyance [and] gives a lusty portrayal of a wily, but essentially ignorant, opportunist who uses his powers of hypnotism, which he does not fully understand, to exact revenge for the brutal killing of his gypsy parents and his own cruel punishment as a boy.
— Thomas M. Pryor, *The New York Times*

Welles plays the part of Cagliostro with enthusiasm and makes the character who finally thought himself a God quite believable. He never lets the Count and his hypnotic power get lost in the elaborate settings. The great number of extras and supporting players all tend to point up the one man. — *Motion Picture Herald*

Orson Welles takes a dive into the part of Cagliostro in *Black Magic* and a very fantastic — and, at times, pathetic — eighteenth century confidence trickster he makes of him. — *Picturegoer*

THE THIRD MAN

1949. LONDON FILMS/
BRITISH LION.

Produced and Directed by Carol Reed.
Executive Producers: Alexander Korda, David O. Selznick. Screenplay: Graham Greene, from his own story. Director of Photography: Robert Krasker. Art Director: Vincent Korda. Music Score: Anton Karas. Film Editor: Oswald Hafenrichter.
Running Time: 104 minutes. (93 minutes in the U.S.)

CAST:

Joseph Cotten (*Holly Martins*); Alida Valli (*Anna Schmidt*); Orson Welles (*Harry Lime*); Trevor Howard (*Major Calloway*); Bernard Lee (*Sgt. Paine*); Paul Hoerbiger (*Porter*); Siegfried Breuer (*Popescu*); Ernst Deutsch (*Kurtz*); Erich Ponto (*Dr. Winkel*); Wilfrid Hyde-White (*Prof. Crabbin*); Hedwig Bleibtreu (*Anna's Housekeeper*).

SYNOPSIS:

Arriving in the ruined splendor of postwar Vienna, Holly Martins (Joseph Cotten), a writer of moderately successful western novels, heads for the apartment of his lifelong friend, Harry Lime, who has offered him a job. There, Holly is told by the porter (Paul Hoerbiger) that Harry's funeral is taking place that day; that he was knocked down and killed a few days earlier.

Reaching the cemetery, Holly is taken aside by Major Calloway (Trevor Howard), a British Army official working in the city. Over a drink in a nearby café, Calloway tells Holly that Harry was involved in black market dealings and deserves to be dead. Incensed, Holly decides to investigate Harry's life and death for himself. Searching out Anna Schmidt (Alida Valli), an actress at the local theater who was Harry's girl, Holly learns more about the accident which killed his friend.

Questioning the porter once again, Holly becomes increasingly suspicious when it turns out that, first, Harry was killed by his own car; second, the incident was witnessed by one of his closest friends; and third, his own doctor was on the scene at the time. The porter insists that there was a "third man" who helped to carry the body across the street.

Holly, meeting those present at the time, uncovers little new information, but returns to Harry's apartment house only to find that the porter has been murdered.

Calloway remains skeptical of Holly's investigations, urging him to leave. To disillusion Holly about his friend Harry, Calloway reveals the extent of the black market dealings in which Lime was involved — selling impure penicillin to hospitals.

Finally deciding he can do no more, Holly visits Anna to say goodbye, but on leaving, he notices a figure in the doorway opposite. Thinking it is one

THE THIRD MAN: Holly Martins (Joseph Cotten) arranges to meet a dead man on the Vienna Ferris Wheel.

of Calloway's men, he calls to him to show himself, and as a light falls across the doorway, it is revealed as Harry Lime (Orson Welles), who slips away as a car passes between them.

Reporting back to Calloway, who first assumes he is drunk, Holly pressures him into conducting a search. A nearby kiosk is found to contain steps leading to the vast underground sewage network below the city. Digging up "Harry's" coffin, the police discover the body of Joseph Harbin,

99

THE THIRD MAN: Joseph Cotten.

THE THIRD MAN: Harry Lime's first appearance: "(The cat) . . . he only liked Harry."

THE THIRD MAN: Anna Schmidt (Alida Valli) and Holly Martins (Joseph Cotten).

THE THIRD MAN: Harry Lime (Orson Welles) enlightens his friend on the intricacies of black marketeering and cuckoo clocks.

another black marketeer who has been missing for some time. Holly confronts Kurtz (Ernst Deutsch) and Popescu (Siegfried Breuer), the other two at the scene of Lime's "accident," and tells them to arrange a meeting between himself and Harry at Vienna's Great Ferris Wheel.

Harry arrives and he and Holly take a ride on the wheel, Lime freely admitting that he is a racketeer, totally unrepentent for the result of his actions. When Holly tells him that the police have discovered Harbin's body and that they know Harry is still alive, the latter shrugs off even this, claiming immunity in the neutral zones of Vienna. Holly refuses his offer of a job and returns to the police, agreeing to help them in bringing Lime in. A trap is set at a local café, but Harry realizes the setup as he enters and escapes into the sewers pursued by Holly and the police.

In an extraordinary chase through the maze of tunnels, Lime shoots dead Sgt. Paine (Bernard Lee), but is himself wounded and finally cornered trying to flee through a solidly jammed manhole cover. It falls to Holly to kill the man who had been his oldest friend. A second funeral is held, and as the parties leave, Holly waits for Anna,

THE THIRD MAN: The climactic chase through the sewers of Vienna at the film's conclusion.

THE THIRD MAN: Harry Lime's entrance into the Mozart Cafe and the police trap.

101

whom he has grown to love. She strides past him, however, without a glance.

NOTES:

Hungarian-born Alexander Korda had been a guiding influence in British cinema before the war. His London Films Studio had closed, however, in 1939 when money problems forced his backers to withdraw support. Reopening in peacetime as the Shepperton Studios, it became the home of independent filmmakers including The Archers (Michael Powell and Emeric Pressburger), David Lean, Frank Launder and Sidney Gilliatt, and Carol Reed.

Reed's success with *Odd Man Out* in 1947 had led to a contract with Korda, and the first project under the new agreement and the newly resurrected London Films banner was 1948's *The Fallen Idol*, from a short novel by Graham Greene. The film was such a success that the winning Korda-Reed-Greene formula was repeated the following year.

For the new picture, Greene wrote an original screenplay, only later published in book form, inspired by a single line which he had written on the back of an envelope some years earlier. Called *The Third Man*, the screenplay was to be coproduced by Korda in collaboration with David O. Selznick, currently involving himself in a number of European projects.

THE THIRD MAN: On the set with director Carol Reed and Joseph Cotten.

Although a British picture, it was filmed entirely on location in Vienna with an international cast. British stars Trevor Howard and Bernard Lee were joined by Selznick's recent Italian discovery, the beautiful Alida Valli whom he previously "introduced" in *The Paradine Case*.

The starring role of the American novelist went to Joseph Cotten, one of Orson Welles' Mercury players whose subsequent career had flourished with a series of fine performances in films like *Shadow of a Doubt, Duel in the Sun* and *Portrait of Jennie*. Now under contract to Selznick, the star insisted on the name of his character being changed from *Rollo* to *Holly* Martins.

The key role of the enigmatic Harry Lime — a mysterious figure who would not even appear in the movie for the first hour — was originally pencilled in for Nöel Coward, but later fell to Orson Welles. After some reported initial reluctance over accepting such a brief role, Welles was delighted to be working again with his good friend Joseph Cotten, and similarly delighted to be

THE THIRD MAN: The end of Harry Lime, trapped in the Vienna sewers.

THE THIRD MAN: Preparing for a scene: for the first time in his career, Welles did not wear any false noses or wigs for the role.

working with director Carol Reed. Unlike some directors who would consider Welles "troublesome," Reed actively encouraged suggestions from his actors and crew, with the result that the film was shot in almost ideal conditions.

Realizing that his character was the central figure in the story, Welles gave a complete and superbly rounded performance as Harry Lime, so much so that despite being seen for only ten minutes, he completely dominated the entire film; some claim that he in fact had more to do with the film than was credited. In a letter to the author, Graham Greene recalls: "Naturally I was very pleased by Orson Welles' performance in *The Third Man*. The only dialogue he wrote during shooting were the few lines about the Swiss cuckoo clock in the scene on the red wheel. I think he was apt to claim that he had done other bits of dialogue but this was not the case. The screenplay was otherwise entirely my own with the collaboration of Carol Reed."

Over suggestions that he actively worked on

THE THIRD MAN: Joseph Cotten during a break in filming. Orson's seat is occupied by two other stars of the film.

THE THIRD MAN: Orson Welles as the public best remembered him: Harry Lime, the Third Man.

The Third Man and the character of Harry Lime would be those associated with Orson Welles for the remainder of his career; more so even than *Citizen Kane*. A huge international success, the picture won an Oscar for the photography of Robert Krasker, as well as a British Academy Award as Best Film. At the Cannes Festival, *The Third Man* was awarded the Grand Prize, and perhaps the most recognizable features of the film, the haunting and dynamic zither music score, made its composer Anton Karas, then a café musician, an overnight celebrity, winning for him invitations to entertain royalty and a series of sell-out concert tours across Europe.

Some years later, Orson Welles was to finally capitalize on the popularity of the movie when he began a BBC Radio series called *The Adventures of Harry Lime*, borrowing the name of the character but otherwise having no resemblance to the original story; Harry in this series was an investigator in the style of *The Shadow*. Similarly, a later BBC Television series starring Michael Rennie as

the direction of *The Third Man*, Welles insisted that this was certainly not so and that it was solely the work of Carol Reed, whom Orson adored. Certainly, if one examines Reed's recent works of the time — *The Fallen Idol* and particularly *Odd Man Out*, there is nothing in *The Third Man* to suggest a definite outside influence. As author of at least part of Harry Lime's dialogue, though, Welles was responsible for the celebrated speech mentioned by Graham Greene. With Machiavellian aplomb, Lime explains: "In Italy for thirty years under the Borgias they had warfare, terror, murder, bloodshed, but they produced Michelangelo, Leonardo da Vinci and the Renaissance. In Switzerland, they had brotherly love; they had five hundred years of democracy and peace, and what did that produce? The cuckoo clock."

Orson was offered either a straight salary of $100,000 or a percentage deal on the profits. Desperate for the cash to begin work on his own movie of *Othello*, Orson took the ready money, only to see *The Third Man* go on to become the biggest-grossing movie of any of which he was a part.

THE THIRD MAN: Offshoot from the film. Anton Karas' theme tune became a worldwide hit, with or without lyrics.

Harry Lime, and called *The Third Man*, used Karas' zither theme, but saw Harry as an internationally respected art dealer who invariably becomes involved in some weekly intrigue *à la The Saint*.

Variety reported in February 1978 that copyright on *The Third Man* had not been renewed and that the film was now in the public domain. The merger of British Lion (of which London Films had been a part) and EMI Films had evidently caused a breakdown in normal efficiency, and the renewal date had passed by unnoticed. It is now available from a variety of tape distributors for home video — both in original black and white and in colorized versions.

REVIEWS:

. . . *The Third Man*, for all the awesome hoopla it has received, is essentially a first-rate contrivance in the way of melodrama — and that's all. It isn't a penetrating study of any European problem of the day. It doesn't present any "message." It hasn't a point of view. It is just a bang-up melodrama, designed to excite and entertain . . . The script is tops. So, too, are the performances of everyone in the cast . . . Even our old and perennially villainous friend, Orson Welles, does a right nice job of shaping a dark and treacherous shadow as the "third man."

— Bosley Crowther, *The New York Times*

The strength and power of the film is Joseph Cotten's manner of facing what he finds out. Orson Welles, as the hunted man, casts a dark shadow over the very atmosphere even before you see him.

— *Daily Graphic*

PRINCE OF FOXES

1949. TWENTIETH CENTURY-FOX.

Directed by Henry King. Produced by Sol C. Siegel. Executive Producer: Darryl F. Zanuck. Screenplay: Milton Krims, from the novel by Samuel Shellabarger. Director of Photography: Leon Shamroy. Art Directors: Lyle Wheeler, Mark-Lee Kirk. Music Score: Alfred Newman. Film Editor: Barbara McLean. Running Time: 107 minutes.

CAST:

Tyrone Power (*Andrea Orsini*); Orson Welles (*Cesare Borgia*); Everett Sloane (*Belli*); Wanda Hendrix (*Camilla Verano*); Felix Aylmer (*Count Verano*); Katina Paxinou (*Mona Zoppo*); Marina Berti (*Angela*); Leslie Bradley (*Estaban*); Joop van Hulzen (*D'Este*); James Carney (*Alphonson D'Este*); Eduardo Ciannelli (*Art Dealer*). WITH: Rena Lennart, Giuseppe Faeti, Adriano Ambrogi, Eva Breuer, Franco Corsaro, Ludmilla Durarowa, Albert Latasha.

SYNOPSIS:

Cesare Borgia (Orson Welles), aiming to extend his control over the whole of Italy, selects Andrea Orsini (Tyrone Power) as his envoy. Orsini already had proven his loyalty by arranging a politically convenient marriage between Cesare's sister, Lucretia, and the Duke of Ferrara (Joop van Hulzen) following the assassination of Lucretia's former husband.

It is Orsini's mission to seek out and murder the elderly Count Verano (Felix Aylmer) in preparation for Borgia's seizing Verano's province. However, once there, Orsini is impressed by the wise and peace-loving Verano. Instead of ordering his aide Belli (Everett Sloane) to assassinate the count, Orsini switches sides and joins Verano in opposition to the invading Borgia army.

Meanwhile, Orsini has fallen in love with Verano's beautiful young wife Camilla (Wanda Hendrix). When Borgia and his army attack, the count is killed and Orsini surrenders in order to save the town and its people. Belli is ordered to gouge out Orsini's eyes, but tricks Borgia into believing he has followed instructions, allowing Orsini to escape. Orsini organizes an army to rescue Camilla and recapture the town, and with Borgia's army defeated, he wins the hand of Camilla in marriage.

NOTES:

Planning a film of *Othello*, Orson Welles began to accept more work as actor only, and this costume adventure was just the type of big-budget feature which would keep him in the public eye while at the same time providing valuable funds for his project.

Prince of Foxes, as directed by Henry King, was filmed in the authentic locations of the story in Italy and served as a starring vehicle for Tyrone Power, the studio's top box-office attraction of the era. Welles' previous encounter with Power had been in the Katharine Cornell production of

PRINCE OF FOXES: With Tyrone Power in one of the film's early scenes.

PRINCE OF FOXES: Belli (Everett Sloane) shows Borgia (Welles) the "blood" on his hands from torturing Orsini.

PRINCE OF FOXES: Orson Welles as Cesare Borgia.

Romeo and Juliet in 1935, when the two young actors had fought for the best role, with Orson coming off best, Tyrone being replaced by him in a second run of the play.

Typical of the grand-scale historical epics of Twentieth Century-Fox, *Prince of Foxes* was unusual in that it was shot in black and white, noted by a number of reviewers of the time. Welles' role in the film was limited. Following a strong opening sequence, he disappeared for much of the picture, as the story follows Orsini (Tyrone Power) on his quest across Italy. However, when he was on screen, Welles created a good impression, leaving his audience to wish he had been allowed a more substantial role.

The film reunited Orson once more with Everett Sloane. Unusually, this fine actor's screen appearances subsequent to his debut in *Citizen Kane* had amounted only to three other films — each of them an Orson Welles movie. From the early fifties onward though, he was to become a much sought after performer and enjoyed a successful and prolific career until his tragic suicide in 1965.

Prince of Foxes was nominated for Academy Awards in the categories of Costume Design (Vittorio Nino) and Cinematography (Leon Shamroy).

REVIEWS:

A picture of stately magnificence, so far as settings and costumes are concerned, and of unbounded generosity in bringing the Italian Renaissance to popular view . . . Tyrone Power as the bold adventurer swashes as much as he can, but the tempo and mood of the picture hold him down . . . Orson Welles's eager performance of Cesare Borgia, whom they called "The Bull," is remarkably appropriate to that distinctive soubriquet.
— Bosley Crowther, *The New York Times*

The cast, headed by Tyrone Power and Orson Welles, is top-grade and performs with all the enthusiasm demanded of it . . . Welles is outstanding in his portrayal of the cruel and power-drunk Borgia.
— *Motion Picture Herald*

THE BLACK ROSE

1950. TWENTIETH CENTURY-FOX.

Directed by Henry Hathaway. Produced by Louis D. Leighton.
Executive Producer: Darryl F. Zanuck. Screenplay: Talbot Jennings, based on the novel by Thomas Costain. Director of Photography: Jack Cardiff. Art Directors: Paul Sheriff, W. Andrews. Music Score: Richard Addinsell. Musical Conductor: Muir Mathieson. Special Effects: W. Percy Day. Film Editor: Manuel del Campo.
Running Time: 120 minutes. Technicolor.

CAST:

Tyrone Power (*Walter of Gurnie*); Orson Welles (*Bayan*); Cecile Aubry (*Maryam*); Jack Hawkins (*Tristram Griffen*); Finlay Currie (*Alfgar*); Michael Rennie (*King Edward*); Herbert Lom (*Anthemus*); Mary Clare (*Countess of Lesford*); Bobby Blake (*Mahmoud*); Alfonso Bedoya (*Lu Chung*); James Robertson Justice (*Simeon Beautrie*); Laurence Harvey (*Edmond*); Torin Thatcher (*Harry*); Gibb McLaughlin (*Wilderkin*); WITH: Hilary Pritchard, Valery Inkijinoff, George Woodbridge, Peter Drury, Ley On, Madame Phang, Carl Jaffe, Rufus Cruikshank, Ben Williams, Alexis Chesnakov.

SYNOPSIS:

In thirteenth-century England, Saxon nobleman Walter of Gurnie (Tyrone Power) refuses to pledge allegiance to Edward (Michael Rennie), the Norman king, and instead leaves for the East with the rebel leader and expert bowman, Tristram Griffen (Jack Hawkins).

Traveling through Antioch, they encounter Bayan (Orson Welles), a Mongol warrior who dreams of conquering the world. Walter and Tristram join with Bayan's troops taking gifts to the

THE BLACK ROSE: As Bayan, the Mongol warlord.

THE BLACK ROSE: Tyrone Power, Orson Welles and Jack Hawkins.

Kublai Khan. Chief gift is *The Black Rose*, a beautiful Eurasian slave girl called Maryam (Cecile Aubry), who pleads with Walter to rescue her from her fate.

While attempting their planned escape, Walter is captured by Bayan and tortured, and soon afterward, Tristram and Maryam are also brought back. Approaching the Chinese border, Bayan's troops attack the royal city.

Tristram is killed during the battle, but Walter escapes and returns to England where he reveals the secrets of the Chinese arts of gunpowder, the compass and paper making. He once again is treated as a nobleman, regaining his lands. Bayan, meanwhile, decides to send Maryam to England as a gift for Walter, despite their differences in China.

NOTES:

Having already proved sympathetic to Welles' plans for filming *Othello* by casting him in *Prince of Foxes*, Darryl F. Zanuck once again teamed Orson with Tyrone Power in the follow-up picture *The Black Rose*. Another starring vehicle for the dashing Power, the film was Orson's first to be made in color, and benefited enormously from the excellent work of the always reliable Jack Cardiff as cinematographer.

Filmed in England and North Africa with a largely English cast, *The Black Rose* was not without its problems for Welles. Director Henry Hathaway evidently attempted to curb what he considered Orson's natural desire to direct himself, with several disagreements resulting. Apart from this, both men genuinely appeared to admire each other, although their relationship on the picture was not always an easy one.

Despite the lavish color and the attention to detail, the film proved to be less popular with audiences than *Prince of Foxes* had been.

Release of the film was delayed in Germany following unfavorable remarks on the German people attributed to Welles in a newspaper article. Orson claimed that he had been misquoted in the report.

REVIEWS:

. . . oddly, the motion picture drama which Talbot Jennings has digested from the [Thomas Costain] book is a woefully unexciting recount of gaudy but static episodes . . . Orson Welles makes a valiant attempt to endow the Tartan general with a wild and bizarre quality, but again we only see him as a fine conversationalist . . . We are afraid that director Henry Hathaway pictured everything but the pulsing drama of *The Black Rose* — and that's a downright shame.
— Thomas M. Pryor, *The New York Times*

Capable performances by Tyrone Power, Jack Hawkins . . . and a suitably sinister one by Orson Welles.
— *Monthly Film Bulletin*

RETURN TO GLENNASCAUL

1951. A DUBLIN GATE THEATRE PRODUCTION.

Directed by Hilton Edwards. Produced by Micheal MacLiammoir and Hilton Edwards. Screenplay: Hilton Edwards. Director of Photography: George Fleischmann.
Running Time: 23 minutes.

SYNOPSIS:

After a day's filming on his production of *Othello*, Orson Welles (playing himself) is driving home when he picks up a young man whose car has broken down. The passenger proceeds to tell Orson a story about his own experience of giving a lift to two ladies who took him to their home. Attracted to the younger of the women, the man returns the following day to find the house derelict and coated with a thick layer of dust.

The house evidently has been unoccupied for many years, yet as a distant clock chimes, the man finds his own cigarette case on the mantel where he had left it the previous evening.

Dropping the man off, Welles continues his journey, but seeing two women in the road ahead, he speeds away as fast as possible.

NOTES:

Return To Glennascaul, made during a break in shooting *Othello*, is a modest and charming short film, produced by Orson's two friends from the Gate Theatre, Micheal MacLiammoir and Hilton Edwards.

Apparently intrigued by their experiences of filming with Welles on his Shakespeare film, they put together this effective ghost story, benefiting substantially from Welles' presence, although he is seen only at the film's beginning and end.

Welles' contribution to it is therefore slight, though he delivers the film's one comedy line: explaining his car's breakdown, the young man remarks, "I'm having trouble with my distributor," to which Orson wryly responds, "I know what you mean, I'm having trouble with mine!"

REVIEWS:

Readers sometimes deplore the quality of short films nowadays; here is something worth looking at for a change.   — Dilys Powell, *Sunday Times*

RETURN TO GLENNASCAUL: Welles stopping to help a stranded motorist.

OTHELLO

1951. A MERCURY PRODUCTION.

Produced and Directed by Orson Welles.
Screenplay: Orson Welles, from the play by William Shakespeare. Director of Photography: Anchise Brizzi, G. R. Aldo, George Fanto. Music Score: Francesco Lavagnino, Alberto Barberis. Film Editors: Jean Sacha, John Shepridge, Renzo Lucidi, William Morton.
Running Time: 91 minutes.

CAST:

Orson Welles (*Othello*); Suzanne Cloutier (*Desdemona*); Micheal MacLiammoir (*Iago*); Robert Coote (*Roderigo*); Hilton Edwards (*Brabantio*); Fay Compton (*Emilia*); Michael Lawrence (*Cassio*); Nicholas Bruce (*Lodovico*); Doris Dowling (*Bianca*); Jean Davis (*Montano*); WITH: Joseph Cotten, Joan Fontaine.

SYNOPSIS:

Learning that Othello the Moor (Orson Welles) has won the hand of Desdemona (Suzanne Cloutier) in marriage, Roderigo (Robert Coote), who had hoped to marry Desdemona himself, tries to destroy their plans by revealing their elopement to her father Brabantio (Hilton Edwards). Influenced by Iago (Micheal MacLiammoir), a cunning soldier who resents Othello's

OTHELLO: As the moor Othello.

promotion of Cassio (Michael Lawrence) in his place, Roderigo begins to plot Othello's downfall.

When Othello leads the Venetian troops to victory against the Turks, he is acclaimed as a great warrior. Iago, meanwhile, aims to take advantage of Othello's nature by convincing first Roderigo and then Cassio that Desdemona is falling in love with the latter. When Cassio is demoted due to his mutinous behavior toward Othello, Iago's wife Emilia is sent to persuade Desdemona to speak to her husband on Cassio's behalf. Unaware of the plot, she asks Othello to reinstate the young soldier. Iago then suggests to Othello that Desdemona is infatuated with Cassio, and although Othello disbelieves him, he nevertheless is made suspicious by Iago's skillful deceit.

Finding one of Desdemona's handkerchiefs, Iago plants it with Cassio's things, and continues to work upon Othello's jealousy. When the handkerchief is found to be in the possession of Cassio, Othello is convinced that Desdemona has betrayed him. Iago then orders Roderigo to kill Cassio. When the plan misfires, Iago himself kills Roderigo to prevent him telling the truth. Emilia rushes to Othello to tell him what has happened, but Othello has murdered Desdemona, convinced of her treachery.

Emilia reveals to Othello that Iago has been lying to him. Iago kills his wife but is captured while attempting to escape. Othello, however, is now completely broken and takes his own life in preference to living on without his beloved Desdemona.

NOTES:

At the suggestion of an Italian producer, Orson Welles began to prepare a movie of *Othello* in 1949 which he would direct as well as star in. The deal, however, fell through, but inspired Welles to continue with the project himself. His film version of *Othello* was to be financed entirely from other Welles acting jobs. In this way, he was certain that he would at last be able to retain complete control over his movie, having been let down by Hollywood studios once too often. At the outset, he could not possibly have guessed that it would be another three years before the film was completed. A saga of financial crises

OTHELLO: Othello with his Desdemona (Suzanne Cloutier).

110

OTHELLO: On set discussion among Desdemona, Othello, Mrs. Iago (Fay Compton) and Iago (Micheal MacLiammoir).

atre in Dublin. MacLiammoir made his film debut as Iago, with Edwards cast as Desdemona's father, Brabantio. Suzanne Cloutier was a late choice as Desdemona, other actresses considered including expatriate American actress Betsy Blair (who was Gene Kelly's wife at the time) and Cecile Aubry, the French ingenue from *The Black Rose*.

With new Italian backers promptly going bankrupt, the crew found itself stranded in Morocco. Costumes being impounded, the killing of Roderigo was immediately rewritten by Welles to take place in a Turkish bath, where the actors would need only to wear towels. This brilliant piece of improvisation provided one of the film's most effective scenes.

Otherwise, *Othello* was a faithful adaptation of Shakespeare's play, although inevitably some critics faulted it. Overall, though, the film is perhaps the most successful version of the play, previously done only once in a sound version — a British 1946 low-budget feature. Later additions included a USSR version in 1955, and the 1965 British film of Laurence Olivier's National Theatre production.

unfolded over the period, with the initially inexpensive production constantly escalating.

To be shot in Italy, partly for economic reasons, *Othello* quickly found its crew, assembled by Welles with his salary from *Prince of Foxes*. Orson then left them almost immediately to appear in *The Black Rose*, but kept his company together in the meantime; he even at one point is said to have "borrowed" some of the equipment used on *The Black Rose*, shooting *Othello* at night before returning the apparatus to the other film's set in the morning! Darryl F. Zanuck also contributed a further sum to Orson's production, which was then hit by a major crisis when the film's Iago, Everett Sloane — Orson's long-time colleague from the Mercury company — left the picture, unhappy over the erratic progress of filming.

This meant some reshooting of scenes, after finding another Iago. Welles solved this problem by calling upon his old friends Hilton Edwards and Micheal MacLiammoir from the Gate The-

OTHELLO: Othello with his treacherous Iago.

Money for the completion of *Othello* came from a variety of sources: Welles' touring version of *Dr. Faustus* with Eartha Kitt and successful radio broadcasts for the BBC in London, as well as a stage version of *Othello* in London, where Orson made his West End debut. Bouncing from one location to another across Europe, filming continued with scenes often beginning in one country and ending a thousand miles away, but skillfully edited to retain continuity.

When finally screened at the Venice Film Festival of 1952, *Othello* was rapturously received, and awarded the Grand Prize. Back in America, however, the major studios remained unimpressed, with, as before, no further offers forthcoming.

A slight technical problem with many release prints of the film means that the sound quality on parts of the film is distorted, although Welles insisted that the original copy did not have this fault.

Unbilled guest appearances in *Othello*: Orson's old friend Joseph Cotten, recruited from a nearby set for *September Affair* in Venice, playing a wealthy Venetian senator, and Joan Fontaine (also from *September Affair*) curiously cast as his page boy! Also glimpsed in the film was Welles' daughter Rebecca from his marriage to Rita Hayworth.

OTHELLO: Othello's Desdemona.

OTHELLO: Impressive location for the film.

REVIEWS:

How much of Shakespeare's *Othello* you are likely to be able to perceive in Orson Welles's motion picture version of it . . . is something this dazzled reviewer would not like to have to guarantee. Shakespeare himself, set down before it, might have a tough time recognizing his play . . . this extraordinary picture, which took more than three years to make and equally as long — or longer — to re-dub and prepare for showing here, is strictly an un-literate, inarticulate and hotly impressionistic film, full of pictorial pyrotechnics

OTHELLO: Othello learns of Desdemona's supposed betrayal.

OTHELLO: "One that lov'd, not wisely, but too well": Othello and Desdemona.

and sinister, shadowy moods . . . Let's be completely forthright about the talent revealed by Mr. Welles. He has a wonderful skill at image-making but a blind spot where substance is concerned . . . There are flashes of brilliant suggestions in this tumbled, slurred and helter-skelter film. But they add up to nothing substantial — just a little of Shakespeare and a lot of Welles.
— Bosley Crowther, *The New York Times* (on the film's New York release in September 1955)

Everything is done with great bravura style . . . Yet, despite the camera tricks, engulfing shadows, dizzying vistas of colonnades and architectural arabesques, the film moves forward at a pulse-quickening stir and bustle. As the jealous Moor, Welles captures the falco look of a Kabyle from the Atlas Mountains.
— *Time*

A few years ago I saw Orson Welles play *Othello* on the stage: a great bewildered bull of a man, heartbreaking in his gullibility, his rage and his remorse . . . I still find this a moving Othello . . . Mr. Welles' stature, gesture, tones make the crumbling of reason, the blind, deaf rage believ-

able. When I think of the Moor now, this is the Moor I imagine . . . At the end of this film . . . I feel that what I have seen is large, noble and tragic.
— Dilys Powell, *Sunday Times*

Orson Welles is such a remarkable actor and director that his failures are worth more than most men's successes. I will not call *Othello* a failure, for there are superb things in it; but few will call it a success . . . The acting? Mr. Welles . . . cuts a magnificent figure as the Moor and, if he doesn't make the most of the poetry, loses none of the sense.
— *Daily Telegraph*

OTHELLO: Iago and Othello.

114

TRENT'S LAST CASE

1952. BRITISH LION FILMS.

Produced and Directed by Herbert Wilcox.
Screenplay: Pamela Bower, from the novel by E. C. Bentley. Director of Photography: Max Greene. Music Score: Anthony Collins. Film Editor: Bill Lewthwaite. Running Time: 90 minutes.

CAST:

Michael Wilding (*Philip Trent*); Margaret Lockwood (*Margaret Manderson*); Orson Welles (*Sigsbee Manderson*); John McCallum (*John Marlowe*); Miles Malleson (*Burton Cupples*); Hugh McDermott (*Calvin C. Bunner*). WITH: Jack McNaughton, Sam Kydd.

SYNOPSIS:

Amateur detective Philip Trent (Michael Wilding) is called in to investigate the death of American-born millionaire Sigsbee Manderson (Orson Welles), following a coroner's inquest verdict of suicide. Trent suspects that Manderson has been murdered by John Marlowe (John McCallum), the millionaire's private secretary, as a means of win-

TRENT'S LAST CASE: Orson stealing the spotlight from supporting star John McCallum.

ning Manderson's wife Margaret (Margaret Lockwood).

The investigation proves Trent partly correct, but a surprise statement by Margaret's uncle, Burton Cupples (Miles Malleson), reveals that Manderson did after all commit suicide but planned to implicate Marlowe, his wife's lover. Margaret meanwhile has fallen for Trent, and the two are married.

NOTES:

Continuing his sojourns across Europe, Orson Welles settled on making a couple of pictures for the British producer/director Herbert Wilcox. Accepting a role in *Trent's Last Case*, a famous though somewhat dated novel, Welles was again acting chiefly for the salary which he would put to use elsewhere. A relatively brief role as the murdered husband offered little challenge to an actor of Orson's capabilities.

John McCallum recalls Welles' often curious behavior on the set: "Herbert Wilcox wanted to retake a whole day's shooting because a lamp had shone in Orson's spectacles. Orson seized on it and said *he* wanted to reshoot the scene with lamps instead of eyes in *both* lenses." Evidently eager to please his star, Wilcox let Orson go his own way. "Herbert offered him the adjoining studio to shoot his close-ups," says McCallum. "He

TRENT'S LAST CASE: Millionaire Sigsbee Manderson (Orson Welles) in a romantic mood with wife Margaret (Margaret Lockwood).

did — and it looked crazy of course and had to be scrapped."

Herbert Wilcox had previously been associated with RKO, which distributed his British-made films in the United States. It was here that Orson Welles first encountered him, over a decade earlier. Wilcox had been at the RKO studios working on *Irene* starring his wife Anna Neagle at the time when Welles was shooting *Citizen Kane*. While RKO was generally less than enthusiastic about the Mercury film, both Wilcox and Miss Neagle were highly vocal in their support for Orson's directorial debut, and made their feelings well known to the RKO heads.

Despite his generosity as a director, often giving huge chunks of scenes to supporting and bit players, Welles' approach to his acting in *Trent's Last Case* was apparently something quite different. John McCallum again: "He was extremely selfish as an actor, very conscious of the best camera angles. In the film he had to hand me a mysterious package to take to Paris at the beginning of a scene. He said it would intrigue the audience more if he kept it until the end of the scene, which he did — knowing the audience would be looking at him and the package in his hand throughout the scene."

Perhaps to add something to the role, Welles insisted on wearing yet another of his false noses: ever since *Citizen Kane*, Orson had reveled in the possibilities of makeup, to the extent that only in *The Third Man* had he been seen devoid of wigs or fake noses.

Filmed in Great Britain, *Trent's Last Case* boasted a strong, all-British cast (though John McCallum, husband of Googie Withers, is actually Australian). Michael Wilding and Margaret Lockwood were both major box-office stars of the period, but despite this, the picture did only moderately well. The film was released by Republic in the U.S., but received only spotty distribution, often on the bottom half of double bills.

REVIEWS:

As the victim who is seen in flashback in the last half of the film, Orson Welles makes the most of his belated appearance. In new makeup — aquiline nose, black homburg, graying hair — he is a tough, brooding schemer, a composite of Machiavelli and a Wall Street tycoon and a jealous conniver who will not stop at anything to thwart his wife's seeming transgressions.
— A. H. Weiler, *The New York Times*

Acquitting himself most favorably is Welles, whose role, although limited to flashbacks, permits him a couple of fine scenes.
— *Motion Picture Herald*

THREE CASES OF MURDER

1954. WESSEX/LONDON FILMS.

Produced by Ian Dalrymple and Hugh Perceval. Director of Photography: Georges Perinal. Art Director: Paul Sherriff. Music Score: Doreen Carwithen. Sound Recording: John Cox. Film Editor: G. Turney Smith. Running Time: 99 minutes.

CREDITS:

In the Picture: Directed by Wendy Toye. Screenplay: Donald Wilson, from a story by Roderick Wilkinson. CAST: Alan Badel, Hugh Pryse, Leueen MacGrath, Eddie Byrne, John Salew, Ann Hanslip.

You Killed Elizabeth: Directed by David Eady. Screenplay: Sidney Carroll, from a story by Brett Halliday. CAST: Elizabeth Sellars, John Gregson, Emrys Jones, Jack Lambert, Alan Badel.

Lord Mountdrago: Directed by George More O'Ferrall. Screenplay: Ian Dalrymple, from a story by W. Somerset Maugham. CAST: Orson Welles (*Lord Mountdrago*); Alan Badel (*Owen*); Helen Cherry (*Lady Mountdrago*); André Morell (*Dr. Audlin*); Peter Burton (*Foreign Affairs Undersecretary*); Arthur Wontner (*Leader of the House*); John Humphrey (*Private Secretary*); David Horne (*Sir James*).

SYNOPSIS:

A portmanteau film of the type popular in Britain since the highly acclaimed Ealing Studios' *Dead of Night* in 1945, *Three Cases of Murder* told three independent stories without a linking theme, although Welsh actor Alan Badel appeared in each episode.

The stories — introduced by British Television personality Eamonn Andrews — all were photographed by ace French cinematographer Georges Perinal, whose previous work included early films by Jean Cocteau and Réné Clair and a series of

THREE CASES OF MURDER: As Mountdrago, the scourge of the House of Commons.

British productions for Alexander Korda. Different directors were assigned to each segment.

In the Picture is set in an art gallery. A mysterious visitor to the gallery, Mr. X (Alan Badel), discusses one of the works with the museum guide, Jarvis (Hugh Pryse). The painting, of a house, fascinates Jarvis, who is transported into the picture along with Mr. X, who reveals himself as the artist. Other inhabitants of the picture include a taxidermist, who claims Jarvis as his next subject. Mr. X meanwhile leaves the picture in search of a new victim.

You Killed Elizabeth concerns a young businessman, Edgar Curtain (John Gregson), prone to attacks of amnesia. Following an argument with his business partner, George Wheeler (Emrys Jones), over George's former girlfriend, Elizabeth (Elizabeth Sellars), Edgar suffers another memory loss. When he recovers, he learns that Elizabeth has been murdered, and that there are bloodstains on his coat. Edgar is accused of murder, but when George commits suicide, a barman (Alan Badel) at their local club discovers Elizabeth's bracelet left at his bar, and George is revealed as the real killer.

The final episode, *Lord Mountdrago*, is the longest of the three. British Foreign Secretary Lord Mountdrago (Orson Welles) is a pompous,

THREE CASES OF MURDER: One of Mountdrago's nightmares.

117

THREE CASES OF MURDER: Mountdrago (Orson Welles) eyes Owen (Alan Badel) suspiciously after another nightmare comes true.

overbearing figure renowned for his incisive, cutting speeches. Victim of his latest attack is opposition MP Owen (Alan Badel), an idealist whose sincerity is brutally mocked by Mountdrago with the effect that Owen's career is in ruins.

Outside the chamber of Parliament, Owen threatens revenge, and Mountdrago begins to suffer a series of nightmares, all of which feature Owen discovering him in humiliating situations. Following each dream, incidents in Parliament convince Mountdrago that Owen is somehow responsible for them. Lady Mountdrago (Helen Cherry) persuades her husband to see Dr. Audlin (André Morell), but the dreams continue until Mountdrago hits on the idea that the waking Owen can be affected by the events of the previous night's dream.

Audlin is deeply concerned when Mountdrago tells him that he intends to kill Owen in his next dream, and so be rid of him. Mountdrago does so that night, but the following day, convinced that Owen is still mocking him from the other side of the House, he rushes from the chamber, stumbling to his death down a huge flight of stairs. Before dying he learns that Owen had indeed died the night before, but has still managed to emerge the victor.

NOTES:

Another of Orson Welles' British films, *Three Cases of Murder* was an interesting if rather low-key movie. Less successful than other portmanteau films, it nevertheless contains some strong acting from Welles, and fine support from the versatile Alan Badel.

Welles adopted his immaculate British accent once again for the role of Mountdrago, and was thoroughly convincing in the part. One is tempted to suspect Welles' hand in the filming, which differs sharply from what has gone before. A number of scenes, most notably in the House of Commons and the interview with Dr. Audlin, seem to bear the stamp of Welles the director, though no real evidence has been put forward to support this.

REVIEWS:

The last is the best, for our money. That is the one by Maugham . . . in which conscience kills a man. The man is a British Foreign Minister, played by Orson Welles, who suffers a fearful obsession of the ruin he has caused an opponent. And the whole thing is a demonstration of this cold and pompous statesman going mad under the imagined taunts of his victim, which is something Mr. Welles does handsomely.
— Bosley Crowther, *The New York Times*

George More O'Ferrall was apparently unable to keep Orson Welles in check, and thus *Lord Mountdrago* is distinguished by his fascinatingly hammy performance in the title role. He casts his enormous shadow over everything in sight, investing his part with considerably more emphasis than is required.   — *Monthly Film Bulletin*

TROUBLE IN THE GLEN

1954. REPUBLIC PICTURES. A WILCOX-NEAGLE PRODUCTION.

Directed by Herbert Wilcox. Produced by Stuart Robertson.
Screenplay: Frank S. Nugent, from a story by Maurice Walsh. Director of Photography: Max Greene. Music Score: Victor Young. Film Editor: Reginald Beck.
Running Time: 91 minutes. Color.

CAST:

Margaret Lockwood (*Marissa*); Orson Welles (*Sandy Menzies, The Laird*); Forrest Tucker (*Lance*); Victor McLaglen (*Parlan*); John McCallum (*Malcolm*); Eddie Byrne (*Dinny Sullivan*); Ann Gudrun (*Dandy Dinmont*); Margaret McCourt (*Alsuin*); Archie Duncan (*Nollie Dukes*); Moultrie Kelsall (*Luke Carnoch*); Mary Mackenzie (*Kate Carnoch*).

SYNOPSIS:

Sandy Menzies (Orson Welles) is a wealthy Argentinian, now living in the Scottish Highlands where, as laird of his grandfather's estate, he still retains his South American ways. When Menzies dismisses one of his workers after a quarrel, the rest of the glen take against him, refusing to work. In retaliation, Menzies closes the road leading through his land.

Major Jim Lansing (Forrest Tucker), a widowed U.S. Air Force pilot, arrives in Scotland to see his crippled daughter, Alsuin (Margaret McCourt). He learns of the road's closure, but when he approaches the laird, he is turned away by Menzies' daughter, Marissa (Margaret Lockwood).

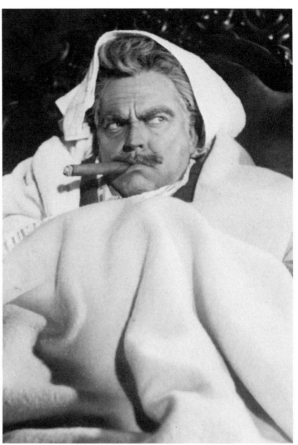

TROUBLE IN THE GLEN: Menzies takes to the blankets to keep off a highland chill.

Unrest grows in the glen, with Nollie Dukes (Archie Duncan) threatening to evict the local tinkers, led by Parlan (Victor McLaglen) and his son Malcolm (John McCallum). A violent confrontation is averted when Lansing comes to blows with Dukes. Menzies, realizing his responsibilities as laird of his people, calls a halt and reopens the road. With the inhabitants of the glen happy once more, Alsuin begins to recover the use of her legs, and at a grand ball, Menzies is seen to adopt the tartan kilt of his ancestors.

NOTES:

The second of Orson Welles' films for British director Herbert Wilcox found him cast rather bizarrely as a kilted Argentinian laird at large in Scotland. Welles was surrounded by virtually the same cast from *Trent's Last Case:* Margaret Lockwood (in that film, Welles' wife; here his daughter), John McCallum and Eddie Byrne, with Victor McLaglen and Forrest Tucker imported from Hollywood to give the film more international appeal. It is from a story by Maurice Walsh, who

TROUBLE IN THE GLEN: Sandy Menzies (Orson Welles) and daughter Marissa (Margaret Lockwood) don't much like what they see from the window.

119

TROUBLE IN THE GLEN: Sandy and Marissa give a cool reception to Jim Lansing. Left to right: Orson Welles, Margaret Lockwood and Forrest Tucker.

... something went wrong in the fulfillment — something that smacks suspiciously of a dismal lack of humor in the characters, and a heavy directorial hand ... Ponderous at the outset is Orson Welles as the laird. Mr. Welles plays this fearful character with a trace of his style as Macbeth.
— Bosley Crowther, *The New York Times*

Welles' portrayal is frequently one of the best things in the picture.   — *Variety*

In Orson Welles' presence, the whole thing is a crazy burlesque of Romantic Scotland.
— *Financial Times*

There is much scenic beauty in the film, and the performance of Orson Welles was so magnificently outsize that he was like Othello wearing the kilt.   — *Evening Standard*

Orson Welles, though a victim of a colour process scarcely sympathetic to the human face, retains a certain dignity as the South American laird.
— *Monthly Film Bulletin*

also wrote *The Quiet Man*, and adapted by Frank S. Nugent, who also adapted that film.

A slight film, *Trouble in the Glen* is little more than another reworking of Dickens' *A Christmas Carol*, with Menzies (Scrooge) being rejuvenated at the end, and even a crippled child (*à la* Tiny Tim) on the road to recovery. In his role, Orson Welles was obliged to give a rather hammy performance, but still managed to make his character probably the most believable in the film. In the U.S., its poor distribution found it, like his previous few, mainly on the bottom half of double bills.

Costar John McCallum says of his two films with Orson Welles, "He had an obsession about makeup, especially noses — he hated his own little button of one." And of acting alongside Welles: "Until you got used to it, his low mumbling delivery of lines was disconcerting — you could hardly hear him two feet away. It was a calculated effect; the sound man had to open the mike so far to pick him up that his voice sounded a much lower growl than it really was."

MR. ARKADIN

(U.K. Title: Confidential Report)

1955. CERVANTES FILMS. A MERCURY PRODUCTION.

Produced and Directed by Orson Welles. Executive Producer: Louis Dolivet. Screenplay: Orson Welles, from his own novel. Director of Photography: Jean Bourgoin. Music Score: Paul Misraki. Sound Recording: Jacques Lebreton. Film Editor: Renzo Lucidi.
Running Time: 99 minutes.

CAST:

Orson Welles (*Gregory Arkadin*); Paola Mori (*Raina Arkadin*); Robert Arden (*Guy van Stratten*); Akim Tamiroff (*Jacob Zouk*); Patricia Medina (*Mily*); Michael Redgrave (*Burgomil Trebitsch*); Mischa Auer (*The Professor*); Katina Paxinou (*Sophie*); Jack Watling (*Marquis of Rutleigh*); Gregoire Aslan (*Bracco*); Peter van Eyck (*Thaddeus*); Suzanne Flon (*Baronless Nagel*); Frederic O'Brady (*Oscar*); Tamara Shane (*Blond Woman*).

SYNOPSIS:

Guy van Stratten (Robert Arden) and his girl Mily (Patricia Medina) go to the aid of the victim of a violent attack on the Naples dockside. The dying man, Bracco (Gregoire Aslan), whispers to Mily a fragment of information consisting of two names: "Sophie" and "Gregory Arkadin."

Van Stratten, a small-time smuggler and adventurer, suspects that this clue may lead to bigger things; Arkadin is one of the wealthiest and most powerful men in the world. Approaching Arkadin (Orson Welles), van Stratten is immediately drawn toward the tycoon's daughter, Raina (Paola Mori), whom Arkadin idolizes. To get van Stratten out of the way, and playing on the younger man's greed, Arkadin offers him a job as an inves-

MR. ARKADIN: Two adventurers bent on seeking out the mystery behind Arkadin: Mily (Patricia Medina) and Guy Van Stratten (Robert Arden).

MR. ARKADIN: The all-powerful Gregory Arkadin.

MR. ARKADIN: Paola Mori as Raina, Arkadin's daughter, with Robert Arden.

tigator on the condition that he must never see Raina again.

The offer of money is too strong for van Stratten, who is then told that the subject of his investigation is to be Gregory Arkadin himself. Arkadin claims to have no memory of his early life or of his own true identity; his earliest memory is of being alone in Zurich in 1927 with 200,000 Swiss francs in his pocket.

Beginning his quest, van Stratten travels across Europe, slowly discovering people who knew Arkadin in his earlier days — each supplying a further link as to where the tycoon and his money came from. A collection of ill-assorted people contribute to van Stratten's dossier — a flea-trainer in Copenhagen (Mischa Auer), an eccentric antique dealer in Amsterdam (Michael Redgrave), a Zurich tailor (Akim Tamiroff). Mily, meanwhile, is conducting her own research and is invited aboard Arkadin's yacht where she drunkenly confronts the millionaire with Guy's discoveries.

MR. ARKADIN: Van Stratten tracks down Arkadin's past through tailor Jacob Zouk (Akim Tamiroff) . . .

MR. ARKADIN: . . . antique dealer Trebitsch (Michael Redgrave) . . .

MR. ARKADIN: . . . and flea trainer The Professor (Mischa Auer).

Van Stratten has discovered a Polish baroness (Katina Paxinou) — the "Sophie" of Bracco's confession — who tells him the real truth about Gregory Arkadin's background. He had been a member of a gang of white slavers before escaping with 200,000 francs, leaving them to be rounded up by the police. Now married to a retired Mexican general, Sophie holds no bitterness toward Arkadin.

When Mily is found murdered, van Stratten discovers that all of his contacts — Sophie included — have since met with violent deaths shortly after he had filed his reports with Arkadin. He realizes that he has been used to trace those figures who might prove embarrassing to Arkadin, who has then systematically had each of them killed in order to prevent Raina from learning the truth about him.

Inevitably breaking his promise not to see Raina again, Guy contacts her at Barcelona Airport where she is waiting for her father's plane. By radio, Arkadin tells his daughter not to listen to anything which van Stratten might have to say, but Guy persuades her to say that he has already spoken to her. Thinking he has been exposed and that all is lost, Arkadin leaps to his death, leaving his plane to crash into the sea.

NOTES:

In the mid-1950s, Orson Welles published two novels — *Un Grosse Legume*, and the thriller *Mr.*

MR. ARKADIN: Welles as Arkadin.

MR. ARKADIN: Van Stratten tells Arkadin he has discovered the truth about his past.

Arkadin. The latter is superficially another variation on the *Citizen Kane* theme, i.e., an investigation into the life of a wealthy and powerful man, sparked by his dying words and revealed through contact with various "witnesses" from his past.

Arkadin himself was apparently an amalgam of armaments millionaire Sir Basil Zaharoff and wealthy tycoon Ivar Kreuge — two men whose deaths had caused major scandals some years earlier. Interestingly, Welles had appeared in a *March of Time* newsreel impersonating Zaharoff back in the late 1930s.

The story had already formed the basis of one of Welles' BBC radio programs in the *Adventures of Harry Lime* series; Welles as Lime investigating Arkadin's background. Expanded first to novel form and then to a feature film, *Mr. Arkadin* was to be financed again largely by Orson Welles' work in other movies, although executive producer Louis Dolivet was recruited to secure extra cash wherever possible.

Shooting began in Madrid, with a remarkable cast assembled including Katina Paxinou, Michael Redgrave, Mischa Auer, Suzanne Flon and Akim Tamiroff, all of whom would make cameo appearances in the film. Some reports suggest that French actor Michel Simon was sought for the role of Arkadin, which may partly explain

Orson Welles' makeup — extraordinary even by his own standards.

Major roles went to Patricia Medina (Mrs. Joseph Cotten) and the Italian Countess di Girfalco, Paola Mori, as Arkadin's daughter. Miss Mori was to become Welles' wife shortly afterward. Cast in the central figure of van Stratten was the relatively unknown Robert Arden. Appearing in *Guys and Dolls* in London, Arden was visited by Carol Reed who told him that Orson Welles wanted him to fly to Madrid to start shooting almost immediately! "I was chosen for the part of van Stratten after having worked with Orson some time previously in a series of radio productions," he says, "as well as several on-off shows. We became fairly good friends during that period, and he offhandedly said that one day he'd like to put me in a film. Two years later, he did."

Filming continued across France, Germany, Spain and Italy, with the inevitable money problems following them as they went. Robert Arden reveals something of working with Welles: "To act with Welles — a little scary at first, until I discovered through conversations with Akim Tamiroff that Orson's concentration was so intense that he couldn't throw off the character until the acting part of his day was done."

With such concentration, Welles continued with what he intended to be the first of his movies since *Kane* to be made completely under his control. Away from the Hollywood studios, *Mr. Arkadin* was undoubtedly *his* film, from his own story and with his own handpicked cast.

With shooting finally completed, Welles retired to the cutting room, while Louis Dolivet set about raising funds to complete the film, selling interests in it in Switzerland and elsewhere. Once again, Welles dubbed the parts of other actors' voices — including Mischa Auer — partly to keep down costs, and also because actors were not always available for recording afterward. What happened next is not entirely clear. Welles later claimed that the picture was taken away from him, recut and completely destroyed — more so, even, than *The Magnificent Ambersons*.

Robert Arden: "No — I was not aware of any interference with the film by anyone. Its only producer was Louis Dolivet, but basically his was a finance-organizing function. Orson was really his own producer — but Louis was a strong arm during the entire period. I am not aware of what, if anything, was done to the finished print by the distributors after Orson delivered it to Warner Brothers, although I know that he always complained that liberties had been taken with his edit. He worked with Renzo Lucidi and Bill Morton on his own edit, but as I say, I don't know what happened afterward."

Whatever Welles' original vision of the film, the distributors evidently were not happy with what they saw. Released in England in 1955 under the title *Confidential Report*, the movie was not seen in America until 1962 and quickly disappeared. Welles was sufficiently appalled by the treatment of his film that even as late as 1982 he claimed that he could not even bear to look at it. Nevertheless, Robert Arden reveals that "interestingly enough, some years later in Paris, the late François Truffaut told me that he thought *Arkadin* was second only to *Kane* in his opinion, and that it had a great influence on his own career."

REVIEWS:

Orson Welles, certainly one of the most fascinating and controversial figures who ever set foot on either side of the camera, is on the screen side once again in another of his extraordinary creations . . . a film that so outraged its European financiers that they sued Mr. Welles for unprofessional conduct during its production. At about the same time, a group of highbrow French critics, writing in the influential little magazine *Cahiers du Cinema*, cited it as one of the 12 best films ever made . . . It is, in turn, baffling, exciting, infuriating, original and obscure. It is also, from start to finish, the work of a man with an unmistakable genius for the film medium. In other words, it is typically Orson Welles.

— Eugene Archer, *The New York Times*
(on the film's New York premiere in
October 1962)

I would sum up *Confidential Report* by saying that it is Welles' best film since *The Magnificent Ambersons* . . . that, given Welles' capabilities, it fascinates, stirs but disappoints. But disappointment with such thrills is worth half a dozen successes. — *New Statesman*

It has much to fascinate the student of film manners . . . A second visit is almost essential.

— Jympson Harman, *Evening Standard*

The basic material of *Confidential Report* is fairly conventional melodrama; it lacks character development — Arkadin himself remains a remote, one-dimensional figure . . . but the style in which Welles has chosen to treat it prepares one for a good deal more ... There is, as one might expect, evidence of a great deal of talent in this film — but it is a talent misapplied, destroying itself, even, in its wilful isolation from anything first-hand. A pity, when the talent itself is obviously so considerable.

— *Monthly Film Bulletin*

MOBY DICK

1956. WARNER BROS. A MOULIN PICTURE.

Produced and Directed by John Huston.
Screenplay: Ray Bradbury and John Huston, based on the novel by Herman Melville. Director of Photography: Oswald Morris. Art Director: Ralph Brinton. Music Score: Philip Stainton. Film Editor: Russell Lloyd.
Running Time: 116 minutes. Technicolor.

CAST:

Gregory Peck (*Captain Ahab*); Richard Basehart (*Ishmael*); Leo Genn (*Starbuck*); Bernard Miles (*Manxman*); Noel Purcell (*Carpenter*); Harry Andrews (*Stubb*); Friedrich Ledebur (*Queequeg*); Orson Welles (*Father Mapple*); Mervyn Johns (*Peleg*); Philip Stainton (*Bildad*); Joseph Tomelty (*Peter Coffin*); James Robertson Justice (*Captain Boomer*); Edric Connor (*Daggoo*); Seamus Kelly (*Flask*); Tamba Alleney (*Pip*); Royal Dano (*Elijah*).

SYNOPSIS:

A young seaman, Ishmael (Richard Basehart), arrives in Dublin looking for a ship. Meeting up with the ferocious-looking but kindly Queequeg (Friedrich Ledebur), he signs for the *Pequod*, a whaling ship due to set sail the next day.

On the quayside, Ishmael encounters a crippled seaman warning the crew of the voyage to come; the ship's captain will be taken by the great whale and beckon his men to follow him to their doom, he says. The crew gathers in the seaman's chapel to receive a blessing on their journey from Father Mapple (Orson Welles), before setting sail.

Captain Ahab (Gregory Peck) makes himself known to his crew after a few days at sea, offering

MOBY DICK: Orson Welles as Father Mapple.

MOBY DICK: Gregory Peck as Ahab.

a golden piece to the man who first catches sight of the great White Whale, Moby Dick. It becomes clear that Ahab is obsessed with killing Moby Dick, the whale which some years earlier had torn off the captain's leg. Forcing his men to press on in fierce weather conditions, the unstable

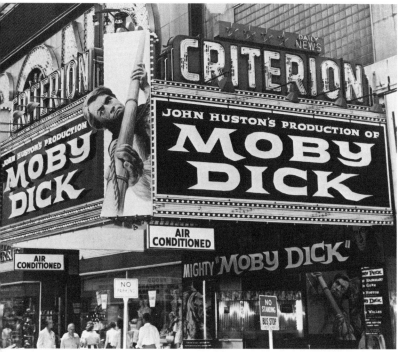

MOBY DICK: Opening of John Huston's film.

The Maltese Falcon appeared the same year as Orson's *Citizen Kane*, and the two men became friends soon afterward, their professional paths crossing on a number of occasions over the years, including a collaboration on the script to *The Stranger*. Huston had made several successful movies in the years between, including *The Treasure of the Sierra Madre*, *The Asphalt Jungle* and *The African Queen*, but this was the first time that Orson Welles had appeared in one of Huston's pictures.

Although many considered that Welles would have made a convincing Captain Ahab, that role had already gone to Gregory Peck. Orson was offered the brief but showy part of Father Mapple, with one scene only, giving a lengthy speech on the perils of the sea and blessing the voyage. Welles wrote this scene himself, since Huston was unhappy with his own treatment, but the director was delighted with Orson's version of the script, and with the performance of the piece itself; a long scene completed in a single take.

The rest of the movie, filmed with particular care by Huston and his cameraman Oswald Morris in an attempt to reproduce the look of old whaling prints, encountered severe difficulties in shooting; a huge model of the whale was lost at sea — evidently never found, and Gregory Peck was at one point nearly drowned filming in the Irish Sea.

Though a solid version of the story, *Moby Dick* was less popular at the box office than had been hoped, its reputation, however, increasing over the years.

REVIEWS:

Moby Dick has been put on the screen by John Huston in a rolling and thundering color film that is herewith devoutly recommended as one of the great motion pictures of our times . . . Orson Welles is good as Father Mapple, but his sermon is nigh superfluous.
— Bosley Crowther, *The New York Times*

Something of the spirit of the whaling men and their views is given in the early part of the picture in a rather long sermon by Orson Welles as Father Mapple. This philosophising of Melville is well delivered by Welles. — *Motion Picture Herald*

Ahab even refuses to help a fellow ship look for a man washed overboard.

Moby Dick is finally sighted, a monstrous creature, more than equal to the efforts of the crew to harpoon him. Many are killed in the confrontation, Ahab himself finally leading a group of longboats out to face the might of the giant. Caught in the ropes and hurling himself onto the back of the whale, Ahab is taken below by the creature, emerging dead but — due to the swirl of the sea — apparently beckoning his men to follow him as the seaman had foretold.

Seized by a sudden rage, Starbuck (Leo Genn) urges his crew forward once again, but the whale proves triumphant, sinking their longboats and the *Pequod* itself: only Ishmael remains, clinging to a wooden coffin as a life raft until rescued by a passing ship.

NOTES:

Orson Welles was already appearing in his own London stage production of Melville's story of *Moby Dick* and planning to film the play when he heard that his old friend John Huston was beginning his own movie of the book. Son of the great American actor Walter Huston, John had begun his career as a writer at Warner Bros. before directing his first movie in 1941.

MAN IN THE SHADOW

(U.K. Title: *Pay the Devil*)

1957. UNIVERSAL-
INTERNATIONAL.

Directed by Jack Arnold. Produced by Albert Zugsmith.
Screenplay: Gene L. Coon. Director of Photography: Arthur E. Arling. Art Directors: Alexander Golitzen, Alfred Sweeney. Music Score: Hans Salter. Film Editor: Edward Curtiss.
Running Time: 80 minutes. CinemaScope.

CAST:

Jeff Chandler (*Ben Sadler*); Orson Welles (*Virgil Renchler*); Colleen Miller (*Skippy Renchler*); John Larch (*Ed Yates*); Joe Schneider (*Juan Martin*); Leo Gordon (*Chet Huneker*); Martin Garraglia (*Jesus Cisneros*); Ben Alexander (*Ab Begley*); Barbara Lawrence (*Mrs. Sadler*); James Gleason (*Hank James*); Royal Dano (*Aiken Clay*); Paul Fix (*Herb Parker*); Mario Siletti (*Tony Santoro*); Charles Horvath (*Len Bookman*); William Schalert (*Jim Shaney*); Harry Harvey (*Dr. Creighton*); Joseph

MAN IN THE SHADOW: Renchler's men give Sadler a rough ride.

MAN IN THE SHADOW: After the townsfolk rally to Sadler's aid, Renchler is brought to justice.

Greene (*Harry Youngquist*); Forrest Lewis (*Jake Kelley*); Mort Mills (*Gateman*).

SYNOPSIS:

When a Mexican laborer is found dead at the Golden Empire ranch, owned by wealthy Virgil Renchler (Orson Welles), local sheriff Ben Sadler

MAN IN THE SHADOW: Marshal Ben Sadler (Jeff Chandler) confronts Virgil Renchler (Orson Welles) after a murder at the ranch.

(Jeff Chandler) suspects murder. Renchler, who owns and controls most of the town, tries to stop Sadler from investigating the incident. Influencing many of the more prominent townsfolk, Renchler increases the pressure on the sheriff, who becomes more determined to solve the case.

A second murder follows, and while searching for evidence, Sadler is ambushed by some of the rancher's men, beaten up and tied to the back of their truck as it drives through the town. This only serves to rouse the townsfolk, who now side with their sheriff. In a final showdown, the ranch foreman is revealed as the original murderer, and Renchler and his mob are rounded up and brought to jail.

NOTES:

For the first time in seven years, Orson Welles found himself employed by an American film studio when producer Albert Zugsmith offered him a role in a fairly routine thriller called *Man in the Shadow*.

Accepting the work to help pay tax bills to the Internal Revenue Service, Welles could not have found the work too stimulating or strenuous, but as was his usual custom, he rewrote certain of his scenes and made suggestions along the way, which director Jack Arnold — whose most notable previous movies had been *Creature From the Black Lagoon* and *The Incredible Shrinking Man* — seemed only too happy to use.

No great work of art, *Man in the Shadow* — retitled *Pay the Devil* in Great Britain — was shot in CinemaScope and proved a modest addition to the Universal catalogue without entirely becoming a box-office sensation.

REVIEWS:

There have been better Westerns than the Jeff Chandler-Orson Welles vehicle, but few, at least recently, as honest. Or as unpretentiously purposeful, as penned by Gene L. Coon and directed by Jack Arnold . . . The [ranch] boss, played as only Orson Welles could, is a big man, murderously watchful of his pretty daughter . . . He owns just about half the state and runs the town. Everybody, that is, but Jeff Chandler.

— Howard Thompson, *The New York Times*
(where the film was reviewed
erroneously as *Man With a Shadow*)

The theme of *Pay the Devil* has turned up, with minor variations, in a number of recent American pictures: the corrupt small town, knuckling under to the Fascist tyrant and aroused to a sense of moral responsibility by the determination of one honest citizen . . . Within its conventions it is sharply and efficiently, if unremarkably made . . . Orson Welles, though, brings little more than his formidable physical presence to the part of the Texan despot. — *Monthly Film Bulletin*

Tough action and good story development . . . Chandler delivers a strong characterization . . . Welles is powerful. — Whit., *Variety*

TOUCH OF EVIL

1958. UNIVERSAL-INTERNATIONAL.

Directed by Orson Welles. Produced by Albert Zugsmith.
Screenplay: Orson Welles, from the novel *Badge of Evil* by Whit Masterson. Director of Photography: Russell Metty. Art Directors: Alexander Golitzen, Robert Clatworthy. Music Score: Henry Mancini. Sound Recording: Leslie Carey, Frank Wilkinson. Film Editors: Virgil Vogel, Aaron Stell.
Running Time: 95 minutes (restored version: 108 minutes).

CAST:

Charlton Heston (*Ramon Miguel "Mike" Vargas*); Janet Leigh (*Susan Vargas*); Orson Welles (*Hank Quinlan*); Akim Tamiroff (*Uncle Joe Grandi*); Joseph Calleia (*Pete Menzies*); Valentin de Vargas (*Pancho*); Marlene Dietrich (*Tanya*); Ray Collins (*District Attorney Adair*); Dennis Weaver (*Night Man*); Joanna Moore (*Marcia Linnekar*); Mort Mills (*Schwartz*); Zsa Zsa Gabor (*Nightclub Owner*); Victor Millan (*Manolo Sanchez*). WITH: Joseph Cotten, Mercedes McCambridge, Keenan Wynn, Gus Schilling, Phil Harvey, Harry Shannon, Wayne Taylor, Ken Miller, Raymond Rodriguez, Rusty Wescoatt, Joe Basulto, Domenick Delgarde, Jennie Dias, Yolanda Bojorquez, Joi Lansing, Michael Sargent, Arlene McQuade, Eleanor Corado.

SYNOPSIS:

Arriving at the Mexican border on his honeymoon, narcotics investigator Mike Vargas (Charlton Heston) witnesses a car bomb explosion which kills a local businessman and his girlfriend. In the confusion, an attack is made on Vargas with a bottle of acid, while his new wife

Susan (Janet Leigh) is confronted by "Uncle Joe" Grandi (Akim Tamiroff), warning her that her husband should keep out of their affairs.

Local detective Hank Quinlan (Orson Welles), a rumpled redneck, takes charge of the car bombing case. He is not happy that Vargas also has been invited to work on the investigation unofficially and announces that he suspects a young Mexican named Sanchez (Victor Millan) of planting the bomb. During an interrogation at Sanchez's apartment, it is clear to Vargas that Quinlan has planted evidence to incriminate the boy, and he sets out to expose the detective's corrupt methods.

Leaving Susan at an out-of-town motel, Vargas returns to town unaware that the Grandi gang, in league with Quinlan, has now abducted her and taken her to another hotel. To conceal his own involvement, Quinlan strangles Grandi and leaves him in the same hotel room with Susan, who is arrested on both narcotics and murder charges.

TOUCH OF EVIL: While his men plant evidence, Quinlan (Orson Welles) interrogates Sanchez (Victor Millan, right) and Marcia Linnekar (Joanna Moore).

Quinlan's devoted partner Pete Menzies (Joseph Calleia) finds the detective's cane in the room and, learning the truth, agrees to help Vargas expose Quinlan. Wired up with a microphone, Menzies confronts a drunken Quinlan at the nearby brothel run by the latter's old flame, Tanya (Marlene Dietrich), Vargas recording a full confession of the methods used by Quinlan over the years to frame suspects.

Realizing he has been set up, Quinlan shoots Menzies, but as he turns his gun on Vargas, he is himself shot by his mortally wounded partner. Susan and Mike drive away, having learned that Quinlan had been right all along — Sanchez has confessed to the car bombing after all. Tanya is left to watch Quinlan's body floating in the river, declaring that "he was some kind of a man."

NOTES:

On completion of *Man in the Shadow*, Orson Welles was offered a role in producer Albert Zugsmith's next film, a crime thriller from a novel by Whit Masterson called *Badge of Evil*. Cast in the leading role of the Mexican agent Vargas was Charlton Heston, already a major star following his work in two movies for Cecil B. DeMille: *The Greatest Show on Earth* and *The Ten Commandments*.

Heston later recalled his first telephone conversation with the producers: "I asked, 'Who's going

TOUCH OF EVIL: One of the notable cameo performances in the film: Marlene Dietrich—reportedly wearing Elizabeth Taylor's wig—with Welles. "Her last great role," according to Orson.

TOUCH OF EVIL: The corrupt cop: Orson Welles as Hank Quinlan.

to direct it?' They said, 'Well, we haven't picked a director yet. . . . we have Orson Welles for the "heavy" though.' After a static-filled pause I said, 'Why don't you have him direct it? He's a pretty good director, you know . . .' The reaction at first was a prolonged silence, as though I had suggested that my mother direct the film."

Having evidently not even considered the possibility, Universal nevertheless agreed to allow Welles to direct his first American movie in almost ten years. Charlton Heston was delighted: "Orson then proceeded to rewrite the entire script in about ten days by himself — which I knew he would — and vastly improved the whole script, and his part — which I knew he would."

The new script bore little resemblance to the source novel or to the first screenplay, with the story shifting from what had seemed a fairly routine thriller. "*Touch of Evil* is really the story of the decline and fall of Captain Quinlan [Orson's part]," says Heston. "My part — the Mexican lawyer Vargas — serves as a witness."

Under Universal's scrutinizing gaze, shooting began in February 1957 with a number of exceptionally long takes designed to soothe the studio executives, before Welles took his crew out to Venice, California, to complete location shooting.

Costar Janet Leigh suffered a broken arm almost immediately, but rather than recast her in the usual sense, Welles had her plaster cast taken off and then replaced whenever necessary, camouflaging or shooting around her for the rest of the time.

During the six weeks of shooting, it became obvious that Welles' standing among Hollywood actors was something special, as a glittering array of guests took cameo roles in the movie. Apart from old Mercury friends Ray Collins, Gus Schilling and Harry Shannon and new "regular" Akim Tamiroff in featured roles, others seen in the film included Marlene Dietrich and Zsa Zsa Gabor, with uncredited appearances by Keenan Wynn, Joseph Cotten as the town doctor and an almost unrecognizable Mercedes McCambridge as a teenage hoodlum. Dennis Weaver, best known then for television's *Gunsmoke*, made a brief but highly effective appearance, improvising with Welles the character of an exceptionally nervous motel worker.

For his own role of corrupt cop Hank Quinlan, Orson Welles created an obscene, monstrous character, increasing his own weight to almost three hundred pounds and virtually disappearing under a gargantuan makeup to look even more obese. In the hands of Welles, Quinlan becomes a figure without a single redeeming feature.

Although the film was edited and delivered to Universal on time, the studio unaccountably took exception to the movie Welles had made, declaring it unmarketable and fragmented. Welles later speculated that they had not liked the "blackness" of the film, something quite out of the ordinary in the mid-1950s.

Offering to reshoot some scenes himself to the studio's specifications, a bewildered Welles found himself barred from the lot. Universal reedited the film, and set to work shooting new sequences. Both Charlton Heston and Janet Leigh initially refused to cooperate on any new shooting, but were ultimately obliged by their contracts to do so. Heston — perhaps assuming the mantle of Welles' representative at this stage — attempted to minimize the interference: "I managed to talk them out of one change I felt would be a mistake," he wrote in his later published *Journal*, but reflected, "I can't honestly say the other additions will seriously harm the quality of the film. What it will be, without Orson's cutting, I don't know. What it would've been had he been allowed to cut on it till the end, I won't know either."

The actual changes made to the film, with additional footage shot by Universal director Harry Keller, are a point of some dispute. Reports suggest that the actual amount of non-Welles material remaining in the film totals only about one minute. More obvious changes involved the renaming of the film *Touch of Evil*, and the placing of the credits over the opening sequence. Welles had originally intended his credits to be shown only at the end of the picture *à la Citizen Kane*.

With post-production delays, the ninety-five-minute film was not released in America until May 1958 without a premiere and badly promoted by the studio. It was quickly forgotten. However, when seen at the 1958 Brussels World Fair, *Touch of Evil* was named Best International Film of the Year. According to Welles, an embarrassed Universal fired its Belgian distributor over his entering the film in the competition without its knowledge.

Opening at a small Paris cinema shortly afterward, *Touch of Evil* then ran for a full two years, becoming perhaps the most commercially successful of all of Welles' works as director. Despite the attention of European audiences and critics,

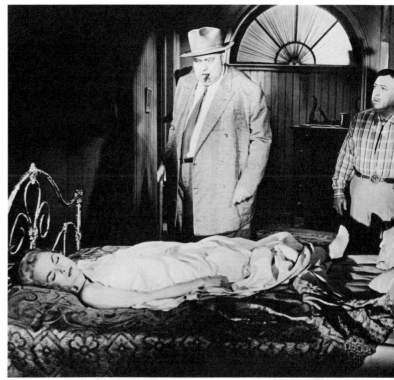

TOUCH OF EVIL: Quinlan prepares to frame Susan Vargas (Janet Leigh), aided by "Uncle Joe" Grandi (Akim Tamiroff).

TOUCH OF EVIL: Mike Vargas (Charlton Heston) convinces Pete Menzies (Joseph Calleia) that Quinlan must be stopped.

131

the Hollywood gates swung shut again on Welles: no further offers were forthcoming for him to work as director. Predictably, the film was further ignored at the American Academy Awards.

Achieving cult status over the years, in 1975 a one hundred-eight-minute version of the film was discovered and made available on 16mm. This version, now the more common print seen on television, is apparently closer to Welles' own original conception of the movie. This "restored" version is now available on home video.

REVIEWS:

Thanks to Orson Welles, nobody, and we mean nobody, will nap during *Touch of Evil* . . . The credits come on, for instance, to a sleepy, steady rhumba rhythm as a convertible quietly plies the main street of a Mexican border town. The car is rigged with dynamite. And so, as a yarn-spinning director, is the extremely corpulent Mr. Welles [who] also adapted the novel by Whit Masterson . . . helping himself to the juicy role of a fanatical Texas cop who frames a Mexican youth for murder and clashes with an indignant Mexican sleuth . . . Any other competent director might have culled a pretty good, well-acted melodrama from such material with the suspense dwindling as justice begins to triumph [but] Mr. Welles's is an obvious but brilliant bag of tricks. Using a superlative camera (manned by Russell Metty) like a black-snake whip, he lashes the action right into the spectator's eye.

— Howard Thompson, *The New York Times*

TOUCH OF EVIL: "I haven't touched a drink in ten years." Quinlan begins his final decline.

TOUCH OF EVIL: On the set cameraman Russell Metty, star Charlton Heston and director Orson Welles.

There is an unpleasant awareness that technical facility is being exploited to gild pure dross — and the suspicion that the dross was chosen because of the opportunities it afforded for virtuoso display . . . But Welles [has] at least managed to keep his audience absorbed in the strange goings-on."
— Arthur Knight, *Saturday Review*

Critics have not been invited to review *Touch of Evil*, the new Orson Welles picture, from which you are free to draw your own conclusions . . . I intend to go to see it as a paying customer, because I am always interested in the Welles eccentricities. — *Observer*

A thriller about a cop who gets his man by framing him, it has the faults we have seen in half a dozen Welles films: the narrative line repeatedly broken, the fluency sliding into confusion. All the same, from the superb opening to the melodrama of the end one feels the presence of one of the cinema's masters . . . The director may exaggerate his own style, but the style is there, and again and again in *Touch of Evil* it gives one a start of delight. The playing — Welles himself, hugely padded and pouched as the cop, Charlton Heston, Joseph Calleia, Akim Tamiroff — has a ferocious edge. — Dilys Powell, *Sunday Times*

TOUCH OF EVIL: Janet Leigh, who broke her arm soon after shooting began, seen here wearing a sling as she discusses a point with Welles and Heston.

TOUCH OF EVIL: Studio portrait of Akim Tamiroff.

TOUCH OF EVIL: A Hollywood director again: Orson Welles with Russell Metty.

TOUCH OF EVIL: The untypical score by Henry Mancini, dictated by Welles' suggestions to the composer, later released as a long-playing record.

Pure Orson Welles and impure balderdash, which may well be the same thing. — *Reporter*

THE LONG HOT SUMMER

1958. TWENTIETH CENTURY-FOX.

Directed by Martin Ritt. Produced by Jerry Wald. Screenplay: Irving Ravetch, Harriet Frank, Jr., based on stories by William Faulkner. Director of Photography: Joseph La Schelle. Art Directors: Lyle R. Wheeler and Maurice Ransford. Music Score: Alex North. Film Editor: Louis R. Loeffler.
Running Time: 118 minutes. Deluxe Color. Cinema-Scope.

CAST:

Paul Newman (*Ben Quick*); Joanne Woodward (*Clara Varner*); Orson Welles (*Will Varner*); Lee Remick (*Eula Varner*); Anthony Franciosa (*Jody Varner*); Angela Lansbury (*Minnie*); Richard Anderson (*Alan Stewart*); Sarah Marshall (*Agnes Stewart*); Mabel Albertson (*Mrs. Stewart*). WITH: J. Pat O'Malley, George Dunn, Jess Kilpatrick, Val Avery, I. Stanford Jolley, Nicholas Kong, Lee Erickson, Ralph Reed, Terry Range, Steve Widders.

SYNOPSIS:

Returning to his ranch from the hospital, Will Varner (Orson Welles) finds that his ineffectual son Jody (Anthony Franciosa) has rented out part of their land to Ben Quick (Paul Newman). Quick has a reputation as a troublemaker, having been driven out of his own hometown after setting fire to a barn. Varner's initial disapproval of him gradually changes to grudging admiration as he sees Quick as a possible husband to his daughter Clara (Joanne Woodward). Clara, however, is half-promised to Alan Stewart (Richard Anderson), who is the complete opposite of Ben's tough, masculine persona.

For Ben's help in selling some wild horses, Varner presents him with a part of the estate including a ruined old house, where it is said a vast sum of money is buried.

Jody becomes increasingly resentful when Ben is offered a job alongside him at the local store.

THE LONG HOT SUMMER: Orson Welles as Will Varner with screen daughter Clara (Joanne Woodward).

Still trying to match Clara with Ben, Varner invites the young man to live in the big house with them. Jody soon confronts Ben with a revolver on his way home, but Ben manages to talk him down and even sells him the ruined house, convincing him that the treasure has been found. Unearthing a bag of coins, Jody is told by his father that he has been tricked: they are newly minted.

Now violently jealous, Jody locks his father in the stables and sets fire to the building, but changes his mind and drags him out in time. The townsfolk meanwhile assume that Ben Quick has started the fire and march on him in an angry mob. Varner placates them, claiming to have caused the fire himself accidentally. Ben decides to leave, but is finally united with Clara, while Varner and Jody are reconciled at last.

NOTES:

While barred from the Universal lot where *Touch of Evil* was still being finalized, Welles accepted a role in Martin Ritt's movie *The Long Hot Summer*, based on three stories by William Faulkner.

Once again cast as a wealthy, powerful rancher,

though noticeably less ruthless than in *Man in the Shadow*, Welles, after struggling with his weight for many years, now allowed himself to fill out; following the gargantuan portayal of Quinlan in his previous picture, he now played a "Big Daddy" type figure complete with Deep South accent and mannerisms.

Far from a challenge, the role of Will Varner was a pleasant diversion for Welles, who now sought to reestablish himself in Hollywood, though as an actor rather than director. (When *The Long Hot Summer* was remade as a television movie in 1985, Jason Robards had the Welles role.)

REVIEWS:

For the first several reels of *The Long Hot Summer* . . . it looks as if they've got themselves a film that will do for the screen what Tennessee Williams did for the stage with *Cat on a Hot Tin Roof* . . . Orson Welles, so help us, does a pretty good hard-hitting job of making a shrewd, fierce, and bloated vulgarian of his small-town tycoon. He even puts on a Southern accent that you can hardly understand.
— Bosley Crowther, *The New York Times*

THE LONG HOT SUMMER: Varner vets Ben Quick (Paul Newman) as a potential son-in-law.

. . . old Will Varner, "thin as a fence rail and almost as long" [from the description by Faulkner] is transmogrified into the Falstaffian figure of Orson Welles — but Welles . . . demonstrates decisively that he is in any case a whale of

135

THE LONG HOT SUMMER: At the ranch barbeque, Minnie (Angela Lansbury) tricks the unfortunate Varner into promising to marry her. Poor Will!

an entertainer, even when he overacts and overaccents his Deep South dialect. — *Time*

No amount of smart dialogue or fine pictures or dramatic incident — not even a fine rumbustious character performance by Orson Welles — can disguise what is finally only an old wooing-the-shrew intrigue. — *Financial Times*

Welles plays high and handsome although he has a tendency to hit some of his lines so hard that they are completely lost. — Whit., *Variety*

THE ROOTS OF HEAVEN

1958. TWENTIETH CENTURY-FOX.

Directed by John Huston. Produced by Darryl F. Zanuck.
Screenplay: Romain Gary and Patrick Leigh-Fermor, from the novel by Romain Gary. Director of Photography: Oswald Morris. Art Director: Stephen Grimes. Music Score: Malcolm Arnold. Film Editor: Russell Lloyd.
Running Time: 125 minutes. Eastmancolor. CinemaScope.

CAST:

Trevor Howard (*Morel*); Juliette Greco (*Minna*); Errol Flynn (*Forsythe*); Orson Welles (*Cy Sedgwick*); Eddie Albert (*Abe Fields*); Paul Lukas (*Saint-Denis*); Gregoire Aslan (*Habib*); Herbert Lom (*Orsini*); Friedrich Ledebur (*Peer Qvist*); Edric Connor (*Waitari*); André Luguet (*Governor*); Olivier Hussenot (*The Baron*); Pierre Dudan (*Major Scholscher*); Francis de Woolf (*Father Fargue*).

SYNOPSIS:

Organizing a petition to the French government to stop the slaughter of elephants in Africa, Morel (Trevor Howard) finds only two supporters, Minna (Juliette Greco), the hostess in a local club, and British ex-officer Forsythe (Errol Flynn). Cy Sedgwick (Orson Welles), an American broadcaster, is about to take part in an elephant safari when he is shot in the rear by some of Morel's party, now determined to take more positive action.

When the Governor (André Luguet) promises Sedgwick that Morel will be severely punished, the influential broadcaster instead tells him to forget the matter, having now sided with the conservationists. Hiding in the hills, Morel is tracked down by Minna and Forsythe, and the three spread their views to newspapers and other media, despite strong opposition.

A battle takes place when Morel's men stampede a herd of elephants in danger of being shot down by hunters. Forsythe and Baron (Olivier Hussenot) are killed and several others are captured but released, thanks to the persuasion of Abe Fields (Eddie Albert), an American photographer who has joined the group. Suffering from a fever, Minna is taken to a nearby hospital, where Morel is treated like a hero before leaving with his men, heading back to continue the fight to save the giant but placid creatures.

NOTES:

Roots of Heaven was Orson Welles' second film for director John Huston, although his role in it was comparatively small. The film itself was made under difficult conditions. Shooting took place mostly in the jungles of French Equatorial Africa, chosen rather unwisely by Darryl Zanuck because the French government would help finance the film.

Many of the cast and crew suffered from a variety of illnesses brought on by heat and inadequate water supplies; some like Errol Flynn and Trevor Howard attempting to solve the problem by drinking only alcohol. Welles' small role enabled him to escape this fate.

Taken from a novel by Romain Gary, the subject of *The Roots of Heaven* — the preservation of elephants in the wild — was considerably ahead of its time, and while this worthy topic well deserved a prominent platform, the film itself was unfortunately not a great success.

Originally intended as a star vehicle for William Holden who was personally genuinely committed to a number of wildlife conservation causes, *Roots of Heaven* eventually starred the fine but no box-office draw Trevor Howard when Holden was unable to disentangle himself from other contracts.

REVIEWS:

There is an embarrassment of riches, as far as pictorial features are concerned. Most of the vivid outdoor action has been shot in Africa, in CinemaScope and color that catches the heat of the sun. And the cast is so large that Paul Lukas, Olivier Hussenot and Orson Welles — the last as an

THE ROOTS OF HEAVEN: Sedgwick recovering in hospital.

THE ROOTS OF HEAVEN: Converted to the cause, Sedgwick makes a television broadcast condemning the slaughter of the elephants.

American television broadcaster — can be beautifully squandered in small roles.
— Bosley Crowther, *The New York Times*

Welles in a brief bit (reportedly done as a favor to Zanuck) is a pinwheel of flashing vigor, his exit to be lamented. — Powe., *Variety*

THE ROOTS OF HEAVEN: Cy Sedgwick (Orson Welles) is accidentally shot where it hurts while on safari.

In a superb vignette of an American television commentator, Orson Welles erupts all too briefly on to the screen.   — *Evening Standard*

There is some wonderful small part playing by Eddie Albert and — for ten marvellous minutes — Orson Welles.   — *Daily Herald*

COMPULSION

1959. TWENTIETH CENTURY-FOX.

Directed by Richard Fleischer. Produced by Richard D. Zanuck.
Executive Producer: Darryl F. Zanuck. Screenplay: Richard Murphy, based on the novel and play by Meyer Levin. Director of Photography: William C. Mellor. Music Score: Lionel Newman. Film Editor: William Reynolds.
Running Time: 103 minutes. CinemaScope.

CAST:

Dean Stockwell (*Judd Steiner*); Bradford Dillman (*Artie Straus*); E. G. Marshall (*State Attorney Horn*); Orson Welles (*Jonathan Wilk*); Diane Varsi (*Ruth Evans*); Martin Milner (*Sid Brooks*); Richard Anderson (*Max Steiner*); Robert Simon (*Lt. Johnson*); Edward Binns (*Tom Daly*); Voltaire Perkins (*Judge*); Wilton Graff (*Mr. Steiner*); Louise Lorimer (*Mrs. Straus*); Robert Burton (*Mr. Straus*); Gavin MacLeod (*Padua*); Terry Becker (*Benson*); Russ Bender (*Edgar Llewellyn*); Gerry Lock (*Emma*); Harry Carter (*Det. Davis*); Simon Scott (*Det. Brown*)

SYNOPSIS:

1924: two psychopathic college teenagers, Artie Straus (Bradford Dillman) and Judd Steiner (Dean Stockwell), plan the perfect murder, as a means of proving their own superiority to society. Soon, the body of Paulie Kessler is discovered in the river, battered to death. Aspiring newspaper reporter Sid Brooks (Martin Milner) discovers a pair of spectacles by the body which turn out to be too large for the boy. Further, the dead boy's uncle confirms that Paulie had never worn glasses. Sid, studying law at the same classes as Straus and Steiner, tells his friends of his discovery, and the two later concoct an alibi for the night of the murder.

Under the questioning of State Attorney Horn (E. G. Marshall), Steiner admits to having lost his glasses but claims he was with a girl that night. When Straus confirms the story, Horn is about to release the boys when Steiner's chauffeur reveals that the car did not move from the family garage that night.

Jonathan Wilk (Orson Welles) is then approached to defend the two boys. Wilk has campaigned against capital punishment in the past and decides to plead his clients guilty, thus dispensing with the jury. The case will now be decided by a judge.

Wilk makes a brilliant closing speech, calling for the death penalty to be set aside and pleading for leniency from the judge. The accused are both given life sentences, but remain unrepentant and ungrateful.

NOTES:

Based on the real-life Leopold-Loeb case of 1924, *Compulsion* was a dramatized version of the headline-making event which also served as the basis for Alfred Hitchcock's *Rope* in 1948. Orson Welles' role as Jonathan Wilk was patterned after Clarence Darrow, defense counsel in the actual trial. A celebrated figure in American legal circles, Darrow summed up his case with a speech lasting two full days and consisting of about 60,000 words.

Welles gave a remarkable performance as the quiet-spoken reasoner of argument, as Darrow had been. To make some approximation to the character, Welles' hairline was shaved back and his hair grayed by the makeup department, while yet another false nose was utilized.

As with *The Third Man*, Orson's entrance was delayed until the final third of the story, but as with the earlier film, his performance was much praised by critics. Darrow's massive oration was condensed for the film to an almost fifteen-minute monologue, caught by three cameras.

Welles' memorable delivery of the speech, said to be the longest ever delivered on screen, was released on record at the time, so popular was it with audiences, and now remains a collector's item.

Welles had, in fact, at one time intended to direct and star in the play of *Compulsion* on Broadway but had been unable to complete a deal with author Meyer Levin. Said to have been slightly acquainted with the elderly Darrow during his childhood in Woodstock, Orson Welles,

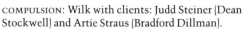
COMPULSION: Wilk with clients: Judd Steiner (Dean Stockwell) and Artie Straus (Bradford Dillman).

COMPULSION: Jonathan Wilk (Orson Welles) arrives at the court flanked by Max (Richard Anderson) and Sid (Martin Milner).

COMPULSION: Orson Welles in one of his finest performances as Clarence Darrow/"Jonathan Wilk" in the bravura court-room speech.

with this film, confirmed once again his true screen star status, completely dominating the entire movie.

At the 1959 Cannes Festival, the award for Best Actor was shared by Orson Welles, Dean Stock-well and Bradford Dillman for their roles in *Compulsion*.

REVIEWS:

In his performance as the defense lawyer, Mr. Welles contributes a comparatively short but the finest portrayal to this searching drama. Heavy-set, beetle-browed, gray hair descending in a drooping cowlick, he is the personification of a wise humanitarian who strongly projects, in one of the longest of film speeches, the need for mercy in the face of public demand for execution.
— A. H. Weiler, *The New York Times*

As delivered by Orson Welles, giving the most moving performance of his career, the trial scene takes on a stature of its own . . . But for Welles, this uncinematic ending to a front-page film might have been fatal.   — *Films and Filming*

Mr. Orson Welles appears in *Compulsion* . . . and the presence of Mr. Welles in a film is enough in itself to rouse expectation. There is a tendency to underrate him both as an actor and a director, perhaps because he is too much of an all-rounder

COMPULSION: As the commanding Jonathan Wilk.

in an age that inclines to worship the specialist. Mr. Welles, however, has gifts that would make him remarkable in any generation — perhaps, being so varied and ingenious, in the old sense of the word, the eighteenth century would suit him best. He is a big man, in more than the physical sense, who touches life and art at a number of points and who, if he sometimes disappoints, has always the capacity to excite.

— *Times* of London

Mr. Welles' 12-minute [sic] speech, delivered quietly, has a noble eloquence; his whole performance is one of the finest in the history of the screen. — *Daily Telegraph*

Welles' concluding speech to the judge employs much of the Darrow rhetoric . . . (no one who pleaded guilty had ever been executed in that state) . . . Welles does very well — with the lines and the line . . . — *Films in Review*

FERRY TO HONG KONG

1959. RANK FILM CORPORATION. (*Released in the U.S. by Twentieth Century-Fox*)

Directed by Lewis Gilbert. Produced by George Maynard.
Executive Producer: Earl St. John. Screenplay: Vernon Harris and Lewis Gilbert, based on the novel by Max Catto. Director of Photography: Otto Heller. Art Director: John Stoll. Music Score: Kenneth V. Jones. Music Conductor: Muir Mathieson. Film Editor: Peter Hunt. Running Time: 113 minutes. Eastmancolor. CinemaScope.

CAST:

Curt Jurgens (*Mark Conrad*); Orson Welles (*Captain Hart*); Sylvia Syms (*Liz Ferrer*); Jeremy Spenser (*Miguel Henriques*); Noel Purcell (*Joe Skinner*); Margaret Withers (*Miss Carter*); John Wallace (*Police Inspector*); Shelley Shen (*Foo Soo*); Roy Chiao (*Johnny Sing-Up*). WITH: Louis Seto, Milton Reid, Ronald Decent, Don Carlos, Nick Kendall, Kwan Shan Lam.

SYNOPSIS:

Mark Conrad (Curt Jurgens), an Austrian in exile, is deported from Hong Kong on board the ferryboat *Fat Annie* bound for Macao. Captain Hart (Orson Welles), however, having won the boat at cards, aspires to respectability and decides to be rid of Conrad as soon as possible.

Macao's authorities refuse to accept the passenger though, and the boat returns to Hong Kong where Conrad is again turned away. Hart is outraged, and sets about looking for somewhere to offload his unwelcome human cargo. Conrad, meanwhile, attracts the attention of Liz Ferrer (Sylvia Syms), an English schoolteacher accompanying a group of children who also fall under the Austrian's spell.

When Hart refuses to help the survivors of a blazing junk, Conrad takes control of the ship. The *Fat Annie*, however, sinks during a storm. Back in Hong Kong, Conrad has found his self-respect once more, while Captain Hart — no

FERRY TO HONG KONG: Orson Welles, looking "startlingly like W.C. Fields," as Captain Hart.

longer obliged to make a pretense of respectability — returns to his former — and happy — ways.

NOTES:

Ferry to Hong Kong was shot entirely on location in Hong Kong; the first of the Rank Organization's attempts at producing a major international blockbuster. The film failed largely through the thinness of the plot rather than due to any fault in the talents involved. Director Lewis Gilbert's earlier successes had included *Reach for the Sky* (he later would direct *Alfie* and several of the James Bond films), while the impressive cast performed well with the material offered.

Orson Welles played much of the film as a comical character, complete with an obviously phony English accent, though this was in keeping with the character of Hart rather than any deficiency on Orson's part as an actor. He had proved several times in the past his command of various accents, not least British.

REVIEWS:

. . . recommended to only the morbidly curious who can see Orson Welles giving his worst performance ever — and we mean ever. As the blustering captain of a boat plying between Hong Kong and Macao, the once distinguished actor, looking like an inflated Buddha, mumbles, growls and simpers as he feuds with an unwanted passenger.

— Howard Thompson, *The New York Times*

Orson Welles, that pudgy old scene-stealer, has quite a time for himself in *Ferry to Hong Kong*, a film mistakenly treated as an action drama. Action there is, but the comical figure of Mr. Welles, who comes across as a caricatured combination of Winston Churchill and Jackie Gleason, outweighs the lightweight drama he's enmeshed in." — Bob Salmaggi, *New York Herald Tribune*

Orson Welles has a makeup startlingly like the late W. C. Fields and an extraordinary "English" accent like nothing else on earth.

— *Times* of London

FERRY TO HONG KONG: Sylvia Sims, Curt Jurgens and Orson Welles.

FERRY TO HONG KONG: Back in port a poorer but happier man, Captain Hart with Joe Skinner (Noel Purcell).

The most fascinating aspect of this slice of hokum is the way Orson Welles has clearly cornered director Lewis Gilbert. Welles seems to have been allowed to write his own dialog and give his own interpretation of his role. He might just as well have taken over the direction . . . Welles, with a magnificently phony makeup and an irritating accent which veers from the "refeened" to the Cockney, has had himself an actor's holiday.
— Rich., *Variety*

DAVID E GOLIA

(David and Goliath)

1959. ANSA. (*Released in the U.S. by Allied Artists*)

Directed by Richard Pottier and Ferdinando Baldi. Produced by Emimmo Salvi.
Screenplay: Umberto Scarpelli, Gino Mangini, Emimmo Salvi, Ambrogio Molteni. Director of Photography: Adalberto Albertini and Carlo Fiore. Music Score: Carlo Innocenzi. Film Editor: Franco Fraticelli. Running Time: 94 minutes.

CAST:

Orson Welles (*King Saul*); Ivo Payer (*David*); Eleanora Rossi-Drago (*Merab*); Kronos (*Goliath*); Massimo Serato (*Abner*); Giulia Rubina (*Michal*); Edward Hilton (*Prophet Samuel*); Pierre Cressoy (*Jonathan*); Furio Meniconi (*King Asrod*); Luigi Tosi (*Benjamin di Gaba*); Ugo Sasso (*Huro*); Umberto Fiz (*Lazar*). WITH: Dante Maggio, Gabriele Tinti, Roberto Miali, Renato Terra, Ileana Danelli, Carlo D'Angelo, Emma Baron, Carla Foscari, Fabrizzio Cappucci.

SYNOPSIS:

King Saul (Orson Welles) rules over Israel when one day a young man, David (Ivo Payer) enters his court. Quickly finding favor, David is appointed equerry and soon finds himself involved in various intrigues and war. Abner (Massimo Serato), the prime minister, becomes resentful as David's position becomes more influential.

A war is declared between Israel and the Philistines, led by the giant Goliath (Kronos). David, however, kills Goliath with a single stone from his sling, and, returning to the court, is thanked by Saul on behalf of the whole of Israel. In gratitude, Saul offers David the hand of his daughter Merab (Eleanora Rossi-Drago).

DAVID E GOLIA: Orson Welles as King Saul.

142

DAVID E GOLIA: With Ivo Payer as David.

NOTES:

At a time when Orson Welles was desperately attempting to raise finance to complete his own project, *Don Quixote*, he accepted the role of King Saul in this biblical epic.

Filmed in Italy, the movie again confirmed Welles' own assessment of his screen persona: French theater recognizes what it calls the "King Actor"; that is to say the man who possesses the necessary authority to play the king. Orson considered himself to be a film "King Actor" — not necessarily the best but the one best suited to play the king.

Welles doubtless directed much of his own performance in *David and Goliath*, working on *Don Quixote* between takes. His commitment to the Italian film was probably less than absolute in this respect, his performance as Saul perhaps reflecting this.

REVIEWS:

Peering over the balustrades as King Saul is a malevolent Orson Welles, whose resonant tones provide occasional relief from the rest of the screeching, but have no relationship to the mouthings of his impressively bearded visage.

Only a lipreader could tell what the formidable Mr. Welles was actually saying to the camera, but it looked to us as if he were expressing his opinion of the picture, in no uncertain terms.
— Eugene Archer, *The New York Times*

Orson Welles strolls nonchalantly through *David and Goliath* giving a brilliant impression of Orson Welles dressed up as King Saul. Very run-of-the-mill stuff, this. — *News of the World*

Orson Welles as King Saul in the last stages of debauchery is got up to look like a Thing from the ancient world. — *Daily Worker*

CRACK IN THE MIRROR

1960. TWENTIETH CENTURY-FOX.

Directed by Richard Fleischer. Produced by Darryl F. Zanuck.
Screenplay: Mark Canfield, based on the novel by Marcel Haedrich. Director of Photography: William C.

Mellor. Music Score: Maurice Jarre. Film Editor: Roger Dwyre.
Running Time: 97 minutes. CinemaScope.

CAST:

Juliette Greco (*Eponine/Florence*); Bradford Dillman (*Larnier/Claude*); Orson Welles (*Hagolin/Lamorciere*); William Lucas (*Kerstner*); Alexander Knox (*President*); Catherine Lacey (*Mother Superior*); Maurice Teynac (*Doctor*); Austin Wills (*Hurtelaut*); Cec Linder (*Murzeau*); Eugene Deckers (*Magre*); Yves Brainville (*Prosecutor*).

SYNOPSIS:

In the poor district of Paris, Eponine Mercadier (Juliette Greco) — mistress of the older Emile Hagolin (Orson Welles) — is really in love with Robert Larnier (Bradford Dillman). Following an uncomfortable dinner together one evening, Hagolin is murdered by the two lovers and his body dumped on a building site. A night watchman witnesses this and Larnier and Eponine are arrested.

Meanwhile, across the city, celebrated attorney Lamorciere (also Orson Welles) keeps his mistress Florence (also Juliette Greco), who herself loves Lamorciere's assistant Claude Lancaster (also Bradford Dillman).

CRACK IN THE MIRROR: First *ménage à trois*: Bradford Dillman, Juliette Greco and Orson Welles on the poor side of town.

Claude is appointed defense counsel to Eponine Mercadier but, jealous of the praise heaped upon his assistant, Lamorciere advises Kerstner (William Lucas) on Larnier's defense and seems certain to win an acquittal. Claude calls only one witness in his defense of Eponine: the Mother Superior (Catherine Lacey) of the prison who says that she believes the girl innocent after hearing

CRACK IN THE MIRROR: The respectable and wealthy Lamorciere (Orson Welles) with mistress Florence (Juliette Greco).

her full confession.

The prosecution privately agrees to a minor sentence, but after Lamorciere overhears Claude and Florence planning to leave together, he makes a dramatic speech calling for the full power of justice to be brought into action, with the result that Larnier receives six years' imprisonment and Eponine life with hard labor.

Arguing with Claude following sentencing, Lamorciere suffers a heart attack and dies, leaving Florence to turn against Claude, feeling that the price of happiness is too great.

NOTES:

Darryl F. Zanuck chose to film *Crack in the Mirror* entirely in Paris, writing his own screenplay under the pseudonym of Mark Canfield, from the novel by Marcel Haedrich. Zanuck also came up with the extraordinary idea of having each of the three leading actors play two roles. The two *menages à trois* each served to illustrate a kind of justice in their own way, with the story jumping back and forth between the elegant world of society lawyers and the squalid, sordid life of the poorer folk.

Once again working under the direction of Richard Fleischer, Orson Welles was unable to repeat the success of *Compulsion*, although one of his roles was again that of an attorney.

An altogether more complex style of filming was evident in *Crack in the Mirror*, and one which found little favor with audiences and critics alike, who found the switching of characters baffling.

REVIEWS:

A determined try for something different — three performers playing six roles, as two adulterous triangles explode in a murder trial — misfires coldly and rather hollowly . . . Mr. Welles is Mr. Welles, both of them — colorful, affected and incisive. And it's a blessed good thing one of him is subtracted early as the corpse. Side by side, two such girths would have split the wide screen long before the mirror cracked.

— Howard Thompson, *The New York Times*

Richard Fleischer's *Crack in the Mirror* is an appalling waste of Orson Welles, Juliette Greco and Bradford Dillman who for no fathomable reason play two roles each in a melodrama . . . Darryl Zanuck deserves seven years' bad luck.

— *News Chronicle*

Some message is intended by the parallel, I suppose. But all it makes clear to me is that the cinema can't afford to saw up its best actors.

— *Observer*

CRACK IN THE MIRROR: Lamorciere and Florence during the trial.

I TARTARI

(The Tartars)

1960. LUX FILMS. *(Released in the U.S. by Metro-Goldwyn-Mayer)*

Directed by Richard Thorpe. Produced by Richard Gualino.
Screenplay: Sabatino Ciuffini, Gaiao Fratini, Oreste Palella, Emimmo Salvi, Ambrogio Molteni, Julian De Kassel. Director of Photography: Amerigo Gengarelli. Music Score: Renzo Rossellini. Film Editor: Maurizio Lucidi.
Running Time: 105 minutes. Technicolor. Metroscope.

CAST:

Orson Welles (*Burundai*); Victor Mature (*Oleg*); Liana Orfei (*Helga*); Bella Cortez (*Samia*); Luciano Marin (*Eric*); Arnoldo Foa (*Chu-Ling*); Furio Meniconi (*Sigrun*); Folco Lulli (*Togrul*). WITH: Renato Terra, Spartaco Nale, Pietro Ceccarelli.

SYNOPSIS:

Tartar leader Togrul (Folco Lulli) prepares to lead an army against the Slavs of the Russias, but Oleg (Victor Mature), the Viking chieftain, refuses to join forces with him. Togrul is killed, his place taken by his brother Burundai (Orson Welles), who swears revenge for the Togrul's death and the abduction by the Vikings of Togrul's daughter, Samja (Bella Cortez).

Oleg's wife, Helga (Liana Orfei), is kidnapped by the Tartars and offered as a hostage for the release

I TARTARI: Lording it over the Tartar court.

I TARTARI: Orson Welles as
Tartar leader Burundai.

of Samja, but Samja has fallen in love with Oleg's
brother, Eric (Luciano Marin), and chooses not to
return to her people. Helga however is returned to
Oleg when she falls from the Tartar battlements
and is carried away by the Vikings.

She dies, and it is now Oleg's turn to seek
revenge against the Tartars and in particular
Burundai. The two meet face to face and Oleg
drowns the Tartar chief in a river but himself falls
victim to a stray arrow. The conflict ended, Eric
and Samja escape together.

NOTES:

Produced by Lux Films in collaboration with
Dubrava Film of Zagreb on location in Yugoslavia

and Italy, *I Tartari* was released in the U.S. and
Great Britain by Metro-Goldwyn-Mayer as *The
Tartars* in a dubbed version cut from 105 to 83
minutes.

As an adventure movie, it was an adequate
entertainment, though no great work of art. The
battle scenes were given what excitement they
had by the use of the Yugoslavian cavalry. By this
time, Orson was already preparing his own next
project, for which his salary from *The Tartars* was
already earmarked.

MGM mounted a publicity campaign to promote *The Tartars* in America and Britain which
included the suggestion to local theater owners to
"Find a burly, bearded character and dress him in
the type of costume worn by Orson Welles in the

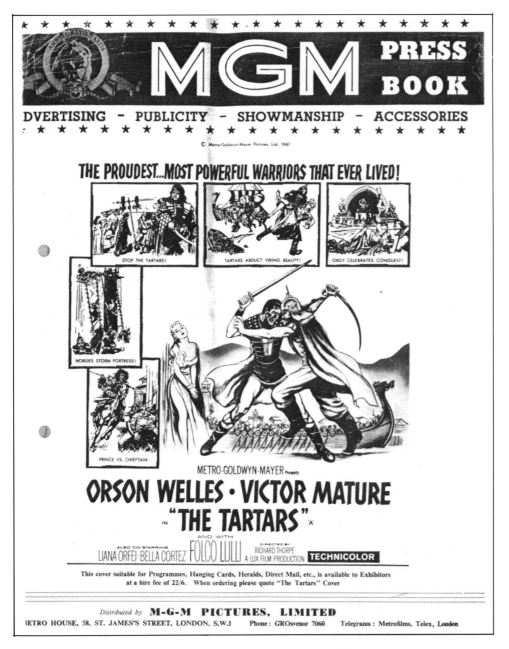

I TARTARI: Press book ad for the MGM release of *The Tartars*.

picture. Hire a horse and have him ride around town, suitably bannered." The press kit also included *Victor Mature's Tips on Self Defense*, perhaps the most sensible of which was No. 9: "The best defense is still to walk away from trouble."

REVIEWS:

Big it is — and loud — and gory, and the biggest thing in sight is Mr. Welles as an evil barbarian chief. At this point in his career he looks like a walking house.
                    — Bosley Crowther, *The New York Times*

Orson Welles rolls his eyes and his bulk, Victor Mature leaps about flashing bare thighs . . . both seem at home in their fancy dress. Amid battles, kidnappings, fire and sword, there is never a dull moment. On the other hand, there is barely an exciting one.   — *Motion Picture Review*

Watching Mature and Welles one feels the same sense of regret as that inspired by the spectacle of viewing two ex-world heavyweight champions battling it out on the comeback trail for the Eastern Yugoslavian title.   — *Variety*

149

BITS: EUROPEAN APPEARANCES 1953–61

Rejected by Hollywood, and facing a huge tax bill from the I.R.S., Orson Welles increasingly turned to European productions as a means of providing much needed funds to continue with his own projects.

Many of these films received only a limited release, and Welles' own involvement consisted of little more than cameo appearances.

EUROPE: Orson Welles as Benjamin Franklin in *Si Versailles m'était conté.*

L'UOMO, LA BESTIA E LA VIRTU (*Man, Beast and Virtue*)

1953. Rosa Films. Directed by Stefano Vanzina. Screenplay: Steno, Brancati, from the play by Luigi Pirandello. Director of Photography: Mario Damicelli.

Orson Welles played "The Beast" in a cast also including Toto, Celia Matania and Franca Faldini.

SI VERSAILLES M'ÉTAIT CONTÉ (*If Versailles Were Told to Me*) a.k.a. *Royal Affairs of Versailles* (IN U.S. IN 1957)

1954. CLM-Cocinex. Directed by Sacha Guitry. Produced by Clément Duhour. Screenplay: Sacha Guitry. Director of Photography: Pierre Montazel. Music Score: Jean Francaix. Film Editor: Raymond Lamy. Running Time: 158 minutes. Eastmancolor.

Orson Welles appeared as Benjamin Franklin in an extraordinary large cast including: Sacha Guitry (*Louis XIV*); Jean Marais (*Louis XV*); Claudette Colbert (*Mme. de Montespan*); Giselle Pascal (*Louise de la Valliére*); Fernand Gravey (*Moliére*); Micheline Presle (*Mme. de Pompadour*); Gérard Philipe (*D'Artagnan*); Daniel Gelin (*Jean Collinet*); Edith Piaf (*Woman of the People*); Jean-Pierre Aumont (*Cardinal de Rohan*).

Financed by the French Government, *Si Versailles m'était conté* was the peak of director/actor/playwright Sacha Guitry's career. The most expensive French film to date retold that country's history through the story of the palace itself, from the mid eighteenth century to the peace conferences of 1919.

The film was intended to raise enough money to restore the palace by illustrating its importance to the French legacy. Outside of France though, the film met with mixed reactions. Initially banned in the U.S., it was held by customs officials under obscenity laws until minor cuts were made.

REVIEW:

Despite the names of Claudette Colbert and Orson Welles, they only make episodic appearances . . . Welles, in astonishing makeup, portrays an owly, aging Ben Franklin who comes for, and gets, aid for the American Revolution.

— *Variety*

NAPOLEON

1954. CLM Films. Produced and Directed by Sacha Guitry. Screenplay: Sacha Guitry. Director of Photography: Louis Née. Film Editor: Raymond Lamy. Music Score: Jean Francaix.
Running Time: 190 minutes. Eastmancolor.

Again, Orson Welles made a cameo appearance as Hudson-Lowe in a huge cast featuring: Daniel Gelin, Raymond Pellegrin, Sacha Guitry, Michéle Morgan (as Josephine), Maria Canale, Danielle Darrieux, Micheline Presle, Simone Renant, Madeleine Lebeau, Yves Montand, Jean Gabin, Jean Marais, Erich von Stroheim (as Beethoven), Marcel Rey, Jean Martinelli, Félix Clément, and Lana Marconi (as Marie Walewska).

An episodic look at the life of Napoleon, played as a young man by Daniel Gellin and as an older one by Raymond Pellegrin; the transformation taking place during a haircut sequence!

At $1.8 million, this expensive film failed to match the success of Guitry's *Si Versailles*, perhaps due in part to a recent American release — *Desiree* — also dealing with Napoleon.

REVIEW:

There is Orson Welles as the beady eyed Hudson-Lowe . . . The bevy of star names and Napoleon theme gives this a chance in America if well plugged and cut.

— *Variety*

AUSTERLITZ *(The Battle of Austerlitz)*

1959. CFPI/SCLF/Galatea/Michael Arthur/Dubrava. Directed by Abel Gance. Produced by Alexander and Michael Salkind. Screenplay: Abel Gance and Roger Richebe. Director of Photography: Henri Alekan and Robert Juillard. Film Editors: Leonide Azar and Yvonne Martin. Music Score: Jean Ledrut.
Running Time: 166 minutes. Eastmancolor. Dyaliscope.

Orson Welles took the role of Fulton, with Pierre Mondy (*Napoleon Bonaparte*); Jean Mercure (*Talleyrand*); Jack Palance (*General Weirother*); Michel Simon (*d'Alboise*); Georges Marchal (*Lannes*); Martine Carol

EUROPE : Scene from Sacha Guitry's 1954 *Napoleon*.

(*Josephine*); Jean-Louis Trintignant (*Segur*); Leslie Caron (*Mlle. de Vaudey*); Jean-Marc Bory (*Soult*); Claudia Cardinale (*Pauline*); Rossano Brazzi (*Lucien Bonaparte*); Jean Marais (*Carnot*); Vittorio de Sica (*Pope Pius VII*).

Another Napoleonic epic, this time directed by Abel Gance, whose previous work on the subject had been a magnificent seven-hour silent movie in 1927. This time he dealt with Bonaparte's victory over the Russians at Austerlitz — the biggest of his career.

A French/Italian/Lichtenstein/Yugoslav co-production, *The Battle of Austerlitz* drew upon a large international cast making cameo appearances, among them top directors Orson Welles as Fulton and Vittorio de Sica as Pope Pius VII.

LAFAYETTE

1960. Copernic/Cosmos. Directed by Jean Dréville. Produced by Maurice Jacquin. Screenplay: Jean-Bernard Luc, Suzanna Arduini, François Ponthier, Jean Dréville, Jacques Sigurd, Maurice Jacquin. Directors of Photography: Claude Renoir, Robert Hubert. Film Editor: René Le Hanaff. Music Score: Steve Laurent, Pierre Duclos.

EUROPE: On the set of *Austerlitz* with director Abel Gance and costar Nelly Kaplan.

Running Time: 158 minutes. Technicolor. Super Technirama 70.

Orson Welles repeated his performance as Benjamin Franklin, with Michel Le Royer (*Lafayette*); Jack Hawkins (*General Cornwallis*); Howard St. John (*George Washington*); Vittorio De Sica (*Bancroft*); Edmund Purdom (*Silas Deane*); Folco Lulli (*Le Boursier*); Liselotte Pulver (*Marie Antoinette*); Jacques Castelot (*Duc d'Ayen*); Albert Rémy (*Louis XVI*).

The first film to deal with the story of Lafayette, the nineteen-year-old pacifist who takes the side of the Colonials during the American War of Independence. The young Frenchman is awarded the highest honor which the United States can give to a foreign citizen when he is invited to tour the country as the nation's guest. Lafayette's tour eventually lasts a full year.

Orson Welles' Benjamin Franklin took the same bizarre makeup as featured in *Si Versailles m'était conté*, an egghead owing much to Mr. Pickwick.

A long film at 158 minutes and with a cost of over $3 million, *Lafayette* was later reissued in a shorter (112 minutes) version not seen in Great Britain until 1963 and received little if any distribution in the U.S.

REVIEWS:

Orson Welles plays Benjamin Franklin like a cracker-barrel character in a television show.
— Bosley Crowther, *The New York Times*

Orson Welles, in two brief scenes as Benjamin Franklin, mouths English and dubs himself in French. — Kenneth Tynan, *Observer**

(*The version reviewed by Tynan evidently differed from that in *Motion Picture Herald*, which said, "The film's dialogue is wholly in English, with the English-speaking actors speaking their own language and that of the French and others dubbed, and unusually well.")

EUROPE: As Benjamin Franklin again in *Lafayette*.

LE PROCÈS

(The Trial)

1962. PARIS EUROPA/HISA/
FI-C-IT.

Directed by Orson Welles. Produced by Alexander and Michael Salkind.
Screenplay: Orson Welles, based on the novel by Franz Kafka. Director of Photography: Edmond Richard. Special Effects: Denise Baby. Pin-screen images: A. Alexeieff and Claire Parker. Sound Recording: Guy Villette. Music Score: Jean Ledrut (Main Theme: *Adagio* by Tomas Albinoni). Film Editor: Yvonne Martin.
Running Time: 120 minutes.

CAST:

Anthony Perkins (*Josef K*); Orson Welles (*Albert Hastler, Advocate*); Jeanne Moreau (*Miss Burstner*); Akim Tamiroff (*Bloch*); Elsa Martinelli (*Hilda*); Romy Schneider (*Leni*); Arnold Foa (*Inspector A*); Suzanne Flon (*Miss Pittl*); Madeleine Robinson (*Mrs. Grubach*); William Kearns (*Assistant Inspector 1*); Jess Hahn (*Assistant Inspector 2*); Wolfgang Reichmann (*Courtroom Guard*); Maydra Shore (*Irmie*); Max Haufler (*Uncle Max*); William Chappell (*Titorelli*); Thomas Holtzmann (*Bert, Law Student*); Fernand Ledoux (*Chief Clerk*); Maurice Teynac (*Deputy Manager*); Michael Lonsdale (*Priest*); Max Buchsbaum (*Examining Magistrate*); Jean-Claude Remoulex (*1st Policeman*); Raul Delfosse (*2nd Policeman*); Karl Studer (*Man in Leather*).

SYNOPSIS:

Josef K (Anthony Perkins) is awakened one morning in his apartment by two men who reveal themselves as policemen placing him under arrest, although no charge is specified. The men tell K that he is free to continue with his normal activities. He finds no sympathy from either his landlady Mrs. Grubach (Madeleine Robinson) or neighbor Miss Burstner (Jeanne Moreau).

At the opera that evening, K is summoned to attend the interrogation commission immediately, where he makes a speech denouncing both the legal system itself and the policemen who had arrested him. The session breaks up in disarray when K is told that he has seriously harmed his chances with his outburst.

LE PROCÈS: Welles with Romy Schneider.

K's uncle Max (Max Haufler) persuades Josef to seek the help of the Advocate, Albert Hastler (Orson Welles), an old school friend of Max's. Hastler tells them that he already knows all about K's case, which he has discussed with the Chief Clerk.

Visiting the law court building again, K discovers hordes of people awaiting news of their own cases; some living out their days in the corridors of the building in the hope of hearing that their case has begun.

Again at the Advocate's apartment, K meets Bloch (Akim Tamiroff), a fellow victim waiting for Hastler to tell him of any new developments. Humiliating Bloch in front of K and Leni (Romy Schneider), the Advocate tells him that his case has not even yet begun.

Increasingly frustrated by Hastler and by the courts, K takes refuge in a cathedral where he is approached by the Advocate, warning him that he

LE PROCÈS: K (Anthony Perkins) with less than helpful neighbor Miss Burstner (Jeanne Moreau).

LE PROCÈS: Anthony Perkins as Josef K.

cannot defy the courts. Still determined not to bow to authority, K goes outside, where he is met by the two policemen who take him to a secluded spot to be executed.

NOTES:

Alexander and Michael Salkind, producers of *The Battle of Austerlitz* in which Orson had appeared, approached him in Paris in late 1959 offering to finance a new movie — his first as director since *Touch of Evil*.

From the list of projects which they offered him — and since they would not allow Orson to film one of his own original scripts — Welles chose Franz Kafka's *The Trial* as the only possible story which he could make.

The Salkinds almost immediately began to run into money problems, so that it was not until the beginning of 1962 that the production got under way in Yugoslavia.

Welles cast Anthony Perkins as Josef K, which caused some disapproval from Kafka purists who had a clear idea of how they imagined the central character. Other roles were taken by Welles himself as the Advocate, Jeanne Moreau — working for the first time with the director — and Welles favorite Akim Tamiroff.

Once completed, *Le Procès* was premiered in Paris in December 1962 to mixed reviews, with several critics commenting on Welles' treatment of the novel. Most contentious was the apparent assumed guilt of K in the film, as opposed to the novel's depiction of K as innocent victim.

Welles also injected some brief scenes of humor into the opening sequence, shot in one continu-

LE PROCÈS: Anthony Perkins in the lengthy opening scene of *Le Proces*.

LE PROCÈS: Hastler (Orson Welles, center background) controls his inferiors: Leni (Romy Schneider), the Chief Clerk (Fernand Ledoux) and K (Anthony Perkins).

Shooting continued in Yugoslavia, with the Salkinds informing their star that the film would have to be shut down through lack of funds. Deeply disappointed, Welles insisted that it be finished and led the crew back to Paris where he set to salvaging his movie.

Although impressive sets had been designed which would have resulted in a very different style of film, these could not now be built. Instead, Orson scouted out new locations, none more effective than the huge Gare d'Orsay in Paris — today a prestigious arts center but at that time an unused railway station.

Improvising almost everything on the spot, Welles managed to keep his film rolling, although often forced to pay his actors and crew out of his own pocket, just as on his previous European movies.

ous take lasting almost eight minutes. Nevertheless, he told *Cahiers du Cinema* that the filming had been a particularly happy experience for him, even claiming *The Trial* as his best film to date.

Two short scenes shot and included in the screenplay but cut from the final release print featured Katina Paxinou and Van Doude as a Scientist and an Archivist respectively. Their roles were eliminated from the film completely.

REVIEWS:

Whatever Franz Kafka was laboriously attempting to say about the tyranny of modern social systems in his novel, *The Trial* is still thoroughly fuzzy and hard to fathom in the film Orson Welles has finally made . . . that is what this viewer gath-

155

LE PROCÈS: Josef K finds he cannot escape the Inspector.

RoGoPaG

1962. ARCO FILMS/CINERIZ/
LYRE.

Produced by Alfredo Bini.

CREDITS:

Illibatezza: Direction and Screenplay: Roberto Rossellini. Director of Photography: Luciano Trasatti. CAST: Rosanna Schiaffino, Bruce Balaban, Maria Pia Schiaffino.

Il Nuovo Mondo: Direction and Screenplay: Jean-Luc Godard. Director of Photography: Jean Rabier. CAST: Jean-Marc Bory, Alexandra Stewart.

La Ricotta: Direction and Screenplay: Pier Paolo Pasolini. Director of Photography: Tonino Delli Colli. CAST: Orson Welles (*The Director*).

Il Pollo Ruspante: Direction and Screenplay: Ugo Gregoretti. Director of Photography: Mario Bernardi. CAST: Ugo Tognazzi, Liza Gastoni.

SYNOPSIS:

A four-episode feature film, tenuously linked by a theme of "human relations," *RoGoPaG* begins with *Illibatezza* or *Chastity:* a tale of an air hostess who must convince her fiancé of her faithfulness while away from him in other parts of the world.

The second episode, *Il Nuovo Mondo (The New World)*, tells of a Paris the day following an atomic explosion. One person only has survived contamination, but quickly learns that the remaining Parisians have lost their sense of values.

La Ricotta (Cream Cheese) stars Orson Welles as a film director shooting the scene of the crucifixion. While he talks to a reporter, the unfortunate actor is actually crucified.

Finally, *Il Pollo Ruspante (The Free Range Chicken)* shows the effects of advertising on Italian consumers. Told by his father that it is almost impossible to find a real farm chicken in Rome, an eight-year-old boy sets out in search of the mythical beast.

ers from the crazy and symbolistic stuff that Mr. Welles and an excellent cast of actors have regurgitated on the screen . . . Mr. Welles himself is a monstrous facade of something sinister as a hero's advocate.
— Bosley Crowther, *The New York Times*

The Trial is Orson Welles' attempt to bring Kafka's dreamlike novel to the screen. It is a nightmare story of a guilt-ridden man's battle to escape the forces which are closing in on him . . . it has its fascinating moments. But not many of them.
— *Daily Express*

Orson Welles' adaption of Kafka's novel *The Trial* is extraordinary, exhausting and often excellent. Loaded with symbolism and topped up with some fiercely Wellesian touches, it is an impressive allegorical nightmare . . . — *Daily Herald*

156

RoGoPaG: On set with director Pier Paolo Pasolini.

NOTES:

RoGoPaG, initially a working title, was devised by taking the surnames of the four directors involved, each of whom wrote and directed his own segment of the movie at various locations: Bangkok (Rossellini), Paris (Godard), Italy (Pasolini) and Rome (Gregoretti).

The film hit trouble largely due to the Pasolini episode. Orson Welles was obliged to speak Pasolini's dialogue, which spoke damningly of the Italian mentality.

Consequently, the film was banned in Italy, and Pasolini charged under obscenity laws. Found guilty in absentia, the director was sentenced to four months penal servitude by the State Attorney, though this was later commuted by the appeal courts.

RoGoPaG was inevitably not a popular film, and even Orson Welles apparently held some reservations over his involvement with the production and with Pasolini himself.

THE V.I.P.s

1960. METRO-GOLDWYN-MAYER.

Directed by Anthony Asquith. Produced by Anatole de Grunwald.
Screenplay: Terence Rattigan. Director of Photography: Jack Hildyard. Art Director: William Kellner. Music Score: Miklos Rozsa. Film Editor: Frank Clarke.
Running Time: 119 minutes. Metrocolor. Panavision.

CAST:

Elizabeth Taylor (*Frances Andros*); Richard Burton (*Paul Andros*); Louis Jourdan (*Marc Champselle*); Elsa Martinelli (*Gloria Gritti*); Margaret Rutherford (*Duchess of Brighton*); Orson Welles (*Max Buda*); Maggie Smith (*Miss Mead*); Rod Taylor (*Les Mangrum*); Linda Christian (*Miriam Marshall*); Dennis Price (*Commander Millbank*); Richard Wattis (*Sanders*); Ronald Fraser (*Joslin*); David Frost (*Television Reporter*); Robert Coote (*John Coburn*); Michael Hordern (*Airport Director*); Stringer Davis (*Hotel Waiter*); Moyra Fraser (*Air Hostess*); Lance Percival (*Airline Official*); Joan Benham (*Miss Potter*); Martin Miller (*Dr. Schwutzbacher*); Peter Sallis (*Doctor*); Clifton Jones (*Passenger*).

SYNOPSIS:

Fogged in at London Airport, the passengers from a New York flight are forced to spend a night at a hotel, where their individual problems only increase.

Frances Andros (Elizabeth Taylor) is planning to leave her husband Paul (Richard Burton) for Marc Champselle (Louis Jourdan). Les Mangrum's (Rod Taylor) business fortunes depend on his reaching an appointment in time, the result of which will also affect his engagement. Film director Max Buda (Orson Welles) is meanwhile hunting for a new location for his next production, while the Duchess of Brighton (Margaret Rutherford) is being forced to sell her ancestral home, unable to pay for its upkeep any longer.

THE VIPS: Welles as Max Buda (center), with Margaret Rutherford and Martin Miller.

THE VIPS: With Richard Wattis.

After a fraught night, Frances decides to leave with Marc but changes her mind when a note from Paul — intended to reach her when the plane landed — tells her he is planning to kill himself.

Mangrum discovers that his secretary Miss Mead (Maggie Smith) is in love with him, and realizes that he feels the same way about her.

Max Buda spots a picture of the exact house needed for his new movie and, offering any amount of money to secure it, discovers it to be the home of the Duchess of Brighton. An agreement is reached between them and everyone is happy as the planned flight finally leaves for New York.

NOTES:

Filmed by MGM's British Unit, and its most expensive British production for many years, *The V.I.P.s*, also known as *International Hotel*, was the studio's latest attempt at recapturing the suc-cess of its all-star *Grand Hotel* of 1932.

Very much designed to exploit the real-life relationship between Elizabeth Taylor and Richard Burton, the film devoted the greater part of its lengthy running time to their on-screen story with other players making the most of what screen time they were allocated.

Orson Welles' Max Buda was a megalomaniac film director loosely based on Alexander Korda. Welles played him with a curious accent, evidently Hungarian, and was a particularly camp, comic figure whose infrequent appearances served as light relief from the melodrama of the Taylor-Burton affair.

The film was nevertheless a huge box-office success, and Welles at least made the acquaintance of Margaret Rutherford, with whom he struck up an immediate friendship. Miss Rutherford won an Academy Award as Best Supporting Actress for her role in *The V.I.P.s*.

Dandy, too, are Margaret Rutherford as a dotty old duchess in tourist class, Orson Welles as a foreign film producer, Martin Miller as his tax counselor, Elsa Martinelli as his companion, and Richard Wattis as the host in the V.I.P. lounge. Under Anthony Asquith's brisk direction, they pack the film with humor and zest.

— Bosley Crowther, *The New York Times*

PARIS BRÛLE-T-IL?

(Is Paris Burning?)

1965. PARAMOUNT/MARIANNE/TRANSCONTINENTAL.

Directed by René Clement. Produced by Paul Graetz. Screenplay: Francis Ford Coppola, Gore Vidal, based on the book by Larry Collins and Dominique Lapierre. Director of Photography: Marcel Grignon. Music Score: Maurice Jarre. Film Editor: Robert Lawrence. Running Time: 165 minutes. Panavision.

CAST:

Jean-Paul Belmondo (*Morandat*); Leslie Caron (*Françoise Labe*); Gert Fröbe (*General Dietrich von Choltitz*); Charles Boyer (*Charles Monod*); Jean-Pierre Cassel (*Lt. Henri Karcher*); George Chakiris (*American GI*); Orson Welles (*Consul Raoul Nordling*); Alain Delon (*Jacques Chaban-Delmas*); Kirk Douglas (*General Patton*); Glenn Ford (*General Bradley*); Anthony Perkins (*Warren*); Simone Signoret (*Cafe Proprietress*); Robert Stack (*General Sibert*); Yves Montand (*Marcel Bizien*); Bruno Crémer (*Colonel Rol*); Pierre Vaneck (*Major Gallois*); Claude Rich (*General Leclerc*); Marie Versini (*Claire*); Wolfgang Preiss (*Ebernach*); Claude Dauphin (*Lebel*); Pierre Dux (*Alexander Parodi*); Daniel Gélin (*Yves Bayet*); Michel Piccoli (*Pisani*); Jean-Louis Trintignant (*Serge*); Sacha Pitoeff (*Joliot-Curie*); Billy Frick (*Adolf Hitler*). WITH: Harry Meyen, Skip Ward, Toni Taffin, Michel Gonzales, Michel Etcheverry, Bernard Fresson, Christian Rode, Georges Géret, Michel Berger, Albert Rémy, Robert Lumont.

SYNOPSIS:

In August 1944, Paris is occupied by German troops while the Allies prepare to liberate the French capital. In the city itself, Communist leader Colonel Rol (Bruno Crémer) attempts to organize a revolt, against the advice of General Chaban-Delmas (Alain Delon). Hitler (Billy Frick) meanwhile charges General von Choltitz (Gert Fröbe) with holding Paris; if the Allies break through he is to burn the city to the ground.

Françoise Labe (Leslie Caron), wife of a leading member of the Resistance movement, approaches Swedish consul Nordling (Orson Welles), whose written authority to release her husband is ignored by SS guards who shoot Labe.

Rol begins organizing his revolt while Nordling attempts to pacify von Choltitz. Rol, however, goes ahead with his plan, and Hitler orders his general to burn the city. Von Choltitz advises the Swedish consul to contact the Allies immediately.

Through the efforts of Nordling and the Gaullist leaders, the Allies, led by General Patton (Kirk Douglas) and Lt. Karcher (Jean-Pierre Cassel) advance and liberate the French capital. Charles de Gaulle returns to lead his people once more.

NOTES:

Another all-star coproduction from France and the United States. *Is Paris Burning?* seemed like a certain box-office success. From a best-selling novel, the film boasted a remarkable star cast working on a massive budget to tell a true and

PARIS BRÛLE-T-IL?: With Leslie Caron.

PARIS BRÛLE-T-IL?: Consul Nordling (Welles) escorts Françoise Labe (Leslie Caron) through Nazi occupied Paris.

moving story. On release, however, the response was lukewarm.

Orson Welles again appeared briefly, this time as a Swedish consul negotiating between the resistance and the German occupying troops, but once more his contribution was limited.

Winning an Oscar nomination for Marcel Grignon's photography, the film contained an early screenplay by Francis Ford Coppola, who later was to share an Academy Award as a writer for another film dealing more prominently with George Patton.

REVIEWS:

Introduced at the outset in the bulging, brutish person of Gert Frobe as a militarist with curious tolerance and possible sensitivities, [Gen. Dietrich von Choltitz] seems to be building toward some stature in mettlesome confrontations with Orson Welles as the interceding Swedish consul general.
— Bosley Crowther, *The New York Times*

Orson Welles effectively underplays as the Swedish consul, and his negotiations with von Choltitz in the confines of the General's kitchen provide one of the few genuinely dramatic moments in the film. — *Motion Film Bulletin*

CAMPANADAS A MEDIANOCHES

(Chimes at Midnight)
(U.S. title: Falstaff)

1966. INTERNACIONAL FILMS ESPANOLA/ALPINE.

Directed by Orson Welles. Produced by Emiliano Piedra, Angel Escolano.
Executive Producer: Alessandro Tasca. Screenplay: Orson Welles, adapted from the plays *Henry IV Part I, Henry IV Part II, Henry V, Richard II,* and *The Merry Wives of Windsor* by William Shakespeare, and *The Chronicles of England* by Raphael Holinshed. Director of Photography: Edmond Richard. Art Director: Jose A. De La Guerra. Music Score: Angelo Francesco Lavagnino. Film Editor: Fritz Mueller.
Running Time: 119 minutes.

CAST:

Orson Welles (*Sir John Falstaff*); Keith Baxter (*Prince Hal, King Henry V*); Sir John Gielgud (*King Henry IV*); Margaret Rutherford (*Mistress Quickly*); Jeanne Moreau (*Doll Tearsheet*); Norman Rodway (*Henry Percy, known as Hotspur*); Marina Vlady (*Kate Percy*); Fernando Rey (*Worcester*); Alan Webb (*Justice Shallow*); Walter Chiari (*Silence*); Michael Aldridge (*Pistol*); Tony Beckley (*Poins*); Andrew Faulds (*Westmoreland*); José Nieto (*Northumberland*); Jeremy Rowe (*Prince John*); Paddy Bedford (*Bardolph*); Beatrice Welles (*Child Page*); Sir Ralph Richardson (*Narrator*); WITH: Julio Pena, Fernando Hibert, Charles Farrell, Keith Pyott, Andres Mejuto.

SYNOPSIS:

The people of England suspect that Henry IV, formerly Lord Bolingbroke (John Gielgud) was responsible for the death of Richard II, who preceded him on the throne. A rebel movement takes as its leader Henry Percy (Norman Rodway), son of Northumberland, known also as Hotspur.

Meanwhile, the new king's son, Prince Hal (Keith Baxter), leads a dissolute life, frequenting taverns where he is heavily under the influence of the roguish Sir John Falstaff (Orson Welles). Fal-

staff takes the prince under his wing and the two continue their life of debauchery while the country divides into two factions over the rights of the throne.

The king's troops take to the field of battle against Hotspur's rebels at Shrewsbury, and in a bitter and bloody encounter, Hotspur is killed by Prince Hal himself. Falstaff, who has spent most of the battle hiding or playing dead, claims to have been responsible for the slaying of Hotspur, and this legend only serves to increase the king's disappointment with Hal, who seeks consolation once more in his old ways.

The king's army is finally victorious over the rebels, but Henry IV dies with Hal at his side, promising that he will become a worthy king. He begins to shake off his past and lead an altogether different life.

At the court, Hal — now King Henry V — makes his first appearance, where he is hailed by Falstaff, come to honor "my boy." However, in keeping with his vow to his father, the king rejects his former friend absolutely, claiming, "I know thee not, old man," and banishing Falstaff from the court.

Abandoned by his king, Falstaff is a broken man. Soon afterward, Mistress Quickly (Margaret Rutherford) announces the sorrowful death of the wretched knight: "The king has killed his heart."

NOTES:

In 1940, Orson Welles had conceived a play made up of extracts from several of Shakespeare's History plays and entitled *Five Kings*. This most ambitious undertaking of the Mercury Theatre closed in heavy debt and was instrumental in Orson Welles accepting RKO's offer to come to Hollywood.

Some twenty years later, a streamlined version of the play, now called *Chimes at Midnight*, opened in Belfast, transferred to Dublin, but again was forced to close at a financial loss before reaching London. Late in 1964, a film version of the play was conceived, with finance becoming available from a variety of sources; as usual including Orson Welles himself.

Shot in Spain in black and white largely for economic reasons, the film once more boasted a starry cast: Welles himself as Falstaff, with Margaret Rutherford, Jeanne Moreau, John Gielgud and Fernando Rey.

John Gielgud, in his book *An Actor and His Time*, later recalled: "Orson Welles was splendid

to work with, although usually in poor health." Like many of the featured players, Sir John was available for only a brief period, with his scenes all being shot within two weeks.

"He engaged a very fine company but he could

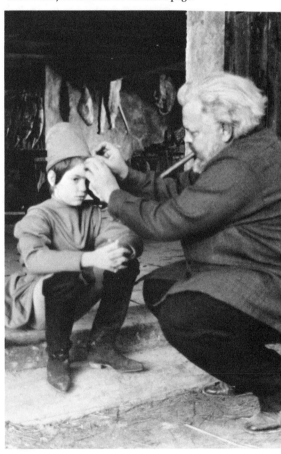

CHIMES AT MIDNIGHT: Falstaff (Orson Welles) with Mistress Quickly (Margaret Rutherford).

CHIMES AT MIDNIGHT: The director adjusts the costume of daughter Beatrice Welles, seen briefly in the film as Falstaff's page.

not afford to keep us all permanently employed," writes Sir John. "I went over for a week's shooting in Spain, then Margaret Rutherford went over for a week, then Jeanne Moreau, and Orson . . . had still not done any of his own scenes. By the time he got round to them, he was tired out and there was nobody left for him to act with. I never even saw him made up as Falstaff until I watched the film in the cinema."

This method of shooting may have seemed

CHIMES AT MIDNIGHT: A wet scene from the film.

impossible to onlookers and crew alike, but Orson the director knew precisely what was needed from each of his performers. Andrew Faulds, recruited as Westmoreland through his previous stage experience in Shakespeare, confirms that Welles "was inclined to be patient, which is strange for someone of his impetuosity and drive. He was marvelous with actors, and very helpful if you wanted to make a suggestion or if you wanted advice."

Despite this attitude toward his actors, Orson was again hard on his crew, as Robert Arden had observed on *Mr. Arkadin*. "He was murder," says Andrew Faulds. "He spoke in five different languages to them and was pretty offensive — very demanding. I suppose he'd worked out that if you bullied actors, you didn't get the best from them whereas, to hell with the technicians. They had to do as they were told, and pretty quick."

The finished movie was assembled through some meticulous editing, since doubles were used extensively for all principal actors whenever their faces were not needed. In the unusually violent and bloody battle scene too, Welles' cutting created an illusion of many more people than were actually used for the sequence. This virtuoso piece of editing would go unnoticed by most viewers and critics, so skillfully was it handled.

Equally as skillful was the choosing of locations to create an authentic English countryside, while of interiors, John Gielgud recalls, "He had found a marvellous setting for the court scenes, a great empty building in the hills above Barcelona, which had been a prison at one time and had a huge hall with a stone floor. However, there was no glass in the windows and the cold November air poured in. I was wearing tights and a dressing gown and practically nothing else for my death scene. I would sit on my throne with a tiny electric fire to warm my feet while Orson spent his last pesetas sending out to buy brandy to keep me going."

Andrew Faulds' more somber impression of that particular setting is of graffiti-covered walls chronicling former inmates' time spent there, together with grim reminders of dates of executions. The building itself is today a luxury Spanish hotel.

Margaret Rutherford was reunited with Welles following their work together on *The V.I.P.s*, and the two evidently hit it off together splendidly. The key role of Prince Hal went to Keith Baxter, a relatively unknown though fine actor, here

repeating his performance from the Irish stage version of the play. Maintaining a family tradition, Welles cast his young daughter Beatrice as a page boy so that each of his Shakespeare films had featured one of his daughters in a small role.

As always with screen adaptations of Shakespeare, there were those who considered that Welles had taken liberties with the text of the

CHIMES AT MIDNIGHT: John Gielgud (right) as Henry IV, with Keith Baxter as Hal.

As Falstaff himself, Welles created a character who is at once a scoundrel yet a lovable rogue whose final rejection by the king is all the more heartrending. One of Shakespeare's most popular figures, Falstaff was evidently based on the real-life Sir John Oldcastle, a leader under Henry V, though his characteristics were supplied by Shakespeare rather than the real historical figure.

In his view of Falstaff as a fundamentally good man, Welles' film is largely intended as a lament for the loss of Merrie England, as symbolized by Falstaff's own deep loss of innocence at the story's conclusion — a loss of all that was good in those days now swept away by a new regime.

On working with Orson Welles the actor, Andrew Faulds again: "He was very interesting to watch at work. A very good actor, oddly enough with limitations because of his physique and his voice, but limitations that he actually made use of. They didn't damage his performance. He didn't have that vocal capacity of Gielgud, but what actor does?" Once again this would confirm Orson's own summation of his persona as a "King Actor."

According to Welles, *Chimes at Midnight* was originally designed to incorporate a definite photographic effect akin to engravings. He later claimed that the film would have been shot entirely differently had he known that the process could not be successfully handled by the laboratory.

Technical problems dogged the film, with the first reel being processed by the Spanish lab slightly out of sync — a particularly upsetting incident for one whose radio background had given him such a view of the importance of sound. Similarly, Margaret Rutherford's key speech on the death of Sir John Falstaff was marred by a background hum which could not be removed.

Finally completed and released in 1966, *Chimes at Midnight* was received well by critics, though distribution difficulties prevented it from becoming a big box-office success. Despite this, it is generally considered to be perhaps Welles' finest screen performance, and the film hailed by many as second only to *Citizen Kane*.

Within the career and life of its director, *Chimes at Midnight* can be seen almost as Orson Welles' lifework — a piece which he had taken some twenty-five years to finally bring to a mass audience. Welles himself later claimed it as a personal favorite among his films, and rightly so.

plays. Andrew Faulds qualifies this: "I think if you're building a film on one character, some liberties with the text are not only required, they are perfectly allowable . . . I thought it was a very skillful job and I don't think the text is sacrosanct when you're creating a specific study. I think Orson knew how much of Falstaff he needed and how little of the rest of the plays he would need."

REVIEWS:

. . . a confusing patchwork of scenes and characters, mainly from Shakespeare's *Henry IV, Parts I and 2*, designed to give major exposure to Jack Falstaff, performed by Mr. Welles. And it is still every bit as difficult as I found it [at the Cannes Film Festival] to comprehend what several of the actors are saying, especially Mr. Welles. This difficulty of understanding Mr. Welles's basso profundo speech, which he seems to direct toward his innards instead of out through his lips, makes it all the more difficult to catch the drift of this great, bearded, untidy man who waddles and cocks his hairy eyebrows and generally bluffs his way through the film.

— Bosley Crowther, *The New York Times*

Inside every fat man there is supposed to be a thin man screaming to get free. Inside Orson Welles there is just another fat man. At the age of 51, the onetime *enfant terrible* of cinema has finally allowed the swollen stranger in him to break loose. The stranger's name is Falstaff . . . Welles is probably the first actor in the history of the theater to appear too fat for the role. Immense, waddling, jowly, pantomiming with great theatrical strawberry nose and crafty, porcine eyes, he takes command of scenes less with spoken English than with body English. In whatever he does, Welles is never entirely bad — or entirely excellent. In this film, there flickers the glitter of authentic genius, along with great stony stretches of dullness and incoherence.
— *Time*

Falstaff's rejection by the newly crowned King, his erstwhile drinking croney, is tremendously moving — a truly great cinema climax.

— *Morning Star*

French critics . . . seemed to see . . . a paradigm of Welles' own career, a too early prodigy never finally accepted as an interpreter of his beloved Shakespeare, never a king but always a curiosity and sometimes a clown. Perhaps for this reason, several of my own French friends seemed uneasy with the film; they found it, they said, unnerving, rather painful. And yet others applauded the empty screen. Why? Partly I think, because of the sheer visual energy in any of Welles' pictures . . . But most of all the applause came for this giant of a man, astride the film like a dictator.

— *New Statesman*

It is beautifully played; a regal Henry IV from John Gielgud, a good wispy Shallow from Alan Webb; Keith Baxter as the Prince . . . and as Falstaff the organ voiced Welles himself, bringing off the jokes with gusto and the bragging knavery with a cheerful enjoyment which makes the final broken attempts at self-reassurance ("I shall be sent for") all the more affecting. A Falstaff . . . of stature. And a film full of visual excitements.

— Dilys Powell, *Sunday Times*

You can hardly accuse Mr. Welles of surrounding himself with lesser lights to illuminate his own brilliance . . . The wonder is that amid the stress of directing the whole thing he stands up as well as he does to so much competition.

— *Daily Mail*

Welles' direction is not only fast moving and full of dazzling shots; it captures all the dirt and squalor, the sweaty shirts and greasy hair of medieval England.
— *Evening News*

CHIMES AT MIDNIGHT: One more false nose: Orson prepares for a scene.

CHIMES AT MIDNIGHT: With Jeanne Moreau.

CHIMES AT MIDNIGHT: For Orson Welles, the film was the final realization of his long cherished *Five Kings* project.

CHIMES AT MIDNIGHT: Welles directs a scene
with Keith Baxter (Prince Hal) and Jeanne
Moreau (Doll Tearsheet).

170

CHIMES AT MIDNIGHT: Falstaff and Doll
Tearsheet.

CHIMES AT MIDNIGHT: As Sir
John Falstaff.

171

A MAN FOR ALL SEASONS:
Orson Welles as Cardinal
Wolsey.

A MAN FOR ALL SEASONS: On the
set with star Paul Scofield and
director Fred Zinnemann (back
to camera).

172

A MAN FOR ALL SEASONS

1966. HIGHLAND FILMS/
COLUMBIA PICTURES.

Produced and Directed by Fred Zinnemann.
Executive Producer: William N. Graf. Screenplay:
Robert Bolt, from his own play. Director of Photography: Ted Moore. Production Designer: John Box. Music
Score: Georges Delerue. Film Editor: Ralph Kemplen.
Running Time: 120 minutes. Technicolor.

CAST:

Paul Scofield (*Sir Thomas More*); Robert Shaw (*Henry VIII*); Wendy Hiller (*Alice More*); Leo McKern (*Thomas Cromwell*); Orson Welles (*Cardinal Wolsey*); Susannah York (*Margaret*); Nigel Davenport (*Duke of Norfolk*); John Hurt (*Richard Rich*); Colin Blakeley (*Matthew*); Corin Redgrave (*William Roper*); Cyril Luckham (*Archbishop Cranmer*); Thomas Heathcote (*Boatman*); John Nettleton (*Jailer*); Vanessa Redgrave (*Anne Boleyn*); Eric Masson (*Executioner*); Molly Urquhart (*Maid*); Yootha Joyce (*Averil Machin*); Anthony Nicholls (*King's Representative*); Eira Heath (*Matthew's Wife*); Paul Hardwick (*Courtier*); Michael Latimer (*Norfolk's Aide*); Matt Zinnermann (*Messenger*); Martin Boddy, (*Tower Governor*); Philip Brack (*Captain of Guard*); Jack Gwilim (*Chief Justice*).

SYNOPSIS:

It is the year 1526. In England, Sir Thomas More (Paul Scofield) is one of the king's most trusted and favored advisers — a devout Roman Catholic. The king, Henry VIII (Robert Shaw), has already been granted special permission by the church to marry Catherine of Aragon, his brother's widow. Now, however, he wishes to divorce her and marry Anne Boleyn (Vanessa Redgrave).

Thomas More is summoned by Cardinal Wolsey (Orson Welles), the Chancellor of England, and urged to seek the Pope's blessing on the king's proposed actions. More, however, refuses on moral grounds.

Nothing can be done for the present, but when Wolsey dies, More is his successor for a brief period. Henry decides to break with the Roman church and forms the Church of England, proclaiming himself its head.

When Henry divorces Catherine and marries Anne, More resigns from his post and aims for a life of peaceful retirement. The king, though, considers More's action to be against him and orders him imprisoned and ultimately beheaded.

NOTES:

A successful stage play by Robert Bolt, *A Man for All Seasons* was filmed in England by Columbia under the direction of Hollywood veteran Fred Zinnemann.

The cast was entirely British with the exception of Orson Welles, who once again demonstrated his flawless English accent and gave a magisterial performance as the dubious Cardinal Wolsey.

Paul Scofield, in one of his all too rare screen roles, recalls that "There was at first some doubt as to whether he [Orson Welles] would accept the part; an important one of course, but not a leading role."

Evidently, Welles considered the cameo worthwhile, and was soon becoming immersed in his performance: "The day came when the Wolsey scenes were to be shot," says Paul Scofield. "Orson arrived and insisted on doing his own makeup — why not? He then most charmingly commandeered me to rehearse with him and help him learn his text. This I most willingly did, and we sat in his trailer/dressing room endlessly going over his lines. He was charming always, but it was hard work."

Welles has often been accused of interfering in the direction of movies in which he was engaged solely as an actor, and the strength of the accusations often lies in the attitude of the named director: some — perhaps for reasons of insecurity over directing such a legend — claim he was "difficult" or "temperamental." Other more experienced and professional directors — men like Carol Reed and Gregory Ratoff — either encouraged or at least allowed Welles to voice his opinions over a scene.

For A Man for All Seasons, director Fred Zinnemann evidently took the latter point of view. Paul Scofield continues: "We shot the scenes, and he stopped acting at any given point and wherever he wished; and required the cameras and his fellow actor (me) to stop and start with him. It was a novel way of working; entirely autocratic and self-absorbed, but not unproductive and certainly not in any way offensive."

A MAN FOR ALL SEASONS: The death of Cardinal Wolsey, as Norfolk (Nigel Davenport) strips him of his office.

Scofield recognized the director's position with regard to Welles: "During his scenes he was in charge, and it is to the eternal credit of Fred Zinnemann, that that situation was sanctioned."

The released film was highly praised, and a great box-office hit; one of the most successful British-produced films for many years. Academy Awards went to Paul Scofield, Fred Zinnemann, Robert Bolt (screenplay), Ted Moore (photography) and it was also voted Best Picture. Other nominations went to Supporting Actress and Actor Wendy Hiller and Robert Shaw. Though not nominated owing to the brevity of his role, Orson Welles was singled out for particular praise by reviewers.

Charlton Heston had evidently been keen on the role of Thomas More, which went to Paul Scofield repeating his stage performance. Heston did the play often over the years in the U.S., though never on Broadway, and was finally to appear in the role on the London stage in the late 1980s, also directing and starring in a film version of the production.

REVIEWS:

Mr. Scofield is brilliant in his exercise of temperance and restraint, of disciplined wisdom and humor, as he variously confronts his restless King or Cardinal Wolsey, who is played by Orson Welles with subtle, startling glints of poisonous evil that, in this day, are extraordinary for him.
— Bosley Crowther, *The New York Times*

Apart from [Paul] Scofield, I think one should pick out from the very good cast John Hurt as Rich, and Orson Welles appearing briefly as Cardinal Wolsey, a puckered, cantankerous clever face drooping over red robes like a deep imprint in sealing wax.
— *Observer*

THE SAILOR FROM GIBRALTAR

1966. WOODFALL FILMS/LOPERT PICTURES.

Directed by Tony Richardson. Produced by Oscar Lewenstein and Neil Hartley.

Screenplay: Christopher Isherwood, Don Magner and Tony Richardson, based on the novel *Le Marin de Gibraltar* by Marguerite Duras. Director of Photography: Raoul Coutard. Music: Antoine Duhamel. Film Editor: Anthony Gibbs.
Running Time: 91 minutes.

CAST:

Jeanne Moreau (*Anna*); Ian Bannen (*Alan*); Vanessa Redgrave (*Sheila*); Orson Welles (*Louis*); Hugh Griffith (*Llewellyn*); Zia Mohyeddin (*Noori*); Umberto Orsini (*Postcard Seller*); Gabrielle Pallotta (*Girl at Dance*); John Hurt (*John*); Arnoldo Foa (*Man on Train*); Erminio Spalla (*Eolo*); Claudio De Renzi (*Jeannot*); *Theodor Roubanis (Theo)*; Wolfgang Hillinger (*Wolf*); Fausto Tozzi (*Captain*); Eleanor Brown (*Carla*); *Massimo Sarchielli (Massimo)*; Guglielmo Spoletini (*Guglielmo*); Brad Moore (*Brad*).

SYNOPSIS:

After quarreling with his girlfriend Sheila (Vanessa Redgrave) on holiday in Italy, Alan (Ian Bannen), a young Englishman, becomes intrigued by a mysterious woman on board a yacht moored out at sea. Beginning an affair with the girl, Anna (Jeanne Moreau), he learns that she is a widow roaming the seas in search of one sailor whom she knew many years ago.

Joining her search, Alan and the crew head for Greece, where Anna expects to find her man, only to be disappointed once more. A further expedition to Africa is heavy with incident but fails to reveal the sailor.

THE SAILOR FROM GIBRALTAR: Happy to be working again with Jeanne Moreau.

THE SAILOR FROM GIBRALTAR: Louis of Mozambique (Orson Welles) and friends.

Louis of Mozambique (Orson Welles) joins the party and suggests that the sailor may never have existed other than in Anna's mind. He takes them to see Legrand (Hugh Griffith) in Ethiopia, who in turn leads them to a native woman who may have known the man. When her description of the man proves to be wrong, Anna finally gives up her search and realizes that in any case she is in love with Alan. She no longer needs to seek out her mystery sailor.

NOTES:

Another British production for Welles, made on location across Europe and Asia. The starring male role went to Ian Bannen, a fine but much underused British actor, while the film once again reunited Welles with Jeanne Moreau.

A modest production, *The Sailor From Gibraltar* provided easy entertainment without being a critical success. Orson Welles' involvement was slight, his mystical, larger than life character absent for much of the film.

REVIEWS:

Certainly Mr. Welles as a fat Mohammedan merchant in one silly sitting-down scene, and Mr. Griffith as a wild-eyed hunter who leads a quick, grotesque foray into the African veldt, are monstrously bizarre. When they come on, you have the feeling that the whole thing is a put-on joke.
— Bosley Crowther, *The New York Times*

Jeanne Moreau appears surrounded by her usual aura of enigmatic worldliness. Orson Welles, wearing a fez and a three day growth of beard, and Hugh Griffith, also turn up in minor roles.
— *Motion Picture Herald*

CASINO ROYALE

1967. FAMOUS ARTISTS/ COLUMBIA PICTURES

Directed by John Huston, Val Guest, Ken Hughes, Robert Parrish and Joe McGrath. Produced by Charles K. Feldman and Jerry Bresler.
Screenplay: Wolf Mankowitz, John Law and Michael Sayers, suggested by the novel by Ian Fleming. Director of Photography: Jack Hildyard. Additional photogra-

CASINO ROYALE: Orson Welles as Le Chiffre.

CASINO ROYALE: At the Baccarat table.

phy: John Wilcox, Nicolas Roeg. Production Designer: Michael Stringer. Music Score: Burt Bacharach. Film Editor: Bill Lenny.
Running Time: 130 minutes. Technicolor. Panavision.

CAST:

David Niven (*Sir James Bond*); Peter Sellers (*Evelyn Tremble*); Ursula Andress (*Vesper Lynd*); Orson Welles (*LeChiffre*); Deborah Kerr (*Agent Mimi*); Woody Allen (*Jimmy Bond*); Daliah Lavi (*Detainer*); Joanna Pettet (*Mata Bond*). WITH: John Huston, William Holden, Charles Boyer, George Raft, Kurt Kasnar, Jean-Paul Belmondo, Jacqueline Bisset, Derek Nimmo, Alexandra Bastedo, Barbara Bouchet, Anna Quayle, Angela Scoular, Duncan Macrae, John Bluthal, Elaine Taylor, Tracey Crisp, Terence Cooper, Bernard Cribbins, Chic Murray, Tracey Reed, Stirling Moss, Peter O'Toole, Geoffrey Bayldon, Richard Wattis, Colin Gordon, Ronnie Corbett, Penny Riley.

SYNOPSIS:

Legendary British agent Sir James Bond (David Niven) is coaxed out of retirement by M (John Huston) and his colleagues (Charles Boyer, William Holden), convinced that SMERSH is about to launch an offensive. Also recruited is Evelyn Tremble (Peter Sellers), a baccarat expert who under the code name James Bond must defeat SMERSH master spy Le Chiffre (Orson Welles) to prevent his gaining enough money to finance the operation.

Defeated by Tremble, Le Chiffre is executed by his own masters, but Tremble is himself then double-crossed and murdered by his contact, Vesper Lynd (Ursula Andress).

Tracing the center of the operation to a secret chamber beneath the Casino Royale, Bond discovers that the brain behind the entire plot is his own nephew Jimmy Bond (Woody Allen), who has always been jealous of his uncle's fame. The plot is defeated, but Jimmy's "time bomb pill" results in all being killed in one final cataclysmic explosion.

NOTES:

The making of *Casino Royale* is possibly more interesting than the completed movie itself: five different directors were involved in the production together with three credited screenwriters. One version claims that each director was hired for specific scenes, while another suggests that each was fired, with John Huston finally being charged to make something of the footage which remained.

Orson Welles may have contributed slightly to the script uncredited, but had little positive to say about the completed picture, which nonetheless was popular at the box office, if not critically, grossing over $10 million in the United States alone.

The story bore virtually no resemblance to the Fleming original, being an attempted spoof on the run of spy thrillers. (It had been done on American television in the late 1950s before the subsequent James Bond craze, with Barry Nelson as Bond.) In general, though, the film was marred by an ineffectual and unfunny script, gimmicky color effects and an irritating Burt Bacharach score. Today it looks very much a film of its time.

Orson Welles did not appear until eighty minutes into the movie, when he had the satisfaction of effortlessly stealing his small scenes with Peter Sellers, even indulging in a few magic tricks, levitating a girl and causing her to vanish above the baccarat table.

REVIEWS:

... it continues to clip along nicely as Peter Sellers, who is supposed to be the world's great authority on baccarat, is recruited to simulate Bond and confront the demon baccarat ace of the evil system, performed stupendously by Orson Welles. The game between these two in the Casino Royale, which is the only thing in the Ian Fleming novel of the same name translated to the film, is a jolly triangle of two notoriously able scene-stealers.

— Howard Thompson, *The New York Times*

Orson Welles is the SMERSH villain who does conjuring tricks at the baccarat table that nostalgically recall the days he used to saw Rita Hayworth in half.

— Alexander Walker, *Evening Standard**

---

*Alexander Walker refers here to the touring *Mercury Wonder Show* of 1943–44 which featured Welles as "Orson the Magnificent." Interestingly, Orson later insisted that he had never sawed Rita Hayworth in half, using a new "victim" each night.

I'LL NEVER FORGET WHAT'S 'IS NAME

1967. SCIMITAR. A UNIVERSAL RELEASE.

Produced and Directed by Michael Winner.
Screenplay: Peter Draper. Director of Photography: Otto Heller. Music Score: Francis Lai. Film Editor: Bernard Gribble.
Running Time: 97 minutes. Technicolor.

CAST:

Orson Welles (*Jonathan Lute*); Oliver Reed (*Andrew Quint*); Carol White (*Georgina*); Harry Andrews (*Gerald Sater*); Michael Hordern (*Headmaster*); Wendy Craig (*Louise Quint*); Marianne Faithfull (*Josie*); Norman Rodway (*Nicholas*); Frank Finlay (*Chaplain*); Harvey Hall (*Maccabee*); Ann Lynn (*Carla*); Lyn Ashley (*Susannah*); Veronica Clifford (*Anna*); Edward Fox (*Walter*). WITH: Stuart Cooper, Mark Eden, Mark Burns, Peter Graves, Josephine Rueg, Roland Curran, Mona Chong, Robert Mill, Terence Seward.

I'LL NEVER FORGET WHAT'S 'IS NAME: With Oliver Reed.

I'LL NEVER FORGET WHAT'S 'IS NAME: On the set with Reed and director Michael Winner.

I'LL NEVER FORGET WHAT'S 'IS NAME: Orson Welles and friend.

I'LL NEVER FORGET WHAT'S 'IS NAME: As advertising executive Jonathan Lute. Would you buy your breakfast from this man?

SYNOPSIS:

Successful advertising executive Andrew Quint (Oliver Reed) arrives for work one morning carrying an axe which he buries in the center of his desk before announcing his resignation.

At the same time, he leaves his wife Louise (Wendy Craig) and breaks off from his two girlfriends Josie (Marianne Faithfull) and Susannah (Lyn Ashley). Quint has decided to give up the rat race and start again at the beginning. Returning to his old college friend, Nicholas

(Norman Rodway), who has retained his youthful principles, Quint becomes assistant editor of the tiny literary magazine run by his friend.

While there he attracts the attention of Georgina (Carol White) and realizes that the old complications are in danger of beginning again.

180

Former boss Jonathan Lute (Orson Welles) periodically contacts Quint offering him his old job back, while Andrew's wife and mistresses also reappear, further impressing on him how difficult it is to leave everything behind. When Lute's agency buys out the literary magazine, Quint's relationship with Georgina is destroyed. In an attempt at revenge, he designs an advertisement for Lute aimed at deliberately sabotaging his campaign. The ad, however, is an unexpected success.

After a fruitless search for his simple past, Quint becomes resigned to his job at the Lute Organization, where at least he understood his problems.

NOTES:

Still in England, Welles went to work with bombastic British director Michael Winner on this improbable socio-comedy-drama which sees Oliver Reed as the archetypal rising executive searching for the meaning of life.

The film was particularly well-received in the United States, and Orson evidently enjoyed working with the director, a flamboyant, larger than life figure perhaps not unlike Welles himself. Michael Winner recalls: "The experience was completely happy and we remained friends for a long time afterwards."

Concerning Welles' supposed reputation for interfering or rewriting, Winner says, "He did not rewrite any of his own scenes. He did have the script retyped each day without any stage directions, and indeed I asked him if he would be rewriting anything as it would be most welcome, but he said he thought the script was so good he did not need to."

Welles himself told Hunter Davies of the *Sunday Times*, "Most films I've been in have been bad. I don't think this one is. It's very funny." And of the director, twenty years his junior: "Michael is a very talented young man with a big future ahead of him."

REVIEWS:

There are several . . . areas of special excellence in the picture: Orson Welles as the suave, powerful head of an advertising agency is monumentally at ease.   — Archer Winsten, *New York Post*

At ease with the effete "Dear boy" dialog, Orson Welles, the designing advertising tycoon, waspishly states, "The new industry of the twentieth century is waste." This hardly applies either to Mr. Welles' suavely pithy portrayal, or to this disturbingly effective picture.
          — A. H. Weiler, *The New York Times*

Orson Welles gives his most striking performance since *Compulsion*.   — *Films and Filming*

HISTOIRE IMMORTELLE

(The Immortal Story)

1968. ORTF/ ALBINA.

Directed by Orson Welles. Produced by Micheline Rozan.
Screenplay: Orson Welles, from a story by Karen Blixen. Director of Photography: Willy Kurant. Art Direction: André Piltant. Music Score: Eric Satie. Film Editor: Yolande Maurette.
Running Time: 60 minutes. Eastmancolor.

CAST:

Orson Welles (*Mr. Clay*); Jeanne Moreau (*Virginie*); Roger Coggio (*Levinsky*); Norman Eshley (*Paul*).

SYNOPSIS:

Mr. Clay (Orson Welles), a rich merchant living in Macao at the end of the nineteenth century, one evening begins to tell an old story to his bookkeeper, Levinsky (Roger Coggio). Levinsky, however, says he already knows the tale, which is still being told, though only a fiction.

Clay decides that the story should come true, so Levinsky is dispatched to find a beautiful girl and a sailor. He approaches Virginie, daughter of the former business partner, Ducrot, who was ruined by Clay some years before.

Initially reluctant to take part, Virginie accepts when Levinsky assures her that this will be her revenge on the old man. A young sailor, Paul (Norman Eshley), is found and offered five guineas to sleep with Virginie, for the sake of the story masquerading as Clay's wife.

The following morning, as Paul leaves the house, he is urged to spread the now true story as no longer mere legend, but the young sailor vows he will not share his story with anyone.

THE IMMORTAL STORY: The arrival of Mr. Clay.

THE IMMORTAL STORY: As Mr. Clay.

Realizing that his plan has failed, and that the true immortal story will never be told, Clay dies leaving Virginie to return to live in the mansion that had been her childhood home.

NOTES:

In 1967, living in a villa just outside Madrid, Orson Welles received an offer from French television to direct a short feature based on a story by Isak Dinesen, alias the Baroness Karen Blixen.*

Welles already had a fondness for the stories of Blixen, and especially this one, eventually titled *The Immortal Story*. In fact, Orson claimed to

---

*The real-life story of Karen Blixen was told in Sydney Pollack's 1985 movie *Out of Africa* starring Meryl Streep.

have heard the story himself many years earlier, before Blixen's version went into print, told by a sailor on a tramp steamer as in the legend.

Casting one of his favorite actresses, Jeanne Moreau, in the female role, and young inexperienced English actor Norman Eshley as the sailor, Welles naturally assumed the role of Mr. Clay himself; yet another in his line of wealthy, powerful, but unloved figures.

Begun in Madrid, in fact at Welles' own home, the production later moved to Paris and was completed within two months. Though conceived for television, the result was so highly thought of that it achieved a theatrical release despite its modest length of just one hour.

Well-received on release, with particular praise

THE IMMORTAL STORY: One of Orson's favorite actresses,
Jeanne Moreau.

for the visual style of the film — Welles' first in color as director — *The Immortal Story* is nevertheless another of Welles' least seen films. *The Immortal Story* proved to be the final complete feature film to be directed and written by Orson Welles.

REVIEWS:

Orson Welles' *Immortal Story* is ineffective in a surprisingly feeble way . . . What goes wrong, I think, is that the acting and the dubbing are so portentous and terrible. The voices, particularly that of the factotum [Welles] are slow and uncertain and flat — as of nonactors, self-consciously reading a script for the first time.
— Renata Adler, *The New York Times*

The Welles film is a perfect evocation of a Baroness Blixen story . . . Welles smoulders away

superbly. Jeanne Moreau plays the young wife . . . with real eloquence and Roger Coggio is remarkable as Levinsky . . . But what atmosphere.
— Derek Malcolm, *Guardian*

The Immortal Story . . . running a serene sixty minutes, as measured and inescapable as the time-passage of an hour-glass.
— Penelope Houston, *Spectator*

HOUSE OF CARDS

1968. WESTWARD. A UNIVERSAL RELEASE.

Directed by John Guillermin. Produced by Dick Berg. Screenplay: James P. Bonner, from the novel by Stanley

HOUSE OF CARDS: With George Peppard and Inger Stevens.

Ellin. Director of Photography: Piero Portalupi. Art Directors: Alexander Golitzen, Frank Arrigo, Aurelio Crugnola. Music Score: Francis Lai. Film Editor: J. Terry Williams.
Running Time: 105 minutes. Techniscope.

CAST:

George Peppard (*Reno Davis*); Inger Stevens (*Anne de Villemont*); Orson Welles (*Charles Leschenhaut*); Keith Michell (*Hubert Morillon*); William Job (*Bernard Bourdon*); Maxine Audley (*Matilde Vosiers*); Peter Bayliss (*Edmond Vosiers*); Rosemary Dexter (*Daniella Braggi*); Ralph Michael (*Claude de Gonde*); Patience Collier (*Gabrielle de Villemont*); Barnaby Shaw (*Paul de Villemont*); Genevieve Cluny (*Veronique*); Raoul Delfosse (*Louis LeBuc*); Perette Pradier (*Jeanne Marie*); Ave Ninchi (*Signora Braggi*); Francesco Mule (*Policeman*); Renzo Palmer (*Monk*); Jacques Stany (*Georges*); James Mishler (*Hardee*); Jacques Rous (*Maguy*); Paule Albert (*Sophie*); Jean Louis (*Driot*).

SYNOPSIS:

Reno Davis (George Peppard), an American former boxer now living in Paris, takes on a job as tutor to the son of Anne de Villemont (Inger Stevens), the widow of a French general killed by a terrorist attack in Algeria. When Reno begins his work at her home, he soon realizes that she is afraid of something, that the atmosphere in the house is tense and unfriendly.

At the de Villemont mansion, he comes to suspect political undercurrents and mysteriously finds himself not only the victim of a number of attacks but also framed for murder. Reno soon uncovers a plot to overthrow the French government, discovering that the family is at the center of a neo-Fascist organization, led by millionaire publisher Charles Leschenhaut (Orson Welles) and the family psychiatrist, Hubert Morillon (Keith Michell).

When Anne's son Paul disappears, Reno begins following a trail that leads him and Anne to Italy where he learns that Morillon is actually Anne's supposedly dead husband, the general, who has faked his own death. Morillon shortly thereafter is shot by one of his own henchmen, and in Rome, Reno and Anne confront Leschenhaut, who agrees to exchange young Paul, whom he has had kidnapped, for a list of the organization's members that Reno has stolen and threatens to give to the press. At the Colosseum, Leschenhaut tries to get Paul to shoot Reno after the list has been turned over, to avenge his father's death, but the youngster instead turns the gun on Leschenhaut himself.

NOTES:

George Peppard had already been directed by John Guillermin in both *The Blue Max* and *P.J.* (in Great Britain, *New Face in Hell*), and the two recruited Orson Welles for their third screen collaboration.

Welles once again took a secondary role to the popular young American actor, with his performance limited to a Hitler-like character which must have at least appealed to his own sense of values, having already dealt with the dangers of fascism in a number of his own earlier productions, notably *The Stranger*.

REVIEWS:

As members of the dastardly crew, Keith Michell, Ralph Michael and Orson Welles help keep a viewer attentive on several occasions. Welles again plays a bearded, malevolent, Buddha-like villain that has become almost a stereotype.
— A. H. Weiler, *The New York Times*

As an arch-conspirator, Orson Welles gives one of his excellent, delightfully hammed-up performances.
— Dick Richards, *Daily Mirror*

L'ETOILE DU SUD

(The Southern Star)

1968. COLUMBIA PICTURES/
EUROFRANCE/CAPITOLE.

Directed by Sidney Hayers. Produced by Roger Duchet. Screenplay: David Purcell and John Seddon, based on the novel by Jules Verne. Director of Photography: Raoul Coutard. Art Director: Pierre Thevenet. Music Score: Georges Garvarentz. Film Editor: Tristam Cones.
Running Time: 105 minutes. Technicolor.

CAST:

George Segal (*Dan Rockland*); Ursula Andress (*Erica Kramer*); Orson Welles (*Roger Plankett*); Ian Hendry (*Karl Ludwig*); Michel Constantin (*José*); Harry Andrews (*Kramer*); Johnny Sekka (*Matakit*); Georges Geret (*André*); Sylvain (*Louis*); Guy Delorme (*Michel*); Van Dooren (*Man in Bar*); WITH: The Senegal National Ballet.

SYNOPSIS:

Kramer (Harry Andrews) is a small-time dictator in French West Africa of 1912, operating his business Kramer Enterprises with the help of Karl Ludwig (Ian Hendry) and a private army. At the engagement party for Kramer's daughter Erica (Ursula Andress) and Dan Rockland (George Segal), a huge 247-carat diamond is stolen during a blackout; Matakit (Johnny Sekka) is the chief suspect, but when he disappears, Rockland is arrested.

Escaping with Erica's help, Dan searches the jungle, followed by Ludwig and his men; all of them converging on a run-down trading station run by Roger Plankett (Orson Welles), an Irish drunkard. Plankett has already captured Matakit, having learned of the theft of the diamond. Ludwig attempts to bargain with the trader but during a struggle, Plankett's partner is killed by Matakit who then escapes.

Meanwhile, Dan and Erica reach the post, and during a gun battle, Ludwig is killed. Returning to Kramer, Matakit protests his innocence but when

THE SOUTHERN STAR: With Ursula Andress.

THE SOUTHERN STAR: Orson Welles as trader Plankett, a man of property.

187

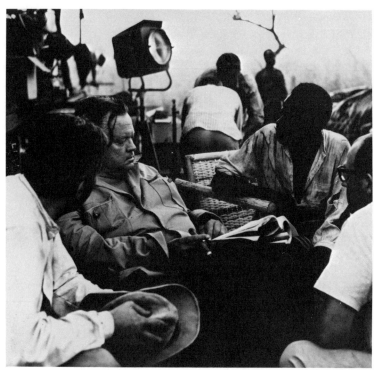

THE SOUTHERN STAR: On location for the adventure.

Kramer's pet ostrich swallows his gold watch, Kramer realizes the truth and chases after the unfortunate animal, while Dan, Erica and Matakit leave for Paris.

NOTES:

Filmed on location in Senegal itself, *The Southern Star* was produced by two French companies, EuroFrance and Capitole, in association with the British arm of Columbia Pictures.

Orson Welles spent only two weeks or so on the film apart from later post-production in London, but reportedly directed the opening sequence of the film at the suggestion of director Sidney Hayers.

REVIEWS:

. . . Mr. Welles, looking like Buddha, swilling cognac, speaking in a pseudo-Cockney accent and perspiring in a white hunter's getup, lazily adds to the lampoon.

— A. H. Weiler, *The New York Times*

Orson Welles, of course, is as usual an entire entertainment in himself as the sluggishly sinister Plankett, oozing lethargic perversity as he fans himself with a petulant hanky, plays draughts with his friend for brimming glasses of whisky,

and inspects his troops with the purse-lipped disdain of a girl guide mistress.

— *Monthly Film Bulletin*

How sad to see actors of the stature of George Segal and Orson Welles reduced to trash like this.

— Clive Hischhorn, *Sunday Express*

Main attraction of *The Southern Star* is Orson Welles playing rather wearily and with an excruciatingly eccentric accent, a villainous gentleman whom everyone seems to keep addressing as Blanket.

— *Spectator*

THE KREMLIN LETTER

1970. TWENTIETH CENTURY-FOX.

Directed by John Huston. Produced by Carter de Haven and Sam Wiesenthal.
Screenplay: John Huston and Gladys Hill, based on the novel by Noel Behn. Director of Photography: Ted Scaife. Art Director: Elven Webb. Music Score: Robert Drasnin. Film Editor: Russell Lloyd.
Running Time: 121 minutes. De Luxe Color. Panavision.

CAST:

Richard Boone (*Ward*); Bibi Andersson (*Erika Boeck*); Max von Sydow (*Vladimir Kosnov*); Orson Welles (*Aleksei Bresnavitch*); Nigel Green (*Janis*); Patrick O'Neal (*Charles Rone*); George Sanders (*The Warlock*); Dean Jagger (*The Highwayman*); Ronald Radd (*Potkin*); Niall MacGinnis (*Erector Set*); Micheal MacLiammoir (*Sweet Alice*); Barbara Parkins (*B.A.*); Raf Vallone (*Puppet Maker*); Marc Lawrence (*Priest*); John Huston (*Admiral*). WITH: Sandor Eles, Anthony Chinn, Guy Deghy, Fulvia Ketoff, Christopher Sanford, Vonetta McGee, Cyril Shaps, George Pravda, Ludmillaa Dudarova, Laura Florin, Hana-Maria Pravda, Dimitri Tamarov, Daniel Smid, Steve Zacharias, Saara Rannin, Pehr-Olof Siren, Sacha Carafa, Rune Sandlunds.

SYNOPSIS:

Lt. Commander Charles Rone (Patrick O'Neal) is sent to Moscow together with a team of agents headed by Ward (Richard Boone) in search of the "Kremlin Letter," a top secret document holding

Russia and the West to an agreement to destroy China's nuclear installations.

In New York, Soviet official Aleksei Bresnavitch (Orson Welles) commandeers the services of agent Potkin (Ronald Radd), who is also working for the Americans holding his family hostage there.

Faking Rone's death, the group further infiltrate Soviet society and intelligence, learning that Bresnavitch is himself involved in smuggling. Using this information, Rone contacts the Russian and blackmails him into helping the remaining Americans escape from the USSR.

Leaving the Soviet Union, Rone and Ward are met by Kosnov (Max von Sydow) and members of the Russian intelligence agency. In a twist, Ward reveals himself as Sturdevent, a top American agent presumed long dead. Ward kills Kosnov and agrees to remain in Moscow under Bresnavitch. The information they have on Bresnavitch's past will be their safeguard against treachery. Rone is dispatched to New York to murder Potnik's family; if not, B.A. (Barbara Parkins) — now his lover — will be killed in Moscow.

NOTES:

Working once again with his old friend John Huston, Orson Welles returned to the studios of Twentieth Century-Fox for *The Kremlin Letter*, a complex spy thriller exploiting the American-

THE KREMLIN LETTER:
Welles looking Russian in Huston's film.

Soviet cold war. An unusually violent film, it is best remembered for the curious appearances of the several guest stars: Micheal MacLiammoir, Welles' old Gate Theatre colleague, as "Sweet Alice," and especially George Sanders as a homosexual female impersonator in a San Francisco nightclub.

Other curiosities include Nigel Green as Janis — "Lord Ashford's Whore" — and Niall MacGinnis as "The Erector Set," whose usefulness to the group is thwarted due to arthritis. Fortunately his daughter B.A. (Barbara Parkins) has followed in his footsteps (literally!) and becomes his replacement after opening a locked safe using only her bare toes!

Orson Welles was effective in the important role of the corrupt Russian official, though the film — perhaps due to its oddness — was not a great success.

REVIEWS:

John Huston's *The Kremlin Letter*, based on Noel Behn's espionage novel, is an extravagant, depressing movie that dimly recalls two early Huston classics, *The Maltese Falcon* and *The Asphalt Jungle* . . . The plot of *The Kremlin Letter* is complicated without being complex . . . The cast is large [and] includes Orson Welles, Bibi Andersson, Max von Sydow, Nigel Green, Raf Vallone and Lila Kedrova.
— Vincent Canby, *The New York Times*

. . . best of all, Orson Welles as Bresnavitch, pacing his luxury apartment, lighting up monstrous cigars, and laying down the law in a magnificently sombre Russian accent.
— Nigel Andrews, *Monthly Film Bulletin*

. . . it offers some rich compensations (Orson Welles as a Soviet agent of unspecified degeneracy; George Sanders as a knitting transvestite).
— *Evening Standard*

MORE BITS:
1964–70

Orson Welles continued to accept minor roles in obscure and largely unseen films during the sixties in order to finance his own projects. Again,

EUROPE: Anthony Quinn as Kublai Khan and Horst Buchholz as Marco Polo in *Marco the Magnificent*.

his involvement amounted to little more than cameo appearances:

LA FABULEUSE AVENTURE DE MARCO POLO
(*The Fabulous Adventures of Marco Polo*)

a.k.a. *Marco the Magnificent* and *L'Echiquier De Dieu*

1964. Ittac/Prodi/Avala/Mounir Rafla/Italaf Kaboul. Directed by Denys De La Patelliere, Noel Howard. Produced by Raoul Levy. Screenplay: Denys De La Patelliere and Raoul Levy. Director of Photography: Armand Thirard. Music Score: Georges Garvarentz. Film Editors: Jacqueline Thiedot and Noelle Balenci.
Running Time: 115 minutes. Eastmancolor. Franscope.

Horst Buchholz (*Marco Polo*); Anthony Quinn (*Kublai Khan*); Omar Sharif (*Sheik Alaou*); Elsa Martinelli (*Girl With the Whip*); Akim Tamiroff (*Old Man*);

EUROPE: Christopher Plummer and Lilli Palmer as Oedipus and his mom in *Oedipus the King*.

Orson Welles (*Ackerman*); Gregoire Aslan (*Achmed*); Robert Hossein (*Nayam*); Folco Lulli (*Spinello*); Lee Sue Moon (*Gogatine*); Jacques Monod (*Nicola De Vicenza*); Guido Alberti (*Pope Gregory X*).

The story of Marco Polo's voyage to spread the word of peace to the Emperor of China, where he helps Kublai Khan defeat his rebellious son thanks to the new invention, gunpowder.

Known in the U.S. as *Marco the Magnificent*, this troubled French/Italian coproduction, filmed in fits and starts by two directors, enabled Orson Welles to continue his own *Chimes at Midnight*, then in production. Like other films of its type, *Marco Polo* relied on the presence of star names in cameo roles, and consequently left their fans disappointed by the brevity of their appearances.

REVIEWS:

Marco the Magnificent looks great on paper. It has a big budget, seven famous names (Anthony Quinn, Horst Buchholz, Omar Sharif, Elsa Martinelli, Orson Welles, Akim Tamiroff, Gregoire Aslan) and a hero who was one of history's great adventurers: Marco Polo. On film, unfortunately, it looks terrible.   — *Saturday Review*

Orson Welles, who plays a Venetian savant, is all dressed up to look like Leonardo da Vinci, but then he queers the pitch by muttering something about a navigational device he calls an "astrolobe."
                                            — *Time*

OEDIPUS THE KING

1967. Crossroads. A Universal Release. Directed by Peter Saville. Produced by Michael Luke. Screenplay: Michael Luke and Philip Saville, based on Paul Roche's translation of the play by Sophocles. Director of Photography: Walter Lassally. Film Editor: Paul Davies. Running Time: 97 minutes. Technicolor.

Orson Welles was Tiresias in a cast which included: Christopher Plummer (*Oedipus*); Lilli Palmer (*Jocasta*); Richard Johnson (*Creon*); Cyril Cusack (*Messenger*); Roger Livesey (*Shepherd*); Donald Sutherland (*Chorus Leader*); Demos Starenios (*Priest*); Friedrich Ledebur (*King Laius*); Alexis Mantheakis (*Palace Guard*); Oenone Luke (*Antigone*).

A crew drawn largely from British television made this first screen version of Sophocles' play.

Director Philip Saville's previous work included a TV version of *Hamlet* with Christopher Plummer filmed on location at Elsinore.

Orson Welles held a brief but pivotal role as the blind oracle Tiresias; central to the plot he reveals to Oedipus the cause of the plague striking the city of Thebes: that Oedipus murdered his father and is now married to his own mother. Jocasta hangs herself while Oedipus blinds himself and is condemned to live a life of torment.

REVIEWS:

Orson Welles appears briefly, and effectively, as the literally mountainous seer, Tiresias.
— Vincent Canby, *The New York Times*

Saville repeatedly cuts away to the landscape when he wants a visual imposing enough to match the words, as when Orson Welles as Tiresias (looking incongruously Falstaffian, as though he had wandered off the *Chimes at Midnight* set) is isolated in long shot high up the bare mountain slope, or when the plague is conveyed by a feeble montage of a gaggle of extras cleansing their Technicolor scars in a stream. But at least Welles has the size to compete with the mountain.
— *Monthly Film Bulletin*

Orson Welles offers one of his best, most powerfully controlled film performances for years.
— John Russell Taylor, *Times* of London

KAMPF UM ROM
(*Fight For Rome*)
a.k.a. *The Last Roman*

1968. CCC/Studioul Cinematografic. Directed by Robert Siodmak. Produced by Artur Brauner. Screenplay: Ladislas Fodor, based on the book by Felix Dahn. Director of Photography: Richard Angst. Music Score: Riz Ortolani. Film Editor: Alfred Srp.
Running Time: Part One: 99 minutes. Part Two: 84 minutes. Later condensed version 94 minutes. Eastmancolor.

Laurence Harvey (*Cethegus*); Orson Welles (*Justinian*); Sylva Koscina (*Theodora*); Honor Blackman (*Amalaswintha*); Robert Hoffman (*Totila*); Harriet Andersson (*Mathaswintha*); Michael Dunn (*Narses*); Ingrid Brett (*Julia*); Lang Jeffries (*Belisar*).

Cethegus, leader of the Roman nobility, travels to Byzantium and its leader Justinian in an attempt to raise an army to march on the Goths under Narses. Cethegus' plan is to set the two sides to war against each other, that his own forces might take control at the outcome.

Another European coproduction, this time between West Berlin's CCC studio and the Bucharest Studioul Cinematografic, *Kampf um Rom* is chiefly notable as the last film to be directed by German-born Robert Siodmak whose forty-year career had produced such diverse Hollywood offerings as *The Spiral Staircase* and *The Crimson Pirate*. Siodmak returned to Germany in the mid-1950s, and his later works consisted of a number of big international coproductions of which this was probably the most ambitious — a two-movie spectacle later telescoped into a single, rather incoherent one.

REVIEW:

As per the many names, ranging from Britain's Laurence Harvey, the U.S.' Orson Welles (who just says a few words) . . . they all could have been substituted by any other players . . . Seriousness often means dullness, which is true here.
— *Variety*

TEPEPA (*Viva la Revolution*)

1968. Filmamerica/SIAP/Roma/PEFSA. Directed by Guilio Petroni. Screenplay: Franco Solinas and Ivan Della Mea. Director of Photography: Francisco Marin. Running Time: 105 minutes.

Orson Welles was Colonel Cascarro, with Tomas Milian, John Steiner, José Torres, Ana Mari Lanciaprima, Paloma Cela, Rafael Hernandez, Luciano Casamonica.

Mexican revolutionary "Tepepa" is wounded during a revolt and is treated by English doctor Henry Price, searching for the Mexican bandit who drove his fiancée to suicide. While they are both on the run from Colonel Cascarro, the chief of police, Price learns more of the peasants' plight, but finally realizes that it is Tepepa who is the object of his search.

192

193

BITKA NA NERETVI
(The Battle of the River Neretva)

1969. Dobrovoljacka/Eickberg/Igor Films. Directed by Veljko Bulajic. Produced by Steve Previn. Screenplay: Ugo Pirro, Patko Djurovic, Veljko Bulajic, Stevo Bulajic. Director of Photography: Tomislav Pinter. Film Editor: Vanja Bjenjas.
Running Time: 175 minutes. Technicolor. Cinema-Scope.

Yul Brynner (*Vlado*); Orson Welles (*Senator*); Curt Jurgens (*General Lohring*); Sergei Bondarchuk (*Martin*); Oleg Vidov (*Nikola*); Milena Dravic (*Nada*); Hardy Kruger (*Colonel Kartzner*); Sylva Koscina (*Danitsa*); Franco Nero (*Captain Riva*); Anthony Dawson (*General Morelli*). WITH: Howard Ross, Ljubisa Samardjic, Boris Dvornik, Charles Millot, Robert Hoffmann, Bata Zivojinovic, Lojze Rozman, Fabijan Sovagovic, Pavlo Viusic.

Resisting German invasion, the People's Liberation Army of Yugoslavia is forced back to the Neretva Valley in this World War II drama. There the Slavs destroy the last remaining bridge across the river. When the German troops head north to block their escape, the partisans build another bridge in a single night and cross the now unguarded river to continue their march through the free territory.

Academy Award nominee as Best Foreign Film, and shot in Yugoslavia and backed by companies from Sarajevo, Monaco and Rome, *The Battle of the River Neretva* — the title given to the film for its British showings — was released in several different versions: originally 175 minutes in length, the U.K. video release runs 127 minutes, with another dubbed print at 106 minutes. In the U.S., the title and the running time were further trimmed — to *The Battle of Neretva* at 102 minutes.

UNA SU TREDICI
(Twelve Plus One)

1970. COFCI/CEF. Directed by Nicolas Glessner. Produced by Claude Giroux. Screenplay: Marc Beham and Nicolas Gessner. Director of Photography: Giuseppi Ruzzolini. Music Score: Piero Poletio.
Running Time: 95 minutes. Eastmancolor.

Sharon Tate (*Pat*); Orson Welles (*Markau*); Vittorio Gassmann (*Mike*); Vittorio de Sica (*Di Seta*); Mylene Demongeot (*Judy*); Terry-Thomas (*Albert*); Tim Brooke-Taylor (*Jackie*).

Mike inherits from his aunt a derelict house and twelve chairs, which he sells. He then finds a note telling him there is a fortune hidden in one of the chairs. Together with Pat he searches for the chairs, eventually finding they have been bought by nuns fundraising for an orphanage.

This Russian story (filmed the same year by Mel Brooks as *The Twelve Chairs*) proved to be the last film completed by Sharon Tate. Orson Welles appeared as a theater manager trying to produce a version of *Dr. Jekyll and Mr. Hyde*.

REVIEW:

. . . a zany interlude in a grand guignol theater run by Orson Welles who has a good time with makeup and a hammy show . . .   — *Variety*

UPON THIS ROCK

1970. Marstan-Rock Corp./Stanley Abrams/Sheldon-Wilson. Directed by Harry Rosky. Screenplay: Harry Rosky. Director of Photography: Aldo Tonti. Film Editor: Donald J. Cohen. Running Time: 90 minutes.

Orson Welles was Michelangelo, with Edith Evans (*Queen Christina*); Dirk Bogarde (*Bonnie Prince Charlie*); Ralph Richardson (*Guide*).

The story of the Basilica of St. Peter in Rome, filmed inside the church itself and told through the characters of those who built it and those who lie buried there. Orson Welles appeared as Michelangelo, the architect of the cathedral.

CATCH-22

1970. PARAMOUNT.

Directed by Mike Nichols. Produced by John Calley and Martin Ransohoff.
Screenplay: Buck Henry, based on the novel by Joseph

CATCH–22: As General Dreedle.

Heller. Director of Photography: David Watkin. Art Director: Harold Michelson. Special Photographic Effects: Albert Whitlock. Film Editor: Sam O'Steen. Running Time: 122 minutes. Technicolor. Panavision.

CAST:

Alan Arkin (*Captain Yossarian*); Martin Balsam (*Colonel Cathcart*); Richard Benjamin (*Major Danby*); Art Garfunkel (*Captain Nately*); Jack Gilford (*Doc Daneeka*); Buck Henry (*Lt. Col. Korn*); Bob Newhart (*Major Major*); Anthony Perkins (*Chaplain Tappman*); Paula Prentiss (*Nurse Duckett*); Martin Sheen (*Lt. Dobbs*); Jon Voight (*Milo Minderbinder*); Orson Welles (*General Dreedle*); WITH: Seth Allen, Robert Balaban, Susanne Benton, Peter Bonerz, Olympia Carlisli, Mar-cel Dalio, Liam Dunn, Norman Fell, Charles Grodin, Jonathan Korkes, Richard Libertini, Eva Maltagliati, Austin Pendleton, Gina Rovere, Elizabeth Wilson.

SYNOPSIS:

In 1944, a small group of U.S. Air Force flyers based on a Mediterranean island are being killed one by one in a variety of bizarre and violent ways. Those remaining are afraid and quietly going crazy when Colonel Cathcart (Martin Balsam) orders yet more bombing missions.

Peace-loving Captain Yossarian (Alan Arkin) decides that he has had enough and requests to be certified insane so that he will not have to fly any

195

CATCH–22: Dreedle attending a briefing session with Major Danby (Richard Benjamin, left) and Colonel Cathcart (Martin Balsam, front).

more, although he is actually the most sane man on the base.

However, Doc Daneeka (Jack Gilford) explains to Yossarian what is known as Catch-22: no sane man would want to fly, so anyone asking to be grounded cannot be insane.

Yossarian's fellow officers continue to be killed. His tent mate Orr (Robert Balaban) fails to return from a mission; wreckage of his plane is found in the sea.

Stabbed by Captain Nately's whore (Gina Rovere), Yossarian is recovering in the hospital when he learns that Orr deliberately crashed his plane and paddled to Sweden. Escaping from the hospital, the flyer sets off in a rubber dinghy for the neutral country.

NOTES:

As early as 1962–63, Orson Welles was enthusiastically announcing his intention to direct a version of Joseph Heller's novel *Catch-22*, for which he hoped to secure the screen rights. Published in 1961, the book was an instant best-seller, coining a new phrase for the language: the "Catch-22" situation. Ironically, having failed to raise the necessary money, he seven years later was offered a role in Mike Nichols' Filmways/Paramount production with a stellar, alphabetically-listed cast.

The situation on set was reportedly tense, with Nicholas telling reporters that the crew was more than a little intimidated by Welles' presence, although the director claimed to use this situation to advantage, this discomfort becoming a feature of Welles' screen character of General Dreedle, the commanding officer.

Whatever the situation during filming, the movie was given a rough ride on release. Most reviewers found it too long and frequently dull, hampered by a weak and loose screenplay.

At a cost of $18 million, all-star *Catch-22* was an instant lossmaker for Paramount, unfavorably compared to the previous year's *M*A*S*H* to which it bore a superficial resemblance.

REVIEWS:

. . . Startling effects . . . here and there, but the picture keeps going on and on, as if it were determined to impress us. — *The New Yorker*

Orson Welles dominates the screen in brief moments as a wartime general, with busty Suzanne Benton ever in tow to relieve combat tension and son-in-law Austin Pendleton to advise him on limits of autocratic behavior.

— Murph., *Variety*

CATCH–22: With (from left) Buck Henry, Austin Pendleton, and Martin Balsam.

WATERLOO

1970. PARAMOUNT/MOSFILM/
CINEMATOGRAFICA.

Directed by Sergei Bondarchuk. Produced by Dino De Laurentiis.
Screenplay: H.A.L. Craig, Sergei Bondarchuk and Vittorio Bonicelli. Director of Photography: Armando Nannuzzi. Music Score: Nino Rota. Film Editor: E. V. Michajlova.
Running Time: 132 minutes. Technicolor. Panavision.

CAST:

Rod Steiger (*Napoleon*); Christopher Plummer (*Wellington*); Orson Welles (*Louis XVIII*); Jack Hawkins (*General Picton*); Michael Wilding (*Ponsonby*); Dan O'Herlihy (*Marshal Ney*); Rupert Davies (*Gordon*); Virginia McKenna (*Duchess of Richmond*); Philippe Forquet (*La Bedoyere*); Sergei Zakhariadze (*Blucher*); Donal Donnelly (*O'Connor*); Ian Ogilvy (*De Lancey*); Terence Alexander (*Uxbridge*); Gianni Garko (*Drouot*); Ivo Garrani (*Marshal Soult*). WITH: Andrea Checci, Charles Millot, Eughenj Samoilov, Orso Maria Guerrini, Oleg Vidov, Charles Borromel, Peter Davies, Vladimir Durjnikov, Orazio Orlando, John Savident, Willoughby Gray, Roger Green, Veronica De Laurentiis, Richard Heffer, Susan Wood, Ghennady Yudin.

SYNOPSIS:

Napoleon Bonaparte (Rod Steiger) announces his abdication as Emperor, heading for exile in Elba, but shortly, King Louis XVIII (Orson Welles) is informed of Napoleon's imminent return, and summons his advisers, Marshal Soult (Ivo Garrani) and Marshal Ney (Dan O'Herlihy), to defend his throne.

Ney — once Napoleon's trusted general — meets Bonaparte on the road where he pledges his

WATERLOO: Welles as Louis XVIII surrounded by court officials. Dan O'Herlihy is at right.

allegiance once more to their former leader. Returning to Paris, they find that the king has fled.

Meanwhile, Lord Wellington (Christopher Plummer) has joined forces with the Austrian, Prussian and Russian armies to face Napoleon. A battle on the Belgian frontier sees the French troops victorious, when Wellington musters the combined troops to Waterloo.

Napoleon's forces, led by Ney, lead an attack on the British. In a lengthy and bloody battle, during which Napoleon is isolated from his men for a time, it looks as though the French will be the victors, until the Prussian troops of Marshal Blucher (Sergei Zakhariadze) combine with Wellington to finally defeat the "little General."

NOTES:

This Italian-Russian coproduction, released through Paramount, was a spectacular and costly movie, supervised by the Russian director Sergei Bondarchuk, whose previous seven-hour version of *War and Peace* was said to be the longest and most expensive theatrical film ever made.

Waterloo contains an interesting mixture of actors; most of the major roles being taken by English and Americans. Rod Steiger gave a thoughtful if not entirely acclaimed performance as Napoleon, while Christopher Plummer's Wellington at least possessed a sense of humor.

Orson Welles, having worked previously with director Bondarchuk when both acted in *Bitka Na Neretvi*, appeared only in the opening sequence as King Louis XVIII, but his tiny cameo was well noted by reviewers. The major portion of the film consisted of the Battle of Waterloo itself, magnificently created by Bondarchuk.

The film however cost over $25 million to produce, being the latest in a long line of costly epics for producer Dino de Laurentiis. Returns were catastrophic, with American losses of almost $24 million.

WATERLOO: Louis, looking less than fit for battle and learning of Napoleon's imminent return, prepares to leave the court.

In matters of record, it seems to follow the encyclopedia. But the sense of the film is another matter, and the particular dullness of Bondarchuk's attempt to translate history into cinema makes *Waterloo* a very bad movie . . . As in most movies of this type, in any 20 lines there is likely to be something laughable . . . which, given the frailties of historical epic, is not the point. Actually much of the film's cast seemed to me pretty good. — Roger Greenspun, *The New York Times*

Then there is a brief interlude with Louis XVIII which Orson Welles points so beautifully that it seems a crying shame when it's cut off at the source.   — Derek Malcolm, *Guardian*

. . . Orson Welles [makes] much of two minor but memorable moments as the King.

— Rich., *Variety*

A SAFE PLACE

1971. A BBS PRODUCTION/ COLUMBIA PICTURES.

Directed by Henry Jaglom. Produced by Bert Schneider. Screenplay: Henry Jaglom. Director of Photography: Dick Kratina. Sound: Fred Bosch. Production Manager: Harold Schneider. Film Editor: Pieter Bergema.
Running Time: 94 minutes. (Premiered at the New York Film Festival in October 1971)

CAST:

Tuesday Weld (*Noah/Susan*); Jack Nicholson (*Mitch*); Orson Welles (*Magician*); Philip Proctor (*Fred*); Gwen Welles (*Bari*); Dov Lawrence (*Larry*); Fanny Birkenmaier (*Maid*); Rhonda Alfaro (*Girl*); Sylvia Zapp (*Susan as a girl*). WITH: Richard Finnochio, Barbara Flood, Jordan Hahn, Julie Robinson, Francesca Hilton, Roger Garrett, Jennifer Walker.

SYNOPSIS:

Noah (Tuesday Weld), living alone in a New York apartment, recalls her childhood and the people she has known throughout her life while constantly searching for her own "Safe Place."

As a child, Noah met a magician (Orson Welles) in Central Park, who gave her magical objects — a

A SAFE PLACE: The deciding factor in Orson's decision to make the film: he played a conjuror. Director Henry Jaglom later used this sequence as opening logo for his International Rainbow Films company.

levitating silver ball, a magic star ring and a Noah's Ark: the "Safe Place" she was looking for.

Noah's memories and dreams involve her learning to fly as a little girl and the two men in her life as an adult: Fred (Philip Proctor) who is practical but dull, and Mitch (Jack Nicholson), her ideal fantasy partner.

As the Magician attempts to make the animals disappear from the zoo, Noah is finally able to fly once again. Leaving her cramped existence behind her, she chooses an escape and Fred discovers her body in the bathtub.

NOTES:

Perhaps the most significant aspect of this movie was that it first brought Orson Welles into contact with one of his greatest admirers, Henry Jaglom, introductions handled by Peter Bogdanovich.

Having just edited the cult movie *Easy Rider*, Henry Jaglom was offered the chance by producer Bert Schneider to write and direct his first feature. Casting his friend Jack Nicholson in a leading role, and Tuesday Weld as the star, Jaglom then set out to entice Orson Welles to play a part written entirely with him in mind.

Initially reluctant, Orson finally became interested when Jaglom mentioned magic. A keen magician himself, Orson's talent as a conjurer had so far surfaced on screen only once — in the 1943 revue *Follow the Boys*. At last offered a role as a magician, Welles' only question apparently was, "Can I wear a cape?"

Contrary to a popular misconception about Orson Welles as a troublesome, difficult actor with no sympathy for his directors, the star took a particular interest in Jaglom, at one point calling him aside when the more experienced members of the crew began to question the first-time direc-

A SAFE PLACE: On location in Central Park with Tuesday Weld.

201

tor's methods. Jaglom recalls Orson telling him: "They'll always tell you it won't cut. You have to tell them it's a dream sequence; they understand that. They're still under the impression that life is real."

From then on, filming largely in Central Park, Jaglom took control of his movie, and a friendship had begun which would last the next fifteen years, during which time Henry Jaglom would be one of Orson Welles' closest friends and staunchest supporters in Hollywood.

A Safe Place, meanwhile, inevitably met with mixed reviews, received only spotty distribution in the U.S., and did not gain a release in Great Britain until four years later.

REVIEWS:

Orson Welles has some terrible moments reading his fortune-cookie lines [with an uncertain Myron Cohen accent], but it's nice to see him alive and well, even if it's in Central Park trying, unsuccessfully, to make a bored llama disappear.

— Vincent Canby, *The New York Times*

Orson Welles moons in and out of the strange proceedings as a magician who is fruitlessly dedicated to the task of making a camel in a zoo disappear. One watches with a kind of fascinated irritation and baffled wonderment that anyone should have the cool nerve to compose such an enigmatic, baffling and pretentious work.

— Dilys Powell, *Sunday Times* (1975)

What makes for loneliness, this film says, is our inability to share our dreams. Those who fail to understand this film will drive themselves and others to the safe place of non-existence.

— Anaïs Nin, *Free Press*

Of the many weirdo roles played in his time by Orson Welles, this may be the prize example. He tries valiantly to read the strange lines written for him by Jaglom. At the start, his accent is Germanic with mannerisms seemingly to match. This veers into Yiddish with the mannerisms modified. All this deliberate experimentation puts a heavy burden upon the viewer. Hardly a scene is fully played out, hardly an explanation provided.   — Land., *Variety*

. . . the pixie-ish magician who surfaces from Susan's childish reveries, to supply some teasing riddles and to sweat ineffectually over his magic, seems a particularly disposable figure, even as incarnated by Orson Welles . . . the major pity of *A Safe Place* is that the not inconsiderable talents

of Weld, Welles, and Nicholson should be allowed to sink, almost without a trace, in the void that Jaglom has left at the center.

— Richard Combs, *Monthly Film Bulletin*

TREASURE ISLAND

1971. MASSFILMS/CCC/LES PRODUCTIONS FDL/EGUILIZ. (*Released in the U.S. by National General*)

Directed by John Hough. Produced by Harry Alan Towers.
Screenplay: Wolf Mankowitz and O. W. Jeeves, based on the story by Robert Louis Stevenson. Director of Photography: Cecilio Paniagua. Art Director: Frank White. Music Score: Natal Massara. Film Editor: Nicholas Wentworth.
Running Time: 95 minutes. Color.

CAST:

Orson Welles (*Long John Silver*); Kim Burfield (*Jim Hawkins*); Lionel Stander (*Billy Bones*); Walter Slezak (*Squire Trelawney*); Angel Del Pozo (*Doctor Livesey*); Rik Battaglia (*Captain Smollett*); Maria Rohm (*Mrs. Hawkins*); Paul Muller (*Blind Pew*); Jean Lefebvre (*Ben Gunn*); Michael Garland (*Merry*); Aldo Sambrell (*Israel Hands*); Alibe (*Mrs. Silver*); Cinchilla (*Anderson*).

SYNOPSIS:

Visited at the Admiral Benbow Inn by two sinister-looking men, old salt Billy Bones (Lionel Stander) collapses and dies after giving an oilskin bag to young Jim Hawkins (Kim Burfield), whose mother runs the inn.

Jim takes the bag to Squire Trelawney (Walter Slezak) and Doctor Livesey (Angel Del Pozo), who discover that it contains a map showing the whereabouts of buried treasure. They set off on board the *Hispanola* in search of the treasure, the crew including a one-legged cook, Long John Silver (Orson Welles), whose control over the men seems greater than that of the captain.

Jim reports to Captain Smollett after overhearing Silver's plot to take over the ship at the island. Smollett sends Silver ashore, planning to counter the mutiny by reaching the stockade first.

TREASURE ISLAND: As Long John Silver.

While Silver's men besiege the stockade, Jim meets up with Ben Gunn (Jean Lefebvre), marooned many years before on the island by Captain Flint. Together they set the *Hispanola* adrift, returning to find that Silver's men have gained control of the map. At the treasure cave, a trap awaits the group and Silver — who has made a deal with Livesey, Smollett and Trelawney — escapes. Ben Gunn then reveals the treasure which he had moved from its hiding place and is now claimed by the party.

NOTES:

Treasure Island, the classic pirate tale by Robert Louis Stevenson, had already been filmed several times, most notably in 1934 by MGM with Wallace Beery and again in 1950 with Robert Newton as the definitive Long John in a Walt Disney production directed by Byron Haskin. More recently, it was done for Italian television with Anthony Quinn and for American TV by Charlton Heston.

A favorite of Orson Welles', the story had been one of the Mercury's radio adaptations in the late 1930s. During the mid 1960s, it seemed that Welles would film the story himself, but instead appeared in this version some years later — yet another international coproduction by Britain, France, Germany and Spain.

The screenplay was written by Welles himself under the name of O. W. Jeeves — a possible reference to W. C. Fields who wrote his own scripts as Mahatma Kane Jeeves. Much of it though was later rewritten by Wolf Mankowitz. The finished film, directed by John Hough — Welles' assistant on *Chimes at Midnight* — was not well received, being poorly dubbed and offering several disappointing performances.

REVIEWS:

Despite Orson Welles' pseudonymous contribution to the script and his attempt to create a Long John Silver in his own tradition of ambiguous villains, this is a lacklustre *Treasure Island*, faithful

TREASURE ISLAND: On Treasure Island: Long John's timbers are completely shivered to find the cave empty. With Walter Slezak, Kim Burfield, Angel Del Pozo and Rik Battaglia.

TREASURE ISLAND: With Kim Burfield as Jim Hawkins.

in a piecemeal fashion to the original but plotted with little colour or spirit.

— Richard Combs, *Monthly Film Bulletin*

The imposing Welles himself alternatives vocally between utter unintelligibility and the croaks of a yawning lion with an Irish brogue, if such can be imagined.

— Murph., *Variety*

MALPERTIUS

1971. SOFIDOC/ARTEMIS FILM/ LES PRODUCTIONS ARTISTES ASSOCIES/SOCIETE D'EXPANSION DU SPECTACLE.

Directed by Harry Krumel. Produced by Pierre Levie and Paul Laffargue.
Screenplay: Jean Ferry, based on the novel by Jean Ray. Director of Photography: Gerry Fisher. Art Director: Pierre Cardiou. Music: Georges Delerue. Film Editor: Richard Marden.
Running Time: 124 minutes. (English language version: 110 minutes at Cannes Film Festival) Color.

CAST:

Orson Welles (*Cassavius*); Susan Hampshire (*Nancy/ Euryale/Alice*); Michel Bouquet (*Dideloo*); Mathieu Carriere (*Yann*); Jean-Pierre Cassel (*Lampernis*); Sylvie Vartan (*Bets*); Daniel Pilon (*Mathias Krook*); Dora Van Der Groen (*Sylvie Dideloo*); Charles Janssens (*Philarete*); Walter Rilla (*Eisengott*); Bob Storm (*Griboin*); Fanny Winkler (*Mother Griboin*); Ward De Ravet (*Abbot Doucedame*). WITH: Jenny Van Santvoort, Jet Naessens, Cara Van Wersch, Hugo Dellas, Gella Allaert, Johan Troch, Cyriel Van Gent.

SYNOPSIS:

Arriving at a Flemish port, Yann (Matthieu Carriere) enters into the debauchery of the local town. A violent fight ends with him being carried to Malpertius, home of his uncle Cassavius (Orson Welles), an old man steeped in black magic and sorcery, who now lies on his deathbed. Gathering his relatives and servants to him, he tells them that they are to receive a fortune, but only on condition that they never leave Malpertius. The inheritance will go to the couple who outlive the rest.

Cassavius dies and Yann is soon planning to leave, but cannot persuade Euryale (Susan Hampshire) to leave with him. Finally, Euryale explains that all of the people of Malpertius are Greek gods whom Cassavius has brought to life again. It was the old man's wish that Yann should fall in love with her and produce a super race, but when she reveals herself as the Gorgon, her gaze turns Yann to stone.

NOTES:

Continuing his European travels, Orson Welles appeared in this, his first screen horror story, a Belgian-French-German coproduction in which, although receiving top billing, he featured only in the first half of the picture. Of the remaining cast, English actress Susan Hampshire performed well in three roles as Cassavius' "nieces" while French singer Sylvie Vartan appeared briefly as a night-club chanteuse.

Released in an English version later cut to 96 minutes, *Malpertius* was screened at the Edinburgh Film Festival in August 1972 where it was

MALPERTIUS: As Cassavius.

well received. The production, though, did not gain a wide release.

REVIEWS:

Uncle Cassavius . . . is a kind of diabolic Franken-stein, played by Orson Welles. He seems to have become typecast as the deity these days . . . I know it's cruel to discuss an end that can't be revealed, but there in the rat-tat-tat triple denouement lies the film's best quality — its ability to send one out of the cinema saying "Wow." But not an enterprise to be taken too seriously.
— David Leigh, *Scotsman*

Though his part is brief, Orson Welles is decid-edly in his element, lording it over another Xanadu.   — Geoff Brown, *Monthly Film Bulletin*

Welles plays a short, telling part as the dying head of a Kafkaesque labyrinthe house surrounded by a strange cohort of relatives and apparently deranged people.
— Mosk., *Variety*

LA DÉCADE PRODIGIEUSE

(Ten Days' Wonder)

1972. FILMS LA BOETIE.

Directed by Claude Chabrol. Produced by André Genovese.
Screenplay: Paul Gegauff, Paul Gardner and Eugene Archer, based on a novel by Ellery Queen. Director of Photography: Jean Rabier. Film Editor: Jacques Gaillard.
Running Time: 108 minutes. Eastmancolor.

CAST:

Marlene Jobert (*Helene*); Orson Welles (*Theo Van Horn*); Anthony Perkins (*Charles Van Horn*); Michel Piccoli (*Paul Regis*); Guido Alberti (*Ludovic*); Giovanni Sciuto (*Preteur*); Tsilla Chelton (*Charles' Mother*); Ermanno Casanova (*Vieillard Borgne*); Vittoria Sani-poli (*Commissionaire*); Sylvana Blasi (*Woman*); Eric Frisdal (*Charles as a boy*); Aline Montovani (*Helene as a girl*). WITH: Corinne Koeningswarter, Fabienne Gauglof, Mathilde Ceccarelli.

LA DÉCADE PRODIGIEUSE: On set with director Claude Chabrol.

SYNOPSIS:

Charles Van Horn (Anthony Perkins) is the adopted son of Theo Van Horn (Orson Welles), a wealthy and generous man of great power married to a much younger woman, Helene (Marlene Jobert). Charles suffers from amnesia and is mentally unstable. Finding himself with bloodied

hands alone in a Paris hotel, he invites Paul (Michel Piccoli) to stay at their house, hoping that his friend, a professor, will be able to bring him out of his depression.

Paul soon realizes that Charles and Helene are in love, that their secret is tormenting them both and that they are now being blackmailed. Charles steals $25,000 from Theo's safe to pay the black-mailer but then hears from Helene that there has

been another demand. She sells her diamond necklace to get the money, telling Theo it has been stolen. Theo suspects that Charles has taken the money, but prefers to ignore the matter since he wants only to see Charles happy.

Paul becomes disillusioned by Charles' tantrums and leaves the house, returning later to find Helene murdered and Charles destroying his work — sculptures of his father — in his stu-

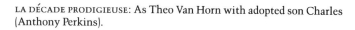

dio before killing himself. Theo finally shoots himself.

NOTES:

French filmmaker Claude Chabrol was one of the young critics who worked on the influential *Cahiers du Cinema* during the 1950s together with François Truffaut and André Bazin; all were great admirers of Orson Welles' work as director. Chabrol's *Le Beau Serge* of 1959 was hailed as the first movie of the *Nouvelle Vague*, and his subsequent films were endlessly analyzed by critics, often to Chabrol's own private amusement.

Orson Welles appeared once again with Anthony Perkins, here as a father and son. Welles was living in France at the time and attempting to finance his latest project, *The Other Side of the Wind*.

REVIEWS:

Everybody in the cast looks uncomfortable, particularly Welles, who either has had a very bad makeup job or has let his nose turn gray. Perkins gives one of his youthful manic performances in a mad cause, and Miss Jobert seems mostly pretty and puzzled.
— Vincent Canby, *The New York Times*

Everything is rather uninterestingly out of control here, including Orson Welles. — *Time*

210

LA DÉCADE PRODIGIEUSE: Strained household: Charles
(Anthony Perkins), Helene (Marlene Jobert) and Theo (Orson
Welles).

Orson Welles, looking cool and faintly amused, plays the urbane head of the household.
— *Sunday Times*

Even the imposing presence of Orson Welles cannot convert an Ellery Queen whodunnit into a Gallic tragedy.
— *Playboy*

GET TO KNOW YOUR RABBIT

1972. WARNER BROS.

Directed by Brian De Palma. Produced by Paul Gaer and Steve Bernhardt.
Screenplay: Jordan Crittenden. Director of Photography: John Alonzo. Music Score: Jack Elliott. Magic Adviser: H. Blackstone, Jr. Film Editor: Peter Colbert. Running Time: 93 minutes. Color.

CAST:

Tom Smothers (*Donald Beeman*); John Astin (*Mr. Turnbull*); Katharine Ross (*The Terrific-Looking Girl*); Orson Welles (*Mr. Delasandro*); Allen Garfield (*Vic*); Hope Summers (*Mrs. Beeman*); Suzanne Zenor (*Paula*); M. Emmet Walsh (*Mr. Wendel*); Samantha Jones (*Susan*); Jack Collins (*Mr. Reese*); Helen Page Camp (*Mrs. Wendel*); Charles Lane (*Mr. Beeman*).

SYNOPSIS:

Tired of working for a large corporation, Donald Beeman (Tom Smothers) decides to "drop out," leaving both his job and his wife for a career in show business. Taking lessons from a professional theatrical conjurer, Mr. Delasandro (Orson Welles), Beeman becomes a tap-dancing magician.

Meanwhile, his erstwhile boss, Mr. Turnbull (John Astin), has lost his position and become an alcoholic. He encounters Beeman and sees an opportunity to regain his former position. Using much of the cutthroat business tactics rejected by Beeman, Turnbull makes the act a hugely successful venture.

Realizing that he is slowly being drawn back into his old ways, Beeman decides once again to get out, but thanks to his magic powers, this time he makes himself disappear.

NOTES:

This was Brian De Palma's third film as director (made in 1970) and his first for a major studio, but despite this, many critics preferred his earlier, independent pictures.

Orson Welles' contribution was limited to a few sequences involving his magic act, which surely must have attracted him to the role in the first place. After some apparent initial conflict, Welles and De Palma got on well together, with the star supporting the young director when Warners objected to the finished picture.

Get to Know Your Rabbit marked the film debut of Tom Smothers, of the popular duo the Smothers Brothers and, partly to please the star, Warners "shelved" the picture for two years before releasing it with extra sequences shot by another director. In De Palma's original version, Beeman was seen — by way of a trick — to slaughter a rabbit on television in order to discredit Turnbull.

De Palma's later works are heavily inspired by Alfred Hitchcock — most notably *Sisters* and *Obsession*, both of which boasted music scores by Bernard Herrmann who, since the days of the Mercury Theatre, had become one of the outstanding film composers in Hollywood.

REVIEWS:

. . . De Palma is a very funny filmmaker. He's most funny, so far, anyway, when he's most anarchic, and *Get to Know Your Rabbit*, though somewhat inhibited by conventional form, has enough hilarious loose ends and sidetracks to liberate the film from its form . . . There's old Mr. Delasandro (Orson Welles) who teaches Donald (Tom Smothers) how to become a seedy, tap-dancing magician . . . It also reinforces my expectation that De Palma will one day make a really fine American comedy.
— Vincent Canby, *The New York Times*

There is a priceless shot of Smothers, surrounded by neophytes of all sizes and shapes, tap-dancing their little hearts out as they learn to master the flowing red and blue foulards that are the classic staples of the magician's art. Orson Welles, their maestro, issues a rabbit to each aspiring prestidigitator with the exhortation, "Get to know it." Only Smothers survives to graduate, receiving a tap-dancing magician's official T-shirt as a diploma.
— Paul D. Zimmerman, *Newsweek*

GET TO KNOW YOUR RABBIT: A brief cameo in Brian De Palma's comedy.

213

NECROMANCY

a.k.a. *The Witching*

1972. ZENITH INTERNATIONAL PICTURES/CINERAMA RELEASING.

Produced and Directed by Bert I. Gordon.
Screenplay: Bert I. Gordon. Director of Photography: Winston Koch. Art Director: Frank Sylos. Music Score: Fred Karger. Film Editor: John Woelz.
Running Time: 82 minutes.

CAST:

Orson Welles (*Mr. Cato*); Pamela Franklin (*Lori*); Lee Purcell (*Priscilla*); Michael Ontkean (*Frank*); Harvey Jason (*Jay*); Lisa James (*Georgette*); Sue Bernard (*Nancy*); Terry Quinn (*Cato's son*).

SYNOPSIS:

Frank (Michael Ontkean) is transferred to Lilith, a small town where the only industry appears to be a factory making and selling objects dealing with the occult.

The factory is owned by Mr. Cato (Orson Welles), a sinister figure who is also responsible for a semi-annual festival in which necromancy is practiced.

With the next ceremony approaching, Frank's wife, Lori (Pamela Franklin), becomes the object of Cato's attention as he attempts to bring back to life his dead young son.

NOTES:

Bert I. Gordon began his movie career playing with special effects during the 1950s and producing a series of low-budget horror movies including *War of the Colossal Beast* and *Attack of the Puppet People*.

After tackling a couple of more serious subjects during the late 1960s, he returned to the horror genre with *Necromancy*, which had a working title of *The Toy Factory*.

Orson Welles, the man who terrified half of America with a single radio broadcast in 1938, dominated the proceedings by his mere presence in this, only his second "horror" film.

REVIEWS:

There appears to be good intent on the part of producer-writer-director Bert I. Gordon as he has topped his cast with the talented Pamela Franklin and the multi-talented Orson Welles, but the pair

NECROMANCY: Welles as Mr. Cato.

of thespians, possibly uninspired by the lackadaisical and erratic script, walk through their parts . . . Welles, in an obviously fake nose, is seen in brief spurts . . . Talent alone isn't enough to bring this cinematic stiff back from the dead.

— Robe., *Variety*

This picture contains a lot of disappointments . . . but at least it makes no stabs at sensationalizing witchcraft. And for a low-budget film (half a million), it achieves the distinction of actually looking as if it were shot and edited by one man instead of a frantic committee . . . Nonetheless, the slow, contrived pace works well here. Welles mumbles but is obviously the only man for the job.

— Anitra Earle, *San Francisco Chronicle*

NECROMANCY: With Lee Purcell as Priscilla.

215

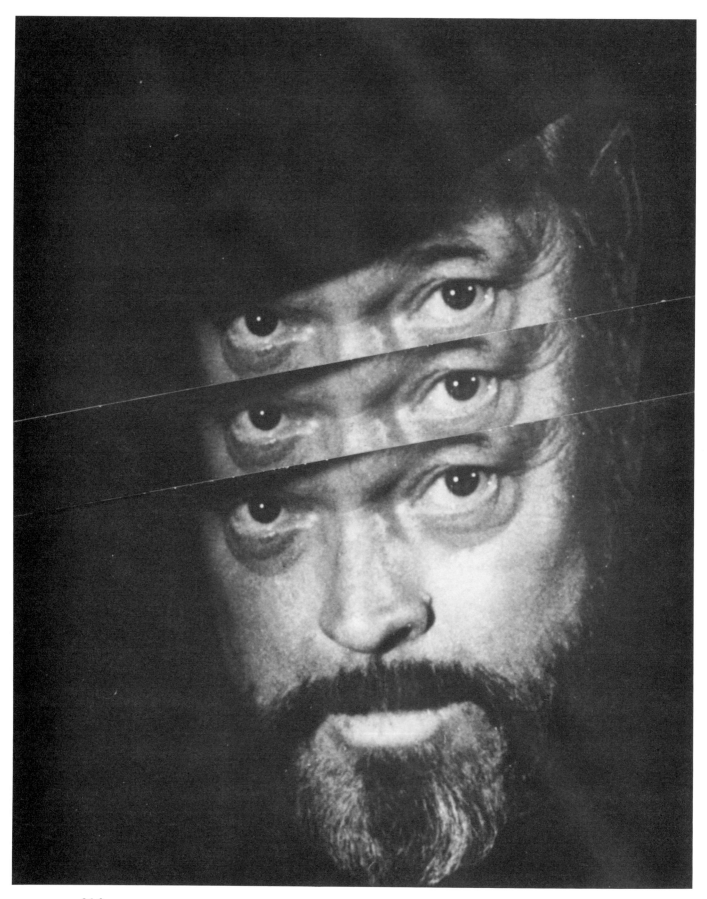

F FOR FAKE

(Verités et Mensonges)
"A.K.A. ?"
and *Stranger Than Fiction*

1973. ASTROPHORE/SACI/JANUS FILMS.

Directed by Orson Welles. Produced by Dominique Antoine and François Reichenbach.
Screenplay: Orson Welles and Oja Palinkas. Directors of Photography: Gary Graver and Christian Odasso. Music: Michel Legrand and Erik Satie. Film Editors: Marie Sophie Dubus and Dominique Engerer.
Running Time: 85 minutes.

CAST:

Orson Welles, Oja Kodar, Elmyr de Hory, Clifford Irving, Joseph Cotten, Edith Irving, François Reichenbach, Laurence Harvey, Howard Hughes, Richard Wilson, Paul Stewart, Gary Graver, Julio Palinkas, Sasa Devcic, Andres Vincent Gomez, Christian Odasso, Françoise Widoff, Peter Bogdanovich, William Alland.

NOTES:

Sometime in 1973, Orson Welles caught sight of a half-hour documentary made for French television by François Reichenbach on the art forger Elmyr de Hory. Reichenbach had already made a similar program on Orson Welles for French TV in 1966.

Viewing the de Hory program, Welles was seized by the thought of expanding the piece into a full-length feature, and bought up the complete footage, including outtakes.

By sublime coincidence, also featured briefly in the film was Clifford Irving, an American journalist whose own book *Fake!* dealt with the de Hory scandal. Irving had been a close friend of the forger but his own exploits were about to outshine anything which Elmyr could have dreamed up.

Revealed as the forger of Howard Hughes' supposed autobiography, purchased by McGraw-Hill for a considerable sum, Irving was as important to the film as was Elmyr. The movie was further extended by adding new material by and about Orson Welles himself.

This was to rebound on him in many ways, since in an early moment of the film, Welles announces, "I am a charlatan," taken as an admission by many reviewers still probing his work for *Significance.* In fact, Welles insisted that he only made the statement in order not to appear a moral judge over his two subjects.

The Welles section of the film involved a reminiscence of his days in Ireland as a sixteen-year-old, the story of the Mercury *War of the Worlds* broadcast and a brief review of Howard Hughes' nonactivities over the years. Joseph Cotten appeared briefly as himself, as did Paul Stewart and Laurence Harvey. William Alland was heard but not seen; a reference to his presence in *Citizen Kane.*

To round off, Welles performed some of his magic tricks at a railway station and elsewhere, and told a story with Oja Kodar of a chance meeting with Pablo Picasso.

This final tale was also the final hoax: at the film's beginning Orson Welles assures us that everything we hear in the next hour will be absolutely true. Revealing the Picasso story as false, Welles tells us that the hour is now up. "For the past seventeen minutes, I've been lying my head off."

F for Fake was a particular joy for Welles and, according to Henry Jaglom, was his own favorite picture. Had it been the success he hoped for, Welles claimed he would have made this his new style of movie — the personal essay, as opposed to the documentary.

The film though, despite many good reviews, was not a hit with the public, and in fairness it is hard to imagine such a picture finding a large audience. For all that, *F for Fake* is an intriguing, thoroughly entertaining piece, which proved to be the last completed film directed by Orson Welles.

REVIEWS:

"I'm a charlatan," says Orson Welles, looking very fit, his manner that of a practicing con artist who knows that if he confesses to everything, he will be held accountable for nothing. Or is it the other way around? This is the beginning of Mr. Welles's latest film . . . a disarming, witty meditation upon fake, forgery, swindling, and art, a movie that may itself be its own Exhibit A.
    — Vincent Canby, *The New York Times*

Yes, within the context *F for Fake* is a masterpiece and a reaffirmation of what a great artist Mr. Welles is.
    — *What's On in London*

218   F FOR FAKE: Subjects of the film: Orson Welles, Elmyr de Hory, Clifford
Irving and Howard Hughes.

BRITISH BOARD of FILM CENSORS
3 Soho Square, London W1V 5DE
President: THE RT. HON. THE LORD HARLECH K.C.M.G.

Secretary: James Ferman

JF/CDM

Telephone: 01-437 2877/8
Telegrams: CENSOFILM, PHONE, LONDON

1st April, 1976.

Managing Director,
Essential Cinema Ltd.,
76 Wardour Street,
London, W.1.

Dear Sir,

<u>F FOR FAKE - Orson Welles</u>

F FOR FAKE has impressed us more than any film ever submitted to the
Board. We would like to issue a unique certificate M (for masterpiece)
to show our enthusiasm for this exceptional work.

Yours faithfully

James Ferman

James Ferman
Secretary

The Incorporated Association of Kinematograph Manufacturers Limited
Registered number 117289 England
Registered Office: 3 Soho Square London W1V 5DE

F FOR FAKE, an authentic masterpiece by and with Orson Welles, has its premiere run at
two London cinemas -
the Essential 76 Wardour Street Soho (439 3657) from Monday 22nd November
& the Electric 191 Portobello Road W11 (727 4992) from Sunday 21st November,
In support at both cinemas, two deceptive shorts: Polanski's THE FAT AND THE LEAN
and Bob Godfrey's WHATEVER HAPPENED TO UNCLE FRED.
Programmes 5.0* 7.0 9.0 (+ 3.0 Saturdays & Sundays)

* No 5.0 show weekdays at the Electric

Press enquiries: Derek Hill, Essential Cinema, 122 Wardour St., London, W.1. Tel: 437 8127

It is good to see that the master's own quirky sense of humour has not left him, as his remarkable film *F for Fake* will prove . . . Tonight it gets its first television showing and should not be missed. — *Evening News*, April 1977

VOYAGE OF THE DAMNED

1976. ITC/ASSOCIATED GENERAL FILMS.

Directed by Stuart Rosenberg. Produced by Robert Fryer.
Screenplay: Steve Shagan and David Butler, based on the novel by Gordon Thomas and Max Morgan-Witts. Director of Photography: Billy Williams. Music Score: Lalo Schifrin. Film Editor: Tom Priestly.
Running Time: 155 minutes. Eastmancolor.

CAST:

Faye Dunaway (*Denise Kreisler*); Max Von Sydow (*Gustav Schroeder*); Oskar Werner (*Egon Kreisler*); Malcolm McDowell (*Max Gunther*); James Mason (*Juan Remos*); Orson Welles (*José Estedes*); Katharine Ross (*Mira Hauser*); Ben Gazzara (*Morris Troper*); Sam Wanamaker (*Carl Rosen*); Lee Grant (*Lili Rosen*); Lynne Frederick (*Anna Rosen*); Wendy Hiller (*Rachel Weller*); Luther Adler (*Prof. Weller*); Nehemiah Persoff (*Mr. Hauser*); Julie Harris (*Alice Fairchild*); Donald Houston (*Dr. Glovner*); Denholm Elliott (*Adm. Canaris*); Victor Spinetti (*Dr. Max Strauss*); Jose Ferrer (*Benitez*); Maria Schell (*Mrs. Hauser*); Paul Koslo (*Aaron Pozner*); Jonathan Pryce (*Joseph Manasse*); Fernando Rey (*President Bru*); Michael Constantine (*Clasing*); Janet Suzman (*Leni Strauss*).

SYNOPSIS:

The true story of 937 Jews lured onto an ocean liner at Hamburg in May 1939 and bound for Cuba, a ploy chosen by the Nazi Propaganda Ministry to convince the world that the Germans were not victimizing the Jews.

Refused entry at Cuba and loath to return to Germany, the ship headed for America. There it also was turned away — officials even refusing to allow the vessel to enter American waters.

Finally, the combined European allies of Britain, Belgium, France and Holland agreed to take the immigrants, but ironically within a few short months, all four countries would be at war with Germany.

NOTES:

Another attempt at a British-produced international blockbuster, *Voyage of the Damned* was another failure for Lord Grade's ITC company, failing to recoup its huge costs. The all-star cast was felt by many reviewers to detract from the true story, similar to the equally stellar *Ship of Fools* from 1965, which coincidentally also starred Oskar Werner.

Orson Welles, in his first screen role in four years, appeared as one of two corrupt Cuban officials surrounded by beautiful young girls.

REVIEWS:

Orson Welles, James Mason, Denholm Elliott and José Ferrer are on and off faster than it takes to type this sentence, while Lee Grant, Julie Harris, Wendy Hiller and Luther Adler might wish they had been so lucky. Movies as clumsy, tasteless and self-righteous as this are worse than merely boring. — Vincent Canby, *The New York Times*

At best, the film turns it into watchable fiction, with indelible star performances from Max Von Sydow, Faye Dunaway, Oskar Werner, Lee Grant, Orson Welles, Wendy Hiller, Ben Gazzara and José Ferrer.   — Margaret Hinxman, *Daily Mail*

Orson Welles and a public school James Mason seem designed to stand out next to José Ferrer . . . as the year's most improbable pair of Cubans.
— *Sunday Times*

The all star cast walks out of the film as fresh and unscathed at the end as they walked into it . . . Faye Dunaway, Max von Sydow, Oskar Werner, James Mason, Orson Welles, Malcolm McDowell and many, many more, act in this extraordinary exercise in non-drama . . .
— Nigel Andrews, *Financial Times*

VOYAGE OF THE DAMNED:
With Victor Spinetti.

THE MUPPET MOVIE

1979. ITC/ASSOCIATED FILM DISTRIBUTORS.

Directed by James Frawley. Produced by Jim Henson. Screenplay: Jerry Juhl and Jack Burns. Director of Photography: Isidore Mankofsky. Music Score: Paul Williams and Kenny Ascher. Film Editor: Chris Greenbury.
Running Time: 97 minutes. Eastmancolor.

CAST:

Orson Welles appeared as "Lew Lord" with other guest appearances from Bob Hope (*Ice Cream Vendor*); Edgar Bergen (*Himself*); Milton Berle (*Mad Man Mooney*); Madeline Kahn (*Woman*); Mel Brooks (*Max Krassman*); James Coburn (*El Sleezo Proprietor*); Dom DeLuise (*Bernie*); Telly Savalas (*Thug*); Richard Pryor (*Balloon Vendor*); Paul Williams (*Piano Player*); Elliott Gould (*Compere*); Carol Kane (*Myth*); Cloris Leachman (*Lord's Secretary*); Steve Martin (*Waiter*); Charles Durning (*Doc Hopper*). WITH: Austin Pendleton, Scott Walker, Ira F. Grubman, H. B. Haggerty, Bruce Kirby, Tommy Madden, Lawrence Gabriel, Jr., Arnold Roberts, James Frawley.

SYNOPSIS:

Kermit the Frog is approached by a Hollywood agent (Dom DeLuise) who convinces him to try his luck in the film capital, and on the cross-country jaunt is joined by other assorted Muppets

THE MUPPET MOVIE: As movie mogul Lew Lord.

along the way. Kermit, constantly trying to avoid the wicked Doc Hopper (Charles Durning) who wants him for a fried-frog-legs commercial, eventually reaches Hollywood with Miss Piggy, Gonzo, and pals, and there movie mogul Lew Lord (Orson Welles) signs them to a contract and they become stars.

NOTES:

Little can be said about this, the first of the Muppet feature films. Orson Welles appears as "Lew Lord," an obvious play on Lord Lew Grade, head of ITC who produced the film.

An overlong extension of the successful Muppets television series, the film was nevertheless a financial success and provided Welles with his first movie salary in two years.

REVIEWS:

. . . the last word in "road" pictures, being the story of Kermit's crazy cross-country trip to Hollywood, much of it in the company of Fozzie the Bear, who drives not well but often . . . The Muppets they meet and take aboard are good company, as are their friends including Dom DeLuise, Mel Brooks, Madeline Kahn, Milton Berle, Orson Welles and Richard Pryor, each of whom turns up briefly. — Vincent Canby, *The New York Times*

Bob Hope, James Coburn, Elliott Gould, Orson Welles and others have guest spots minute enough to be near fraudulent.

— *New Statesman*

TAJNA NIKOLE TESLA

(The Secret of Nikole Tesla)

1980. ZAGREB FILM/ KINEMATOGRAFI.

Directed by Krsto Papic.
Screenplay: Ivo Bresan and Ivan Kusan. Director of Photography: Ivica Rajkovic.
Running Time: 120 minutes.

CAST:

Peter Bozovic (*Nikole Tesla*); Orson Welles (*J. P. Morgan*); Strother Martin (*George Westinghouse*); Dennis Patrick (*Thomas Edison*). WITH: Oja Kodar, Charles Millot, Boris Buzancic, Ana Kavic.

SYNOPSIS:

Nikole Tesla (Peter Bozovic) is fascinated by the powers of electricity and, stumbling across the alternating current system, he heads for America where Thomas Edison (Dennis Patrick) is interested in Tesla's work but eventually dismisses it as unworkable. Refusing Edison's offer of a job, Tesla becomes a road laborer.

Ultimately, however, he is "discovered" by George Westinghouse (Strother Martin) who, together with John Pierpont Morgan (Orson Welles), pushes for legislation to adopt Tesla's alternating current across the country. Tesla becomes famous and rich almost overnight.

When Tesla begins work on harnessing solar energy, though, Morgan realizes that its implementation will lose him a great deal of money through his investments in other power sources, so he puts an end to the experiment. Tesla's work is destroyed and his papers kept under lock and key.

BUTTERFLY

1981. PAR PAR PRODUCTIONS.

Produced and Directed by Matt Cimber.
Screenplay: John Goff and Matt Cimber, based on the novel by James M. Cain. Director of Photography: Eddy Van Der Enden. Art Director: Dave De Carlo. Music Score: Ennio Morricone. Film Editors: B. A. Schoenfeld and Stan Siegel.
Running Time: 108 minutes. Metrocolor.

CAST:

Stacy Keach (*Jess Tyler*); Pia Zadora (*Kady*); Orson Welles (*Judge Rauch*); Lois Nettleton (*Belle Morgan*); Edward Albert (*Wash Gillespie*); James Franciscus (*Moke Blue*); Stuart Whitman (*Reverend Rivers*); June Lockhart (*Mrs. Gillespie*); Ed McMahon (*Mr. Gillespie*); Paul Hampton (*Norton*); Buck Flower (*Ed Lamey*); Ann Dane (*Janey*); Greg Gault (*Bridger*); John O'Connor White (*Billy Roy*). WITH: Peter Jason, Kim Ptak, Leigh Christian, Abraham Rudnick, John Goff, Dylan Urquidi.

SYNOPSIS:

Jess Tyler works as caretaker of a rundown silver mine in Arizona, having been deserted by his wife Belle (Lois Nettleton) ten years ago when she left with her lover Moke Blue (James Franciscus), taking Jess' two young daughters with her. It is 1937 and suddenly he is confronted by his daughter, Kady (Pia Zadora), now seventeen.

Kady, however, shows very undaughterly feelings toward her father and soon persuades him to reopen the mine and make money for her to live in luxury, while at the same time cheating the mine's owners, the Gillespies (Ed McMahon and June Lockhart), who disapprove of her.

Driven by Kady, Jess becomes involved in fights and theft and plots murder when Ed Lamey (Buck Flower) accuses them of improper relations with Kady.

A lengthy trial takes place, held by Judge Rauch (Orson Welles), which clears them both, but complications follow when Wash Gillespie (Edward Albert), father of Kady's baby, announces that he is taking her away. Belle and Moke also reappear, and Jess must now decide to face Moke and settle their futures once and for all.

NOTES:

The Butterfly, a 1946 novel by James M. Cain, had shocked readers upon its first publication, as had Cain's other works, *Double Indemnity* and *The Postman Always Rings Twice*.

Matt Cimber, husband of the late Jayne Mans-

BUTTERFLY: With Pia Zadora.

224

field, wrote, produced and directed this reasonably faithful version of the story which served to introduce Pia Zadora to the cinema audience.

Orson Welles, as the lecherous judge, appears in two courtroom scenes and was singled out for praise by most reviewers. The film itself was given a mixed reception; some critics found it too seedy while others thought it entirely appropriate to the subject matter.

REVIEWS:

Mr. Cimber has . . . pulled together a good cast, including Mr. Keach; Orson Welles, who has two, brief, funny scenes as a small town judge.
— Vincent Canby, *The New York Times*

Outclassing everything else is Orson Welles as the High Court Judge. — *Western Mail*

It is significant that the only time the film comes alive is during Lois Nettleton's brief appearance on screen: her part is mangled and her lines atrocious, but here, at least, is an actress. The rest of the cast — including Orson Welles and Stuart Whitman in cameos as a crackerbarrel judge and a hellfire preacher — seem bemused by having to act as foils to Ms. Zadora's monotone performance. — Tom Milne, *Monthly Film Bulletin*

WHERE IS PARSIFAL?

1983. SLEDERLINE.

Directed by Henri Helman. Produced by Daniel Carrillo.
Screenplay: Berta Dominguez D. Director of Photography: Norman Langley. Production Designer: Malcolm Stone. Music: Hubert Rostaing. Film Editors: Russ Lloyd and Peter Hollywood.
Running Time: 87 minutes. Color.

CAST:

Tony Curtis (*Parsifal Katzanella-Boden*); Cassandra Domenica (*Elba Katzanella-Boden*); Erik Estrada (*Henry Board III*); Peter Lawford (*Montague Chippendale*); Donald Pleasence (*Mackintosh*); Orson Welles (*Klingsor*); Ron Moody (*Baron Gaspard Beersbohm*); Christopher Chaplin (*Ivan*); Nancy Roberts (*Ruth*);

Ava Lazar (*Sheila*); Anthony Dawson (*Ripple*); Vladek Sheybal (*Morjack*). WITH: Jay Benedict, Edward Burnham, Victoria Burgoyne, Stuart Latham, David Baxt, Simon Cloquet, Peter Poll, Sally Cranfield, Christina Artemis, Pamela Trigg, Arthur Beatty.

SYNOPSIS:

Parsifal Katzanella-Boden (Tony Curtis) is a former tycoon, a whiz-kid who has somehow lost the secret of being a success. When he meets up with the inventor of a skywriting machine, he quickly purchases the rights. He plans to use the machine — which will write with colored 3-D lasers in the sky right across the world — to make his fortune. His wife, Elba (Cassandra Domenica), sees the invention as a means of spreading peace to the corners of the globe by transmitting messages of love and hope.

Various tycoons and interested parties arrive at their home, including Klingsor (Orson Welles) and Henry Board (Erik Estrada), who try to outbid each other for the machine.

The situation develops into a farce as the assembled group await the first demonstration of the wondrous invention.

NOTES:

Alexander Salkind, coproducer of Orson Welles' 1962 film of *The Trial*, approached Orson again in 1983 with an offer of financing a modest-budget version of *King Lear* if he would accept a small role in the current Salkind production, *Where Is Parsifal?*

Orson Welles contributed three days' work, or more accurately, three nights since his scenes were filmed between dusk and dawn, his actual appearance in the film limited to the closing reel. He rewrote much of his script and made suggestions over the shooting of the scene which were accepted by the director and crew, but otherwise his involvement was minimal.

On release the film (which premiered at the 1983 Cannes Film Festival) was poorly received, many reviewers bemoaning the waste of talent on such an enterprise. It seems never to have had a U.S. showing.

REVIEWS:

Ludicrous beyond belief . . . Structurally, the film is a variation on *You Can't Take It With You* except someone forgot to put in any funny lines.
— *Variety*

225

Just when you thought Central Casting had been exhausted, the magnificent Orson Welles is ferried in at the denouement as the wily King of the Gypsies.   — P. Bergsin, *What's On in London*

SOMEONE TO LOVE

1987. AN INTERNATIONAL
RAINBOW PICTURE.

Directed by Henry Jaglom. Produced by M. H. Simonsons.
Screenplay: Henry Jaglom. Director of Photography: Hanania Baer. Original Music: Diane Bulgarelli, Stephen Bishop, Dave Frishberg. Editor: Ruth Wald. Running Time: 110 minutes. Color.

CAST:

Henry Jaglom (*Danny Speir*); Orson Welles (*Danny's Friend*); Andrea Marcovicci (*Helen Eugene*); Michael Emil (*Mickey Sapir*); Sally Kellerman (*Edith Helm*); Oja Kodar (*Yelena*); Stephen Bishop (*Blue*); Dave Frishberg (*Harry*). WITH: Geraldine Baron, Ronee Blakley, Barbara Flood, Pamela Goldblum, Robert Hallak, Kathryn Gould, Monte Hellman, Jeremy Kagan, Michael Kaye, Miles Kreuger, Amnon Meskin, Sunny Meyer, Peter Rafelson, Ora Rubens, Katherine Wallach.

SYNOPSIS:

Filmmaker Danny Speir (Henry Jaglom) meets with his brother Michael (Michael Emil), a businessman who tells Danny he has just made a successful deal involving the sale of a property. The building turns out to be a 1911 theater, due to be demolished to make way for yet another shopping center.

Puzzled by his relationship with Helen (Andrea Marcovicci), Danny decides to hold a party at the doomed theater the following Sunday — Valentine's Day. He sends invitations to his unmarried and seemingly alone friends.

On Valentine's Day, the theater is filled with Danny and his group, plus a film crew to record what Danny hopes will be a useful record of his friends' views on loneliness and the search for romance.

At the back of the theater, Danny's Friend (Orson Welles) has been watching the progress of

SOMEONE TO LOVE: "I'm speaking from the cheap seats": Orson Welles in Jaglom's film.

SOMEONE TO LOVE: With director and friend Henry Jaglom.

the film and the state of the guests' personal lives. Prompted by Danny, he gives his own views on the film itself and on the problems of the new generation.

Many of the women return to the stage to join in the conversation, the latest guest offering his opinion on women's liberation and other topics. Finally, Danny tells Helen that the film is to be his Valentine gift to her, but continues filming until his Friend finally orders the cameras to "Cut!"

NOTES:

For a time it seemed that *Where Is Parsifal?* would be an inglorious finale to the screen career of Orson Welles. At his death in October 1985, he left unfinished several promising new projects.

Already half-completed was Henry Jaglom's *Is It You?* in which Orson appeared. Released some eighteen months later as *Someone to Love,* the movie has a greatly improvised feel to it, most apparent during Welles' discussions with "Danny" during the closing section of the picture.

"Yes, Orson's comments in *Someone to Love* were entirely his own," Henry Jaglom says. "We created a script together, which he memorized and used as a basis for his part — although he

departed from that script on the spot quite frequently and quite wonderfully."

Watching the film, it seemed to me that, had it not been for Orson on occasion calling Jaglom "Danny," we could be eavesdropping on a private conversation. Again, Jaglom agrees: "Your suspicions were correct: The scenes with Orson were in the nature of a conversation between ourselves, from which I selected and rearranged the parts you see in the film. We created the script entirely from lunches we had together preceding the making of the film, in which we discussed the subject at hand and Orson came up with the thoughts which we later formalized into the screenplay."

Since *A Safe Place* in 1970, Orson Welles had taken a keen interest in Jaglom's work, sitting with him during editing and offering suggestions. This practice was to have been followed on *Someone to Love,* since Jaglom recalls, "He made many suggestions about its final shape in person, on the phone and in many memos which he sent me during and after the making of the film."

Despite his usual deferment to Welles in the cutting room, Jaglom nevertheless says, "Had he lived, of course, he would never have allowed me the ending, in which he says that I should stop the cameras rolling as the conversation has gotten

SOMEONE TO LOVE: (*Opposite page*) Video release of the film.

SOMEONE TO LOVE: Orson with his pet poodle Kiki.

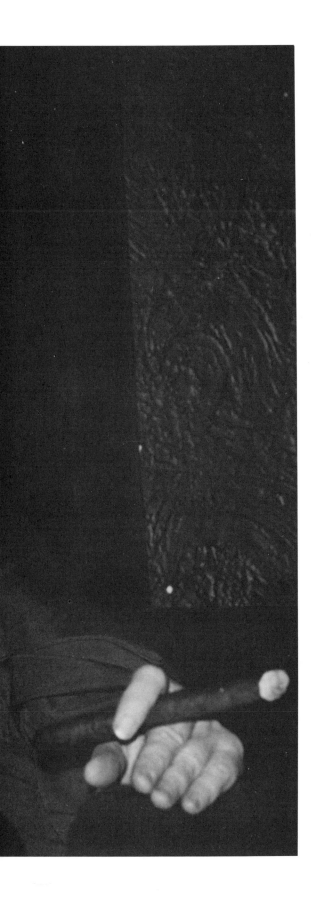

'too sweet.' I felt it correct to give Orson the final word and I thought that 'Cut!' was the best final word with which to end his on-screen career; and even after that, I felt the desire, as you saw, to give him the Last Laugh."

Someone to Love is Henry Jaglom's tribute to his friend, and the film is dedicated "To Orson Welles, with Love." As with most of Jaglom's pictures, reviews were mixed. In general, British critics were less enthusiastic, while the American press seemed to recognize the feeling behind the work: a true and fitting finale to the screen career of a Giant of American Cinema, Orson Welles.

Others in the cast include Michael Emil as Danny's Brother — in real life Henry Jaglom's own half-brother—and, as Yelena, Oja Kodar, Orson Welles' companion for many years.

REVIEWS:

Welles, as ever, is a treat to watch and hear, even when he is reduced to pontificating about the sexual revolution. As for the rest, it's mainly lifestyle patois from interchangeable characters.
— Walter Goodman, *The New York Times*

Orson Welles adds a superb last performance speaking lifetime words of wisdom — about men, women, films, life — in a most human and amusing way.   — Jerry Tallmer, *New York Post*

Welles's ascerbity from the stalls provides a mesmeric commentary on men and women, post-liberation . . . Monumental, witty and wise, he tempers his strictures on life and the movies with a final dragon-slaying dictum: 'I am speaking from the cheap seats, not Mount Sinai.'
— Victoria Mather, *Daily Telegraph*

Someone to Love is aptly dedicated to the rotund genius who acted as sounding board, friend and father figure throughout Jaglom's striking career. Orson Welles can rest assured that his influence and guidance live on in one of the most original talents in Hollywood.
— Tom Crow, *Star-News*

For Jaglom to have given Welles this last opportunity to shine is a wonderful thing, like a son giving a perfect last send-off to a father. Yet it is not forced but belongs to the film . . . Not even the final credits end the occasion, although Welles speaking through them remarks that by now the audience will be up the aisles and away. But we are not. How could we be when witnessing a moment so fine: for Welles, for Jaglom and, thanks to them, for us.   — *What's On in London*

ORSON WELLES IN THE THEATER

GATE THEATRE, DUBLIN

Between October 1931 and February 1932, Orson Welles appeared in Ashley Dukes' *Jew Süss* (as Karl Alexander), David Sears' *The Dead Ride Fast* (as Ralph Bentley), *The Archdupe, Mogu of the Desert* by Padraic Colum, *Death Takes a Holiday* by Alberto Cassella and Shakespeare's *Hamlet* (as the Ghost, and Fortinbras) at the Gate Theatre, Dublin.

KATHARINE CORNELL COMPANY

1933–34. Touring as Mercutio in Shakespeare's *Romeo and Juliet*, Octavius in Rudolph Besier's *The Barretts of Wimpole Street* and Marchbanks in Shaw's *Candida*. Later played Tybalt in *Romeo and Juliet* when the production reached New York.

PANIC

By Archibald MacLeish. The play produced by John Houseman. Directed by James Light. Orson Welles played MacGafferty at the Imperial Theatre in New York for a scheduled three performances in March 1935.

MACBETH

1936. William Shakespeare. Adapted and Directed by Orson Welles. A Federal Theatre Production opening at the Lafayette Theatre on April 14, 1936, later transferred to the Adelphi Theatre, New York. Music by Virgil Thomson. Cast included Jack Carter (*Macbeth*); Edna Thomas (*Lady Macbeth*); Service Bell (*Duncan*); Wardell Saunders (*Malcolm*); Maurice Ellis (*Macduff*); Canada Lee (*Banquo*).

HORSE EATS HAT

By Edwin Denby and Orson Welles, based on *An Italian Straw Hat* by Eugene Labiche and Marc-Michel. Directed by Orson Welles. A Project 891 Production at the Maxine Elliott Theatre, New York, from September 26 to December 5, 1936. Music by Paul Bowles. Cast included: Orson Welles and Edgerton Paul (alternating as *Mugglethorpe*); Joseph Cotten (*Freddie*); Virginia Welles (*Myrtle Mugglethorpe*); Hiram Sherman (*Bobbin*); Arlene Francis (*Tillie*); Dana Stevens (*Queeper*).

TEN MILLION GHOSTS

Written and directed by Sidney Kingsley. One performance only at St. James Theatre, New York, October 23, 1936. Orson Welles played André Pequot.

DOCTOR FAUSTUS

By Christopher Marlowe. Directed by Orson Welles. A Project 891 Production at the Maxine Elliott Theatre, New York, for 16 weeks from January to May 1937. Music by Paul Bowles. Cast included: Orson Welles (*Faustus*); Charles Peyton (*The Pope*); Jack Carter (*Mephistopheles*); Myron Paulson (*Cornelius*); Bernard Savage (*Valdez*).

THE SECOND HURRICANE

Music by Aaron Copland; Libretto by Edwin Denby. Produced by the Music School of the Henry Street Settlement. Three performances only in April 1937 at Henry Street Playhouse. Directed by Orson Welles. Cast included: Joseph Cotten (*Mr. MacLanachan*); Vivienne Block (*Queenie*); Arthur Anderson (*Gyp*); Estelle Levy (*Gwen*).

Directing Joseph Cotten and Arlene Francis in the Mercury *Horse Eats Hat.*

THE CRADLE WILL ROCK

By Marc Blitzstein. Directed by Orson Welles. A Project 891 Production at the Venice Theatre, New York, for two weeks in June 1937. Later revived for four performances at the Mercury Theatre, November–December 1937. Cast included: Olive Stanton (*Moll*); Guido Alexander (*Dick*); Will Geer (*Mr. Mister*); Robert Farnsworth (*Cop*); Hiram Sherman (*Professor Skoot*); Howard da Silva (*Larry*).

JULIUS CAESAR

By William Shakespeare. A Mercury Production. Adapted and Directed by Orson Welles at the Mercury (Comedy) Theatre, New York, November 11 to December 24, 1937. Later transferred to the National Theatre, New York, April–June 1938. Music by Marc Blitzstein. Cast included: Joseph Holland (*Julius Caesar*); Joseph Cotten (*Publicus*); Orson Welles (*Brutus*); George Coulouris (*Marcus Antonius*); Martin Gabel (*Cassius*); Hiram Sherman (*Casca*); William Alland, Norman Lloyd, John Hoysradt.

THE SHOEMAKER'S HOLIDAY

By Thomas Dekker. A Mercury Production. Adapted and Directed by Orson Welles at the Mercury (Comedy) Theatre, New York, opening January 1, 1938. Later in repertory at the National Theatre, New York, April–June 1938. Music by Lehman Engel. Cast included: George Coulouris (*The King*); Joseph Cotten (*Rowland Lacy*); Vin-

The modern dress *Julius Caesar*. Welles as Brutus (left) and Martin Gabel as Caesar (third right).

cent Price (*Master Hammon*); Norman Lloyd (*Roger*); Hiram Sherman (*Firk*); William Alland (*Serving Man*); John Hoysradt (*Sir Roger Oteley*); Whitford Kane (*Simon Eyre*).

HEARTBREAK HOUSE

By George Bernard Shaw. A Mercury Production. Directed by Orson Welles at the Mercury (Comedy) Theatre, New York for eight weeks, opening April 29, 1938. Cast included: Orson Welles (*Captain Shotover*); Geraldine Fitzgerald (*Ellie Dunn*); Brenda Forbes (*Nurse Guinness*); Erskine Sanford (*Mazzini Dunn*); Vincent Price (*Hector Hushabye*); George Coulouris (*Boss Mangan*); John Hoysradt (*Randall Utterword*); Eustace Wyatt (*Burglar*).

TOO MUCH JOHNSON

By William Gillette. A Mercury Production. Adapted and Directed by Orson Welles for two weeks beginning August 16, 1938 at Stony Creek Summer Theatre, Connecticut. Cast included: Eustace Wyatt (*Faddish*); Joseph Cotten (*Augustus Billings*); Anna Stafford* (*Lenore Faddish*); Edgar Barrier (*Dathis*); Erskine Sanford (*Frederic*); Richard Wilson (*Cabin Boy*); Ruth Ford (*Mrs. Billings*). John Houseman, Arlene Francis, Marc Blitzstein.

DANTON'S DEATH

By Georg Büchner. Translated by Geoffrey Dunlop. A Mercury Production. Adapted and Directed by Orson Welles at the Mercury (Comedy) Theatre, New York for 21 performances, opening November 1938. Cast included: Orson Welles (*St. Just*); Anna Stafford* (*Julie*); Martin Gabel (*Danton*); Edgar Barrier (*Camille Desmoulins*); Arlene Francis (*Marion*); Joseph Cotten (*Barrere*); Ruth Ford (*Rosalie*); Vladimir Sokoloff (*Robespierre*); Richard Wilson (*Mercier*); Eustace Wyatt (*Fourquier*).

*"Anna Stafford" was the professional name used on occasion by Orson Welles' wife Virginia during the days of the Mercury Theatre.

FIVE KINGS

Directed and Adapted from William Shakespeare's *Henry IV, Henry V, Henry VI, Richard II, Richard III* by Orson Welles. A Mercury Theatre Production in association with the Theatre Guild. Music by Aaron Copland. On tour Boston and Philadelphia, February–March 1939. Cast included: Orson Welles (*Falstaff*); Burgess Meredith (*Prince Hal*); Eustace Wyatt (*Northumberland*); Morris Ankrum (*Henry IV*); John Emery (*Hotspur*); Edgar Barrier (*Archbishop of Canterbury*); Gus Schilling (*Bardolf*); Erskine Sanford (*Lord Chief Justice*); William Alland (*Peto*); Eustace Wyatt (*Pistol*).

THE GREEN GODDESS

By William Archer. A 20-minute vaudeville act performed by Orson Welles. RKO vaudeville circuit opening June 8, 1939, at the Palace Theatre in Chicago.

NATIVE SON

By Richard Wright. Directed by Orson Welles. St. James Theatre, New York. Opened March 17, 1941. Cast included: Orson Welles, Canada Lee, Ray Collins, Erskine Sanford, Everett Sloane, Paul Stewart.

THE MERCURY WONDER SHOW

A touring variety production visiting U.S. army bases during 1942 and featuring Orson Welles, Rita Hayworth, Joseph Cotten, Marlene Dietrich and Agnes Moorehead.

AROUND THE WORLD IN EIGHTY DAYS

By Jules Verne. A Mercury Theatre Production. Adapted and Directed by Orson Welles, with a

The impossibly extravagant *Around the World in Eighty Days* of 1946. Arthur Margetson, Orson Welles and Mary Healy.

In London, rehearsing the 1955 *Moby Dick*. Joan Plowright is at left.

score by Cole Porter. 75 performances at the Adelphi Theatre opening on May 31, 1946, following tryouts at Boston, New Haven and Philadelphia. Cast included: Orson Welles, Larry Laurence, Arthur Margetson, Julie Warren, Mary Healy, Victoria Cordova, Stefan Shnabel.

MACBETH

By William Shakespeare. Adapted and Directed by Orson Welles. A Mercury Production at the Utah Centennial Festival, Salt Lake City, May 1947. Cast included: Orson Welles (*Macbeth*); Jeanette Nolan (*Lady Macbeth*); Daniel O'Herlihy (*Macduff*); Roddy Macdowall (*Malcolm*).

TIME RUNS

Revue presented at the Théâtre Edouard VII, Paris, June–August 1950. Including *Doctor Faustus* by Christopher Marlowe, adapted by Orson Welles, and *The Unthinking Lobster* by Orson Welles. With Orson Welles, Hilton Edwards, Eartha Kitt and Suzanne Cloutier. Music by Duke Ellington.

AN EVENING WITH ORSON WELLES

German touring version of *Time Runs*, with Oscar Wilde's *The Importance of Being Earnest* replacing *The Unthinking Lobster*. Also featuring passages from *Henry VI* by Shakespeare; music by Duke Ellington and Eartha Kitt. Cast included: Orson Welles, Micheal MacLiammoir, Eartha Kitt, Suzanne Cloutier, Lee Zimmer. Opened August 7, 1950, in Frankfurt, followed by Hamburg, Cologne, Dusseldorf and Berlin.

OTHELLO

By William Shakespeare. Adapted and Directed by Orson Welles. St. James Theatre, London, opening October 18, 1951, following tryouts in Manchester and Newcastle. Cast included: Orson Welles (*Othello*); Gudrun Ure (*Desdemona*); Peter Finch (*Iago*); Maxine Audley (*Emilia*).

THE LADY IN THE ICE

A ballet with decor and costumes by Orson Welles. Music by Jean-Michel Demase. Choreography by Roland Petit. Performed by the Ballet de Paris. Opened at the Stoll Theatre, London, on September 7, 1953.

MOBY DICK

By Herman Melville. Adapted and Directed by Orson Welles. Presented at the Duke of York's Theatre, London, for four weeks, opening June 16, 1955. Cast included: Orson Welles (*Captain Ahab*); Gordon Jackson (*Ishmael*); Patrick McGoohan (*Starbuck*); Kenneth Williams (*Elijah*); Joan Plowright (*Pip*); Peter Sallis (*Flask*); Jefferson Clifford (*Peleg*).

A version of Welles' *Moby Dick*, also known as *Moby Dick Rehearsed*, starring Rod Steiger, opened at the Ethel Barrymore Theatre, New York, on November 28, 1962, and closed on December 8. It had a tryout earlier in Boston.

KING LEAR

By William Shakespeare. Adapted and Directed by Orson Welles at the City Center Theatre, New York, opening January 12, 1956. Cast included: Orson Welles (*King Lear*); Geraldine Fitzgerald (*Goneril*); Viveca Lindfors (*Cordelia*).

LAS VEGAS

Orson Welles appeared as a headline act at Las Vegas Riviera performing a magic act and reading passages from Shakespeare for one week in March 1956.

CHIMES AT MIDNIGHT

From William Shakespeare's *Henry IV, Parts I and II, Henry V, Merry Wives of Windsor*. Adapted and

Directed by Orson Welles. Opened at the Theatre Royal, Belfast, February 13, 1960, for one week, then at the Gaiety Theatre, Dublin. Cast included: Orson Welles (*Falstaff*); Keith Baxter (*Prince Hal*).

RHINOCEROS

By Eugene Ionesco. Directed by Orson Welles at the Royal Court Theatre, London, opening April 1960; later at the Strand Theatre. Cast included: Laurence Olivier, Joan Plowright, Alan Bates, Maggie Smith, Alan Webb.

ORSON WELLES ON THE AIR

PRE-MERCURY

First appearing in 1934 on the *March of Time* radio newsreel, Orson Welles contributed anonymously to the series for the next three years, impersonating anything from foreign statesmen to six-week-old quintuplets!

He read poetry on *The Alexander Woollcott Show* and during 1935–36 adapted and starred in *Les Misérables* for Mutual and *Hamlet* and *Macbeth* both for CBS.

Making up to four broadcasts per day, Orson hired an ambulance to rush him across the city from one station to another before being whisked off to his theater rehearsals. With so many broadcasts — mainly uncredited and on various stations — a complete list of his work in the medium is virtually an impossibility.

In 1937, Welles appeared as Lamont Cranston, *The Shadow*. This successful series ran for several months until CBS offered Orson a weekly series each Monday evening at 9:00: classics to be adapted, written, produced and directed by Welles, who was also to star.

THE MERCURY THEATRE ON THE AIR

First Person Singular premiered on July 11, 1938, with *Dracula*, featuring most of the current Mercury Theatre players plus Bernard Herrmann, head of the CBS music department, contributing the score. The series ran for ten weeks: other broadcasts including *Treasure Island, The Thirty-Nine Steps, A Tale of Two Cities* and *Julius Caesar*.

A further thirteen programs were commissioned by CBS, which considered the series a prestige production. Now renamed *The Mercury Theatre on the Air*, its new season — now slotted at 8:00 on Sunday evenings — began with *Jane Eyre, Sherlock Holmes* and *Oliver Twist*. As yet without a sponsor, the series continued, with Paul Stewart, John Houseman and later Howard Koch contributing to the writing, but Orson Welles retaining overall control of each show, rewriting constantly and directing each broadcast.

Surviving recordings retain a remarkable sharpness and dramatic intensity over half a century later, each introduced by Welles who then assumes character and leads the audience into the play.

THE WAR OF THE WORLDS

It was the Mercury show of October 30, 1938, that was to become the single most famous broadcast in American history and to catapult Welles and his players onto the nation's front pages.

The adaptation of *The War of the Worlds*, H. G. Wells' extraordinary 1895 novel describing an invasion from the planet Mars, was, according to several of those involved with the show, rather dull during early rehearsals. The crucial changes came with the decisions to update the story from 1890s England to 1938 midwest America and — more importantly — to present the play as a series of news bulletins, unfolding the story over sixty minutes.

From a program of dance music from "Ramon Raquelle" (Bernard Herrmann) interrupted by an item about gas explosions on Mars to an interview with Professor Pierson (Orson Welles) on the

One of the many commercially released recordings of the
legendary *War of the Worlds* broadcast.

significance of the sightings and on through reports of space objects crashing in New Jersey — an abruptly halted "outside broadcast" revealing that the "meteors" are, in fact, metallic cylinders which open to reveal murderous alien beings intent on destruction — the drama escalates rapidly as the aliens cross country, finally advancing on New York itself. Impudently enough, the final assault takes place on the CBS building!

A chilling rooftop broadcast — brilliantly performed by Joseph Cotten as the reporter finally overcome by poisoned smoke — is apparently followed by a radio ham breaking into the frequency with the plea "Isn't there anyone on the air? Isn't there . . . anyone?"

By this time — a mere twenty minutes into the broadcast — CBS was inundated with calls from terrified listeners convinced that an invasion was under way. Later reports spoke of thousands taking to the streets and heading for the countryside. John Barrymore was said to have dashed out to his kennels where he released his beloved dogs, shouting, "Fend for yourselves!"

Today's observers are inclined to play down the effects of the broadcast, but it is worth noting that during those days of unrest in Europe, unscheduled news bulletins were becoming a feature of everyday listening and it is quite possible that some sections of the audience — particularly the Jewish community — were panicked by thoughts of a German invasion.

Whatever the cause, Orson Welles found himself on the front page of *The New York Times* the following morning, despite the usual credits having been observed at the end of the Halloween broadcast — Welles describing the show as "the Mercury's own radio version of dressing up in a sheet and jumping out of a bush and saying *Boo!*"

Apologies were duly made, with the 23-year-old star innocently telling newsreel cameras of his shock over the effect the Mercury company's play had had on its audience, though many years later Welles claimed that the group knew what it was doing; the purpose of the broadcast had been to demonstrate the possible dangers of the power of the media — making the public believe something truly impossible before telling them, "It's only radio."

Incredibly, a repeat of the original broadcast on American radio in 1978 produced a similar though less frenzied response, as did a further transmission on Portuguese radio on the fiftieth anniversary of the original broadcast in October 1988.

A 1975 Paramount television movie, *The Night That Panicked America*, reconstructed the broadcast, with the studio scenes particularly well handled. Orson Welles was played convincingly by Paul Shenar, although of other participants only Howard Koch and Paul Stewart were portrayed; the real Paul Stewart acting as executive producer on the film.

Otherwise the movie was a dramatized version of the panic and its effects on the audience, in particular "Hank Muldoon" (!) and his family. These scenes were rather predictable and heavy-handed.

In 1938, though, the Mercury series continued on radio, later shows including *Rebecca* (which strongly influenced David O. Selznick's screen version of the story shortly afterward), *Pickwick Papers*, *Our Town*, *Les Misérables*, *Lost Horizon*, *Dodsworth* and *The Magnificent Ambersons*.

Soon after the *War of the Worlds* broadcast, the series attracted its all-important sponsor and became the rather less grandly titled *Campbell Playhouse*, as it remained until the final broadcast, a repeat of *Jane Eyre* on March 31, 1940.

AFTER MERCURY

With Orson and the Mercury in Hollywood, radio appearances became fewer, though Welles guested on variety shows and produced a series of fifteen-minute broadcasts in 1945 as part of his own political ambition, but billed as an entertainment program.

A 1946, half-hour version of *The Mercury Theatre on the Air* was Orson's last American broadcast. In 1951 in England, he recorded 26 half-hour BBC shows entitled *The Adventures of Harry Lime*. The resurrection of the characater was an astute move, as it was his most popular and acclaimed film role to date. The shows themselves bore no resemblance to *The Third Man*, with black marketeer Harry Lime transformed into a respectable figure involved in international intrigue. It was on one of these programs that *Mr. Arkadin*, from Welles' own original story, was first heard.

A later series, again for the BBC, saw Welles introducing *The Black Museum*, stories from the casebook of Scotland Yard. His final contact with BBC Radio Drama was in 1955 as Professor Moriarty in an adaptation of Conan Doyle's *The*

Final Problem. Sir John Gielgud was Sherlock Holmes with Sir Ralph Richardson as Doctor Watson.

TELEVISION

Orson Welles first appeared on American television in a 1953 CBS *Omnibus* production of *King Lear* directed by Peter Brook. The live broadcast was rapturously received by American critics, who had seemingly forgotten the power of Welles as an actor.

However, his next television was for the BBC in England in 1955. A modest series, cocreated by Wolf Mankowitz, *The Orson Welles Sketchbook*, was followed almost immediately by a series for the newly-formed rival ITA network, *Around the World with Orson Welles*, prompting one critic to describe him as "easily the most powerful personality ITV has presented up to date."

Back in New York in 1956, Orson played in a CBS television production of *Twentieth Century* as the megalomaniacal Oscar Jaffe. That same year he guested as himself on *I Love Lucy* with Lucille Ball, performing magic tricks and reciting Shakespeare. Lucille Ball — in 1940 considered too inexperienced by RKO to star in Orson's *Smiler With a Knife* — was soon to find her Desilu company in possession of the very studio lot formerly owned by the now defunct RKO, and offering Orson Welles a drama series as director.

The pilot show, *Fountain of Youth*, was however considered too "sophisticated" for the television audience and the series was canceled. To compound the insult, *Fountain of Youth* materialized two years later under the banner *Colgate Theatre* and won the Peabody Award for Excellence.

In 1972, Orson starred in the Hallmark Hall of Fame production of *The Man Who Came to Dinner* which, he told reporters, had been originally written for him by George S. Kaufman and Moss Hart in 1939. Welles had been offered both the stage and the film but declined, the role of the monstrous Sheridan Whiteside — based on Welles' benefactor Alexander Woollcott — making a star of Monty Woolley.

A 1972 British series made for Anglia Television, *Orson Welles' Great Mysteries*, traded on the celebrity of the star, who introduced each half-hour drama in his current apparel of wide-brimmed hat and flowing black cape, but overall had little artistic control of the series.

Otherwise, Orson's work for the small screen involved guesting on such as *The Dean Martin Show*, *The Jackie Gleason Show*, *ABC Comedy Hour*, *The Marty Feldman Comedy Machine* and as a talk show guest and sometime host of *The Tonight Show* or *The Merv Griffin Show*. A 1979 pilot show promised a new departure: *The Orson Welles Show* was not picked up by the networks.

The real Orson Welles however was seen at his most entertaining and charming in an extensive interview filmed in Las Vegas in 1982 and screened by the BBC in its *Arena* arts series. The two-part, three-hour program included some revealing comment from Welles himself, and contributions from Anthony Perkins, Charlton Heston, Jeanne Moreau, John Huston, Peter Bogdanovich and Robert Wise.

As narrator, as in the cinema, Welles was much in demand, contributing to a great many productions including *Out of Darkness* (CBS 1955), *The Method* (BBC 1958), *An Arabian Night* (ATV 1960), *Around the World of Mike Todd* (ABC 1968), *The Name of the Game* (NBC 1970), *A Woman Called Moses* (a dramatization of the life of Harriet Tubman starring Cicely Tyson) (NBC 1978), *Shogun* (NBC 1980) and *Jack London's Tales of the Klondike* (CBC 1982).

Apart from a series of commercials for Paul Masson Wines, Sherry and Carlsberg Lager, probably Orson's final television appearance was in autumn 1985 when he introduced an offbeat episode of the popular series *Moonlighting* filmed in 1940s Monochrome with Cybill Shepherd in a Rita Hayworth-style song and dance number.

Welles himself also was portrayed in three television movies. In addition to *The Night That Panicked America*, there were *Rita Hayworth: The Love Goddess* in 1983 (Edward Edwards was Orson to Lynda Carter's Rita) and the 1985 *Malice in Wonderland*, a lighthearted recounting of the celebrated feud between Hedda Hopper (Jane Alexander) and Louella Parsons (Elizabeth Taylor), which featured an amusing interlude about an incident at one of Louella's parties involving Welles (played by Eric Purcell) and Joseph Cotten (portrayed by Tim Robbins).

Although only an occasional performer in the medium, it is worth nothing the reaction of one American critic in 1953 following Orson's *King Lear*. Discussing what was needed to raise the standards of television entertainment, he unhesitatingly pronounced, "*More of Orson Welles.*"

TILTING AT WINDMILLS: OTHER CREDITS AND UNRELEASED PROJECTS

VOICE ONLY

A much sought-after narrator, Orson Welles was heard in the following:

1940:   Swiss Family Robinson
1942:   The Magnificent Ambersons
1946:   Duel in the Sun
1949:   Desordre
1955:   Out of Darkness*
1958:   The Vikings; South Sea Adventure*; Come to the Fair*
1959:   Les Seigneurs de la Forêt
1961:   King of Kings
1963:   River of the Ocean*
1964:   The Finest Hour (UK)*
1969:   Barbed Wire (UK)*
1970:   Start the Revolution Without Me**; A Horse Called Nijinsky (UK)*
1971:   Sentinels of Silence (UK),
        Directed by John Ford*
1975:   And Then There Were None***; Bugs Bunny Superstar
1976:   The Late Great Planet Earth****
1977:   The Greatest Battle*****
1978:   Filming Othello

----

  *   Documentary
  **   OW listed as actor, had a walk-on part in the movie
  ***   Listed as actor, OW was the voice of the unseen U. N. Owen in this German/French/Spanish coproduction of the Agatha Christie novel, also known as Death in Persepolis and Ten Little Indians
  **** OW also credited as cowriter
  ***** Narrated the cut and English-dubbed version of this Italian-made World War II drama

EARLY FRAGMENTS AND "LOST" MOVIES

One Sunday afternoon in spring 1934, as a reaction against Luis Bunuel's *Un Chien Andalou* and Jean Cocteau's *Le Sangue du Poet*, Orson Welles, his future wife Virginia Nicholson, and their friend William Vance made a short (four minute) "home movie" of vaguely symbolic images under the title *Hearts of Age*.

Reminded forty years later of *Hearts of Age* — a copy of which survives at the Library of Congress Film Archives in Washington — Welles was horrified that it should be considered his "first" film. "Some dumb stuff" was his comment. His opinion of the Bunuel and Cocteau films however was completely reversed many years previously when he acknowledged them as classics.

Too Much Johnson, a Mercury Theatre production of 1938 closed during its out-of-town run without ever having screened its filmed prologue in public. Shot in a quarry and other locations around New York, it is chiefly significant as the first piece of film actually directed and edited by Orson Welles. Its content, quality and potential cannot however be measured since the only known copy of the film was destroyed by a fire at Welles' house in Spain some years later.

RKO

The first Mercury film at RKO was to have been *Heart of Darkness*, from the novel by Joseph Conrad. A screenplay was written and sets designed; the picture cast with Welles himself taking two parts, Marlow the storyteller and Kurtz the object of his search. Welles had intended that Marlow never be seen in the movie, the camera itself being his "eye." Although used briefly at the opening of Rouben Mamoulian's *Dr. Jekyll and Mr. Hyde* in 1932, this technique would not be adopted again until, with limited success, 1947's *Lady in the Lake*, when Robert Montgomery played another Marlowe, this time Raymond Chandler's detective.

Canceled for either political or financial reasons, *Heart of Darkness*, the novel, later served as a basis for Francis Ford Coppola's *Apocalypse Now*.

A second project was *Smiler With a Knife* from a story by C. S. Lewis, starring Joseph Cotten in a role loosely based on Howard Hughes. Carole Lombard refused the female lead, claiming that

Welles would receive all credit if the picture were to be a success, but that she would be blamed for any failure. Rosalind Russell also backed out, and Welles' third suggestion, Lucille Ball, was not considered enough of a "name" by the studio.

Proposed follow-ups to *Citizen Kane* included *Pickwick Papers* with W. C. Fields, who proved unavailable, and *Jane Eyre*.

"IT'S ALL TRUE"

In the midst of completing *The Magnificent Ambersons* and *Journey Into Fear* in 1942, Orson Wells was dispatched to South America by Nelson Rockefeller to make a movie as part of the war effort.

In Rio, Welles began three episodes of *It's All True*, his portmanteau feature. *My Friend Bonito*, directed by Norman Foster, was a tale of a boy's pet bull spared from his fate in the ring. The second episode, *The Story of the Samba*, told the story of the native dance using footage of the Rio Carnival, and the third sequence, *Jangadeiros*, was based on a true story. Four fisherman became national heroes, sailing two thousand miles from Brazil to Rio by raft without a compass in 1941 to bring to the attention of the president their poor working conditions.

With the change of management at RKO, the film was canceled, and despite desperate efforts by Welles to complete the film at his own expense, *It's All True* was confiscated by the studio with legend telling of its mysterious dumping into Santa Monica Bay by order of RKO bigwigs, while others assumed that the nitrate base footage had decomposed over the years.

Forty years later, however, several reels were discovered at Paramount, new owners of the old RKO lot. Richard Wilson, longtime associate of Orson Welles and assistant director on the Rio shoot, put together a twenty-two-minute documentary on the episode. It was seen at the Venice Film Festival in 1986 under the title *It's Not All True*. Wilson's footage contains the black and white sections of the *Bonito* and *Jangadeiros* episodes, while color footage of the Rio Carnival shot for the *Samba* story has also been discovered. It seems possible that some version of *It's All True* may yet see the light of day under Richard Wilson's supervision.

AFTER RKO

Orson Welles received screen credit as supplying the original idea for Charles Chaplin's *Monsieur Verdoux* in 1947. Welles had wanted to direct the picture, but the collaboration was not accepted by Chaplin, as was the case on a later proposed project with Walt Disney.

Welles discussed several projects with Alexander Korda in England, including a version of *War and Peace* to be directed by Welles who would star alongside Laurence Olivier and Vivien Leigh. *Cyrano de Bergerac* was also proposed, as were

Scenes from the *Jangadeiros*
episode of *It's All True*.

Crime and Punishment, Ulysses and Homer's
Iliad.

A film version of his own London stage version
of *Moby Dick* was begun, with Welles as Ahab, but
this was abandoned probably because of the John
Huston version which went into production
almost immediately. Gordon Jackson, Ishmael in
the West End production, recalled the few days of
shooting before the film was abandoned: "We
started filming the production at the end of the run
in London — but, sadly, Orson had to leave after a
week's shooting! That unfinished project must be
in a vault somewhere — together with his other
unfinished projects!"

Of the actual filming, Mr. Jackson said: "I
remember, during filming one day, Orson shouting, 'Roll 'em!' and the poor cameraman saying, 'I
haven't got a setup yet!' Orson shouted back, 'Find
one and surprise me! Roll 'em!!'"

Welles contributed uncredited as writer of the
Abraham episode in John Huston's 1966 production of *The Bible.* He also cowrote and narrated an
ecological film *The Late Great Planet Earth* in
1976.

Orson Welles in Rio.

"DON QUIXOTE"

Perhaps the most celebrated of the unfinished Orson Welles movies, *Don Quixote* — originally conceived for television — began shooting in 1955 and was still officially in production at the time of Welles' death thirty years later.

Charlton Heston was to have played Quixote, with the crew entering Mexico as visitors and completing filming within five or six days. Unfortunately, Heston's commitments forced him to leave for Rome and *Ben Hur* at the crucial moment, and the project was shelved.

Beginning in earnest soon afterward, Welles cast his friend Akim Tamiroff as the faithful Sancho Panza and a virtually unknown Spanish player, Francisco Riguera, as the Don. Entirely financed by Welles, the film opens with a young girl, Patty McCormack, asking Welles about the book he is reading. He then tells her the story of Don Quixote, updating it so that the child can understand Cervantes' work.

Filming took place as and when money was available and the two actors could be found. A break of three years was not unusual; Akim

Opening of *Don Quixote*. Patty McCormack asks Welles to explain the book he is reading. It took him thirty years!

Francisco Riguera as Don Quixote.

Tamiroff told reporters in 1964, "Any time, I think I may hear from Orson saying, 'Drop everything, we make some more.'"

In 1965, Riguera urged Welles to finish the apparently three-quarters completed film as soon as possible, having already warned Tamiroff that he feared his own death before the film was finished. In any event, both actors died before *Don Quixote* was completed. Yet even in 1982, Welles still intended to complete the picture even without his stars. All dialogue apparently was to be dubbed by Welles himself, and skillful editing would solve any other problems. Weary of being questioned on its progress after a quarter of a century, he had now retitled the film *When Are You Going to Finish Don Quixote?*

One apparent cause for the film's noncompletion was the need to film a huge nuclear-type explosion, from which the Don and Sancho would emerge unharmed. The cost of such a shot evidently proved prohibitive.

"DEAD CALM"

A similar problem hampered the completion of a new project *The Deep*, also known variously as *Dead Reckoning* or *Dead Calm*, the title of the source novel, a thriller by Charles Williams. Filmed in Yugoslavia in 1968, the movie starred Laurence Harvey as a psychopathic murderer picked up by a honeymoon couple at sea. Orson Welles and Jeanne Moreau also were featured in the movie, financed and actually filmed by Welles himself.

The state of *Dead Calm* is not entirely clear. One report suggests that one final scene — an explosion of the yacht at sea — had yet to be filmed, another that Welles was simply not satisfied with the picture. A third possibility is that the film was never completed following the death of Laurence Harvey in 1973.

Dead Calm did finally reach the screen in 1989, but not Orson Welles'. Australian director Philip Noyce acquired the rights to the novel and released a new version starring Sam Neill. The film was well promoted but critical reaction was mixed, some reviewers even comparing it unfavorably to the unseen Welles production! Of the unfinished or "lost" films of Orson Welles, *Dead Calm/The Deep* appears to be the most elusive in terms of possible release in the future.

Akim Tamiroff as Sancho Panza.

248

Quixote sets out to rediscover the age of chivalry.

TESTS AND NON-STARTERS

A television documentary on the life of Gina Lollobrigida was discussed and then dropped just as quickly. Orson made an unbilled appearance in a 1968 Romanian film called *Mihai Viteazul (Michael the Brave)*. A 1989 Oja Kodar movie, *Jaded*, contains previously unseen tests for a version of Shakespeare's *The Merchant of Venice*, evidently filmed in Morocco during the making of *Othello*. Ms. Kodar — Orson's companion for the past twenty years of his life — is dedicated to the completion and release of as many of Welles' "lost" films as is possible.

"THE OTHER SIDE OF THE WIND"

Perhaps the most publicly seen of the unreleased movies, *The Other Side of the Wind* was viewed by an audience of millions when two clips were introduced by Orson at the 1975 American Film Institute Life Achievement ceremony.

John Huston (left) as director Jake Hannaford in Welles' *The Other Side of the Wind.*

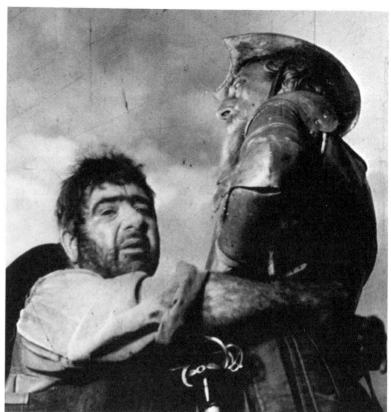

Sancho and the Don.

The Other Side of the Wind stars John Huston, with Lilli Palmer and Peter Bogdanovich. Also in the film were longtime friends and colleagues Norman Foster, Henry Jaglom, Edmond O'Brien, Mercedes McCambridge, Oja Kodar and Susan Strasberg. Also scheduled at one point for roles in the movie were Marlene Dietrich and Jeanne Moreau, but both were finally unavailable.

In his autobiography, *An Open Book*, John Huston noted that there was a two-year delay between Welles first mentioning the project and commencing filming.

Summoned to Arizona in 1973, Huston recalled, "Orson received me with open arms and a great show of affection. I'm very fond of Orson. I have enormous admiration for him as an actor and a director, and the figure he cuts delights me." As for the story of the film, Huston wrote, "The plot concerns a director (my role in the film) who comes to the end of his rope. Orson denied that it was autobiographical in any way . . ."

The director, Jake Hannaford, has almost completed a new movie (the film-within-the-film starred Oja Kodar) but needs *end money* which his assistant, Norman Foster, is attempting to extract from a Hollywood producer.

"Orson had come up with·an ingenious idea," wrote Huston. "It was to tell the story through cameras being held in the hands of persons being filmed by the major cameras . . . Most of the action took place during a big party to celebrate the director's birthday . . . There was always a camera on the director during the course of the festivities . . . It's through these various cameras

— what they see — that the story is told. The changes from one to another — color, black and white, still and moving — make for a dazzling variety of effects."

Finance was sought from several quarters; this more than anything caused problems later on. A Spanish contact apparently made off with large amounts of cash, but worse was to follow. Desperate to squash rumors of his being unable to complete his film, Welles accepted further financing from Iran with the result that when the Shah of Iran fell, prints of the film — now virtually completed — were confiscated by the Ayatollah Khomeini's men in Iran and the Shah's brother-in-law in Paris.

Word of the film's imminent return to Welles circulated regularly until in 1982 Orson met with the French Government to discuss the release of the print to him. Newspaper reports suggested that it would be only a matter of weeks before the problem was finally solved, yet time rolled on and still no film.

Back in 1973, John Huston "left, having had a wonderful time, and admiring Orson and his whole *modus operandi*. Some months later the incomplete picture was shown to a selected audience. Orson still didn't have the funds to finish it. I didn't get to see it, but those who did tell me it is a knockout."

WELJAG

Following their work on *A Safe Place* in 1970, Orson Welles and Henry Jaglom became firm friends, with Jaglom one of Orson's most vocal supporters in Hollywood, arranging endless meetings in the hope of attracting finance from producers for a new Welles project.

With Henry Jaglom as executive producer, Orson Welles was reported in *Variety* (June 18, 1980) to have signed to direct and star in Isak Dinesen's story *The Dreamers*. Dinesen — the pseudonym of Karen Blixen — was a favorite author of Welles', who had already filmed her *Immortal Story* in 1968. The movie, at a modest cost of $6 million, was to be produced by Northstar International as the first of a two-picture deal with Weljag, the partnership formed by the two maverick directors.

For whatever reason — supposedly Welles' screenplay was "too poetic"(!) — *The Dreamers* fell through, although Orson apparently shot about twenty minutes of the film featuring Oja

Kodar in 1985. Again, Ms. Kodar is custodian of the footage, hailed by those who have seen it as of a rare beauty indeed.

Henry Jaglom's tireless efforts continued to arrange meetings with producers, many promising to be in touch but somehow never managing it once lunch was over. At Jaglom's urging, Orson wrote an entirely new screenplay, *The Big Brass Ring*. Described as a "bookend to *Citizen Kane*," the plot was an examination of the American dream as seen through the relationship between a presidential candidate and an older, retired politician. Welles was to be the elder statesman, while Jack Nicholson was said to have agreed to the other leading role.

The $8 million movie was to be produced by Arnan Milchan, with several studios keen to distribute the picture. What happened next is probably known fully only to Henry Jaglom, who says that seven major Hollywood stars in turn rejected the leading role. Each star's excuses ranged from not working for less than $4 million in case it damaged his reputation, to only accepting the movie if he could rewrite, produce and cut the film himself, and, worst of all, one agent snidely replied that his client was "busy for the next four years doing real movies."

Henry Jaglom was understandably disgusted at such a reaction. Without a second recognized leading actor, the film could not be made. Despite Arnan Milchan's admiration for Welles and his eagerness to work with the star, the deal fell through. Henry Jaglom, custodian of the screenplay, refuses to entertain the possibility of the film being made by anyone else, although shortly after Welles' death, he told reporters that he intended to see the script, which he describes as a "masterpiece," published. "But no one else could make it," he added.

LAST YEARS

On August 28, 1984, *Variety* reported that Orson Welles would direct his first American film in many years, *The Cradle Will Rock*, produced by Circle Theatre and telling the story of the Welles-Houseman 1937 New York production of Marc Blitzstein's play of the same name.

A screenplay was prepared by Welles and Ring Lardner, Jr., with British actor Rupert Everett cast as the twenty-two-year-old Orson Welles. Coproducer Michael Fitzgerald was highly enthusiastic about the film. "Orson Welles has put it into the

Orson himself acted as cameraman for some of *The Other Side of the Wind*.

perspective of the time, showing the hopes and ideals of the period as they exist in his memory," he said. Within months the project had foundered. Not entirely abandoned, funds were sought from various sources, reportedly including Steven Spielberg whose then-wife Amy Irving was to have played Welles' first wife, Virginia.

With *The Cradle Will Rock* shelved, Welles prepared his fourth Shakespeare film, and what perhaps would have been his greatest — *King Lear*, Orson felt that he was now the right age to play Lear "properly." (Laurence Olivier recounted a similar conviction when preparing his own *King Lear* for British television in 1982 at the age of seventy-five.)

A deal was struck with Alexander Salkind, producer of *The Trial*, who would finance the $5 million *Lear* after Orson appeared in the latest Salkind production, *Where Is Parsifal?* Orson dutifully obliged, only for the *King Lear* deal to fail due to poor profits on Salkind's *Superman III*. French backers offered to finance the production, although their sincerity was later questioned by Oja Kodar, claiming it as a political maneuver aimed at the American industry. Nevertheless, Orson remained optimistic over *King Lear*, which promised to be a highly personal interpretation of a story which has proved notoriously difficult to film successfully.

Although death took Orson Welles at the age of seventy in 1985, it is still far too early to say that we have seen the last of his works. Oja Kodar insists that many of his unreleased films as possible will finally be seen. Rumors circulated in the mid-1970s that the missing reels from *The Magnificent Ambersons* had been found, and given the subsequent discovery of footage from *It's All True*, who can discount the possibility?

This book may not be *The Complete Films of Orson Welles*, since I am far from alone in believing that there is yet more of Orson Welles' cinematic artistry still to be seen and enjoyed.

ORSON WELLES' FAVORITE MOVIES

Although *Citizen Kane* topped the polls of *Sight and Sound* magazine as "Best Movie of All Time" in 1962, 1972 and 1982, at the first poll in 1952 it was mentioned only as a runner-up outside the first ten.

In that year of 1952, Orson Welles named his own "12 Best Movies of All Time" at the Brussels Film Festival. Significantly, the list includes work by notably individualistic and unconventional directors. Unlike several other directors polled, Welles did not include any of his own movies.

The list is:

1. *City Lights* (Charles Chaplin)
2. *Greed* (Erich Von Stroheim)
3. *Intolerance* (D. W. Griffith)
4. *Nanook of the North* (Robert Flaherty)
5. *Shoeshine* (Vittorio De Sica)
6. *The Battleship Potemkin* (Sergei Eisenstein)
7. *The Baker's Wife* (Marcel Pagnol)
8. *La Grande Illusion* (Jean Renoir)
9. *Stagecoach* (John Ford)
10. *Ninotchka* (Ernst Lubitsch)
11. *The Best Years of Our Lives* (William Wyler)
12. *Bicycle Thieves* (Vittorio De Sica)

END REEL

One of Orson Welles' favorite stories concerned a birthday party given for Louis B. Mayer, head of MGM studios and ironically one of the men who tried to block the release of *Citizen Kane* in 1941. At the country club dinner, Welles — a keen magician — had brought along a rabbit which he intended to produce out of Mayer's hat during the party. As the evening wore on, stars like Al Jolson and Danny Kaye were asked to entertain the guests while Orson sat in growing discomfort as the unfortunate rabbit proceeded to piddle all over him.

In the early hours of the morning as the party broke up, Orson left with the other guests — his rabbit still in his pocket. No one had asked him to do a magic trick the entire evening.

As a magician of the cinema, it has to be said that Orson Welles was forced to spend far too long waiting for someone to ask him to produce the rabbit from that particular hat. So many tricks left unseen . . .

FREE!

Citadel Film Series Catalog

From James Stewart to Moe Howard and The Three Stooges, Woody Allen to John Wayne, The Citadel Film Series is America's largest film book library.

Now with more than 125 titles in print, books in the series make perfect gifts—for a loved one, a friend, or yourself!

We'd like to send you, free of charge, our latest full-color catalog describing the Citadel Film Series in depth. To receive the catalog, call 1-800-447-BOOK or send your name and address to:

**Citadel Film Series/Carol Publishing Group
Distribution Center B
120 Enterprise Avenue
Secaucus, New Jersey 07094**

447-2665

The titles you'll find in the catalog include:
The Films Of...

Alan Ladd
Alfred Hitchcock
All Talking! All Singing!
  All Dancing!
Anthony Quinn
The Bad Guys
Barbara Stanwyck
Barbra Streisand:
  The First Decade
Barbra Streisand:
  The Second Decade
Bela Lugosi
Bette Davis
Bing Crosby
Black Hollywood
Boris Karloff
Bowery Boys
Brigitte Bardot
Burt Reynolds
Carole Lombard
Cary Grant
Cecil B. DeMille
Character People
Charles Bronson
Charlie Chaplin
Charlton Heston
Chevalier
Clark Gable
Classics of the Gangster
  Film
Classics of the Horror Film
Classics of the Silent Screen
Cliffhanger
Clint Eastwood
Curly: Biography of a
  Superstooge
Detective in Film
Dick Tracy
Dustin Hoffman
Early Classics of the
  Foreign Film

Elizabeth Taylor
Elvis Presley
Errol Flynn
Federico Fellini
The Fifties
The Forties
Forgotten Films
  to Remember
Frank Sinatra
Fredric March
Gary Cooper
Gene Kelly
Gina Lollobrigida
Ginger Rogers
Gloria Swanson
Great Adventure Films
Great British Films
Great French Films
Great German Films
Great Romantic Films
Great Science Fiction Films
Great Spy Films
Gregory Peck
Greta Garbo
Harry Warren and the
  Hollywood Musical
Hedy Lamarr
Hello! My Real Name Is
Henry Fonda
Hollywood Cheesecake:
  60 Years of Leg Art
Hollywood's Hollywood
Howard Hughes in Hollywood
Humphrey Bogart
Ingrid Bergman
Jack Lemmon
Jack Nicholson
James Cagney
James Stewart
Jane Fonda
Jayne Mansfield

Jeanette MacDonald and
  Nelson Eddy
Jewish Image in American
  Films
Joan Crawford
John Garfield
John Huston
John Wayne
John Wayne Reference
  Book
John Wayne Scrapbook
Judy Garland
Katharine Hepburn
Kirk Douglas
Lana Turner
Laurel and Hardy
Lauren Bacall
Laurence Olivier
Lost Films of the
  Fifties
Love in the Film
Mae West
Marilyn Monroe
Marlon Brando
Moe Howard and The
  Three Stooges
Montgomery Clift
More Character People
More Classics of the
  Horror Film
More Films of the '30s
Myrna Loy
Non-Western Films of
  John Ford
Norma Shearer
Olivia de Havilland
Paul Newman
Paul Robeson
Peter Lorre
Pictorial History of Science
  Fiction Films

Pictorial History of Sex
  in Films
Pictorial History of War
  Films
Pictorial History of the
  Western Film
Rebels: The Rebel Hero
  in Films
Rita Hayworth
Robert Redford
Robert Taylor
Ronald Reagan
The Seventies
Sex in the Movies
Sci-Fi 2
Sherlock Holmes
Shirley MacLaine
Shirley Temple
The Sixties
Sophia Loren
Spencer Tracy
Steve McQueen
Susan Hayward
Tarzan of the Movies
They Had Faces Then
The Thirties
Those Glorious Glamour Years
Three Stooges Book of Scripts
Three Stooges Book of Scripts,
  Vol. 2
The Twenties
20th Century Fox
Warren Beatty
W. C. Fields
Western Films of John Ford
West That Never Was
William Holden
William Powell
Woody Allen
World War II